A Century of
Higher Education for American Women

A Century of
Higher Education

for American Women

By *MABEL NEWCOMER*

EMERITUS PROFESSOR OF ECONOMICS,
VASSAR COLLEGE

Harper & Brothers Publishers, New York

With this book the author pays tribute
to Vassar College on the occasion of its
Centennial.

A CENTURY OF HIGHER EDUCATION FOR AMERICAN WOMEN

To all the students in my classes over a period of forty years from whom I learned much about the higher education of women that I have not found in print.

Contents

Tables

Acknowledgments

THIS STUDY was prepared at the request of the Committee on Publications for the Vassar College Centenary Celebration. I am indebted to the members of this committee, and particularly to its chairman, Mr. Russell Lynes, for permitting me to extend the scope of the study beyond that originally envisaged.

For assistance in obtaining materials for the work I am greatly indebted to many members of the Vassar College Library staff, past and present, who have accumulated and made easily available a superb collection of materials, not only on Vassar College but covering the whole field of women's education. I am particularly grateful to Dorothy Alice Plum for giving me many helpful suggestions as to sources and for making materials easily available to me. I also wish to thank Mrs. Opal D. David, Director of the Commission on the Education of Women of the American Council on Education, and all the college officials throughout the United States who took the trouble to answer my inquiries. Many officers of Vassar College have helped greatly by collecting special data for me and discussing particular phases of the study with me. These include Miss Julia Grant Bacon, Mrs. Elizabeth M. Drouilhet, Miss Jean L. Harry, and Mrs. Eleanor M. Murtaugh. Mrs. Frank H. Ellis, Secretary of the Committee on Publications for the Vassar College Centenary Celebration, has also been helpful in answering inquiries and furthering the progress of the work.

Friends among the faculty and administration of Vassar College have read the manuscript and made valuable suggestions. These include President Sarah Gibson Blanding, Professor Helen Codere, Dr. Mervin Freedman, Professor Josephine Gleason, Professor Margaret Myers, Dean Marion Tait, and Dr. Sydnor H. Walker. Among these I am particularly indebted to Helen Codere and Sydnor Walker, who not only read the manuscript but discussed many of the problems with me as the work progressed. Needless to say, the responsibility for any errors of judgment or fact are entirely mine.

Outside of the college community, from Muriel C. Haynes of Compton Advertising, Inc., Russell Lynes, and Dr. Ordway Tead of Harper & Brothers, have come suggestions that have led to substantial reorganization of the entire study, to its great improvement. For these I am most grateful.

Finally, I wish to thank President Blanding, not only for her deep interest in this study, but for all that she has done to extend and improve the higher education of women at Vassar College and in the country as a whole.

Mabel Newcomer

July 1959

A Century of

Higher Education for American Women

IT OCCURRED TO ME THAT WOMAN, HAVING RECEIVED FROM
HER CREATOR THE SAME INTELLECTUAL CONSTITUTION AS
MAN, HAS THE SAME RIGHT AS MAN TO INTELLECTUAL CUL-
TURE AND DEVELOPMENT.   MATTHEW VASSAR*

1. Introduction

IN THE FALL of 1957 the number of women enrolled in American
colleges exceeded one million for the first time. This was just one
hundred twenty years after Oberlin admitted women to its college
courses—the first authentic instance of women being permitted to
obtain a college education equivalent to that of men. There were
many at that time who doubted the value of higher education for men,
but the men's right to knowledge was not questioned. Women's right
to knowledge, however, was not yet accepted. This was a male pre-
rogative, and only when men deemed it safe—that is, that it would
neither kill the women or seriously impair their attractiveness and
usefulness to men—was the right reluctantly extended to all human
beings. "Man is the yardstick of the human race."[1]

The education of women has been endlessly discussed. When I
look up "women's education" in the library catalogue I find between
two and three hundred entries. It has a special number in the Dewey

* From Matthew Vassar's first address to the Trustees of Vassar College, February 26, 1861.

1

classification system. "Men's education," on the contrary, has no entry and no catalogue number reserved for it. This is further evidence that education has been for men. Women have succeeded in getting their share only through perseverance and luck.

The debate has long since died away. It is taken for granted today that women have the right to go all the way through to the doctor's degree in any field at all. There is no field of knowledge that some woman has not tried. The question of what women should study has been fairly well settled by the students themselves since the introduction of the free elective system opened the door to every field of knowledge. But it is still of interest to know what women have chosen to study, what they have done with their education, and what contribution college women have made to society and to the development of education itself. What kind of women have gone to college? And why? More particularly, what is the current trend—why do they go to college today? Why don't more of them go? For the fact is that the increase in the number of women enrolled in college, large though it is, has not kept pace with the increase in the number of men. And then there are questions concerning the women's colleges, which have played such an important part in the history of women's college education in this country. What has been their contribution? Now that the pioneering is over do they still serve a useful purpose?

There has been a marked change in recent years in what women do with their lives. They are less likely than women of a generation ago to choose between marriage and the job; they are now almost sure to marry, and when the children are grown, to seek employment too. Moreover, in our urban society the homemaker's activities cannot be limited to the home. The welfare of her family depends in ever increasing degree on conditions in the community and beyond. How can a college education assist her to meet these varied demands? And how will she find time for the education she needs when she marries so young?

That women are physically and mentally capable of being educated like men is an accepted fact. But whether it is useful to educate them in the same manner as men is still an open question. In fact, with the threatened overcrowding of the colleges, the right of women to take places that men might use to "better advantage"—that is, for more obvious professional purposes—is now being challenged. And many coeducational colleges are in fact accepting a much larger proportion of the men who apply than of the women. Women's rights are still of a lesser order than men's.

Most of the literature in this field has consisted, since the controversy has abated, of histories of individual colleges, or special studies of college women—their roles as homemakers, their professions, and all their interests and achievements. Thomas Woody's *History of Women's Education in the United States*[2] can be accepted as the definitive history in this field. But it is now thirty years old, and thirty years is a long time in the brief span of women's higher education.

This study does not pretend to present a carefully documented history of the higher education of women. It is much too brief for this purpose. But I hope that it may give some perspective on the development of women's college education over the hundred and twenty years of its existence. If the reader finds the emphasis on older women's colleges to be out of proportion to their number and enrollment, it is because these have served to isolate and emphasize factors which have differentiated women's education from men's. Also, they have played a role in advancing higher education of women that has been, in fact, out of proportion to their size. This will appear in later discussion.

I shall have to plead guilty of drawing on Vassar College materials more than the importance of this or any single college seems to justify; this is only because the data have been easily accessible to me, and because I have been acquainted with the college over a period of forty years. I have not intended, however, to inflate its importance; on the contrary, I believe that it is fairly representative of the resident women's colleges and the liberal arts education. Such comparative data as I have been able to find confirm this position.

The questions I have raised cannot be answered with any degree of finality at this time. Some of the changes noted are too recent to allow anyone to measure their effects. And one can never be sure that present trends will continue for any considerable period of time. I have found it impossible to make this study without forming some strong convictions that will be apparent to the reader. But it is only fair to say that these convictions are not the ones with which I started. They have grown out of the facts as my investigation has proceeded. I trust that I have presented enough of the facts, with sufficient objectivity, that the reader can arrive at his own conclusions independently. That, after all, is what the liberal arts education is for!

NOTES

[1] M. Jahoda and J. E. Havel, "Psychological Problems of Women in Different Social Roles," *Educational Record*, October 1955.

[2] T. Woody, *A History of Women's Education in the United States* (New York, 1929).

THE WORK OF FEMALE EDUCATION MUST BE CARRIED ON IN
SOME FORM, AND IN A MUCH MORE EFFICIENT MANNER THAN
IT HAS BEEN HITHERTO, OR OUR COUNTRY WILL GO TO
DESTRUCTION.
PHILO STEWART—COFOUNDER OF OBERLIN COLLEGE*

2. The Beginnings

Two HUNDRED and one years after Harvard College opened,
four young women enrolled at Oberlin College. Three of them received the A.B. degree four years later, in 1841. This is the first un-
disputed instance in this country of women receiving bachelor's
degrees equal to those granted to men.

The explanation for the great lag between the establishment of
institutions of higher learning for men and the recognition of women's
claims to such opportunities is not far to seek. The original impetus
for establishing colleges in America was the desire for an educated
clergy, and colleges appear early in our history in consequence.
Harvard was founded in 1636, and William and Mary was established
before the close of the seventeenth century. Nine colleges still in existence trace their origins to the pre-Revolutionary era. Most of these
were established primarily for the education of the clergy, and every
college president appointed prior to the Revolution was a clergyman.
So, also, were a large proportion of the members of the faculty.

Ends other than the ministry were recognized from the beginning.
Harvard included the law and teaching as professions for which it

* From F. J. Hosford, *Father Shipherd's Magna Charta* (Boston, 1937), p. 7.

should prepare its students; 48 per cent of its seventeenth century graduates never entered the ministry.[1] Only one in four of the Princeton students in the early years of its history later became clergymen; and Yale's charter cited preparation for employment "both in Church and Civil State" as its aim.[2] Many of our early statesmen were college men. Only Washington among the early presidents was without a college education; and more than half the signers of the Declaration of Independence had some formal college training either in America or abroad. Only one of this group seems to have been ordained as a minister and he abandoned the profession early for the law. The law occupied more than half of the signers, at least in part. It is clear that college education was useful both for the law and for government service. Other professions demanding higher education included medicine, and to a lesser extent teaching.

Thus college education was primarily professional education; and the professions, including teaching, were men's occupations. Consequently, there was no apparent need for including women in the small and privileged student bodies of the colleges. The early founders of these institutions would probably have scoffed if any one had predicted that by mid-twentieth century eight of the nine pre-Revolutionary institutions would be admitting women to some or all of their courses of instruction. For of this group to date only Princeton has made no concessions to the coeducational trend.

The great majority of institutions of higher learning continued to be church founded until after the Civil War. Nine out of ten of the college presidents were selected from the clergy up to this time, although the first lay president, John Wheelock of Dartmouth, had been appointed as early as 1779.[3] But as the colleges multiplied, their objectives broadened, and the reason for excluding women was no longer clear. Women as well as men were concerned with religious beliefs. And women began to teach in public schools. The value of higher education for women began to be debated, as it had not been in the earlier period.

Prior to the nineteenth century the desirability of *any* formal schooling for girls was not generally accepted. Free public education was exceptional, and such money as parents felt they could spend for schooling was likely to be reserved for boys, where its economic value was recognized. Small boys aged four to seven usually learned to read and write in the dame schools, that small sector of the educational world conceded to women. Boys were not admitted to masters' schools until they could "stand up and read words of two syllables and keep their places."[4] Once they became reasonably proficient in reading and writing they were transferred to the masters' schools for further training—arithmetic, and whatever else might be regarded as important at the time.

Girls, too, might attend the dame schools, but it was considered sufficient for them to read a little. Even writing was not regarded as essential. In fact, there were some who feared that if women learned to write, they might forge their husbands' signatures; and if they could read easily, they would neglect their household tasks. The girls who lingered on in the dame schools after their brothers had been transferred to the masters' schools were more likely to be taught sewing or some other household art than the basic subjects being taught to the boys. Here and there, however, where the dame's education was adequate and the girl eager, she not only mastered the subjects taught the boys, but stayed to study arithmetic and even Latin. The dame schools continued well into the nineteenth century. Harriot Stanton Blatch notes in her autobiography that she learned to read at the age of four in a dame school in Johnstown, New York. This was in 1860.[5] But the public school systems gradually took over even the most elementary instruction.

The town schools of New England opened to girls slowly. Although an agreement was made by the town fathers of Hampton, New Hampshire, as early as 1649, for the instruction of boys and girls together in the three R's, this seems never to have been put into effect. The first clear record of girls attending a master's school with boys was in Ipswich in 1769.[6] By the end of the eighteenth century, however, there were a number of instances of girls being allowed to go to school.

The economic motive was working in favor of the girls, particularly in the more sparsely settled areas. Having hired a master, the parents wanted to get their money's worth, and if there were not enough boys in the school to occupy the master fully, the girls could be educated without additional cost. Thus girls might attend school in summer, while the boys were busy with farm work; or for two hours in the afternoon after the boys had been dismissed, as in Medford in 1766; or two hours before the boy's classes began, as in New London in 1774, where the girls were admitted from five to seven in the morning.[7]

The pattern was not uniform, of course, since schools were a purely local affair. In the Central Colonies, where the Society of Friends was influential, there were more opportunities for girls than in New England. And here and there in the South private girls' schools began to appear. Also in the South, wealthy families isolated on plantations often hired tutors, and daughters as well as sons were likely to receive instruction.

Some girls profited at second hand by the increasing education of fathers and brothers. In 1783 Lucinda Foote, at the age of twelve, having studied with her brothers as they prepared for Yale, was examined by the president of this institution and received a Latin certificate stating that she was qualified for admission to Yale in every respect *except* sex. Hannah Adams, growing up in the latter half of the eighteenth century, read alone in her father's library, acquiring faults of pronunciation that she said she was never able to overcome. Sarah Josepha Hale of *Godey's Lady's Book* was tutored by her Dartmouth brother. Almira Phelps, sister of Emma Willard, studied with her brother-in-law's nephew while he attended Middlebury. Sometimes the girls' fathers tutored them. And if the fathers happened to be school masters or college professors, the girls might even attend classes, although not for credit. Mary Lyon spent weeks in Professor Hitchcock's home in Amherst sudying science under his guidance, and Elizabeth Cady Stanton studied Greek with the local minister in a vain attempt to console her father for the fact that she was not a son.

These cases represent a rare combination of ability and initiative on the part of the girl, and a degree of tolerance, education, and wealth on the part of the family. The importance of such instances in the total development of women's education lies in the fact that they provided some evidence that women might be capable of learning at these higher educational levels. They also provided leaders in the early nineteenth century as the movement for secondary education spread.

Provision for secondary education of girls started, as it had somewhat earlier for boys, with private schools. Most of the early girls' schools were designed to teach the social graces rather than to prepare for college, or even for homemaking, or teaching. John Eliot, describing schools in Boston in 1782, says: "We don't pretend to teach ye female part of ye town anything more than dancing. . . ."[8] But in the same decade in Philadelphia the Young Ladies' Academy was founded with more serious ends in view, and one of its supporters, Benjamin Rush, was urging a serious and substantial education for girls. He argued that American women had greater responsibilities than English women, not the least of which was to educate their sons in "the principles of liberty and government."[9] Their education was to prepare them for their function as homemakers, but in addition to the three R's—the usefulness of which, for girls, could still be debated at this time—he proposed a substantial education in the sciences, history, English literature, and moral philosophy. And the developments that followed indicate that such an education was welcome.

Only isolated instances of private schools for "young ladies" are to be found at this time and in the years immediately following. Woody cites only six incorporated in the thirty-year period from 1790 to 1820. But in the next thirty years, 1820 to 1850, he finds 104. And 96 more were established in the single decade just preceding the Civil War.[10] Most of these schools featured such accomplishments as painting, musical performance, elocution, the best drawing room manners, and perhaps a little French. But they at least insured literacy, and there is a good deal of evidence that the girls were exposed to more science than the boys. Botany might not go beyond the accumulation of herbariums, and geography was likely to consist largely of memorizing place names. But these sciences were still in their infancy. It is worth noting that the greatest improvement in teaching in geography and botany at this time, and the best texts in these fields, were contributed by Emma Willard and Almira Phelps, neither of whom had the benefit of attending any institution of higher learning.

The fact that the private girls' schools did not have to prepare their charges for college gave them a real advantage in experimenting with new subjects and different methods of teaching. And it cannot be assumed that the resulting education was inferior. Not only did the girls get more science than the boys did; they were often taught more history and more modern languages, and they were exposed to more English literature. They did not, of course, go on with higher mathematics. They rarely studied Greek. And if Latin was offered it was not likely to be carried beyond a year or two.

The first public high school for girls was opened in Worcester in 1824. Two years later, one was opened in New York City and another in Boston; but the latter was promptly closed because of the overwhelming demand![11] As public high schools spread, however, there was a tendency to accept girls in the same school with boys, particularly when the numbers were small. The authorities could be tolerant if it did not cost too much. The public high schools were designed to prepare boys for college, and in the coeducational schools the girls were receiving the same training as the boys. They too were prepared for college and some of them wanted to go. The next step was inevitable.

Higher education for women in the United States began during the first half of the nineteenth century. It is not possible to cite the earliest instances, partly because of the fragmentary nature of the records, but even more because of the uncertainty as to standards in the days before government officials and private accrediting agencies began to concern themselves with these matters. Clear instances can be found, however, in the 1830's. Even earlier some of the private academies for young ladies were beginning to interest themselves in preparing their students for teaching. In fact, some of them were founded primarily for this purpose. This required something more than the courses which the ordinary schools of the time were offering to girls.

Emma Willard emphasized the role of women as teachers, both at home with their own children and in the schools. Mary Lyon's Mount Holyoke Female Seminary was oriented to this end—how successfully is indicated by the fact that more than 70 per cent of the alumnae of the first forty years had teaching records.[12] And Catherine Beecher devoted her life to establishing, and persuading others to establish, better teacher training programs. She was not satisfied with the academies. She wanted real colleges. She had much to do with the development of the Milwaukee Institute and High School which in time became Milwaukee-Downer College.

Most of the academies and seminaries were offering a high school education at best; but a number of them clearly achieved junior college status. Mount Holyoke Seminary gave courses comparable to those offered at Amherst, using the same texts. One Amherst student of the early period is on record as testifying that in many ways it was equal to Amherst.[13] The less well known Hudson Female Seminary had a collegiate department before the Civil War that offered three years of college work, judging by the names of the courses, the texts listed, and the age of the students admitted. It did not, however, offer a four year course leading to the bachelor's degree. The name "college" was rarely applied to women's educational institutions in the North. In fact, Emma Willard, when presenting her "plan to improve female education" to the New York State Legislature in 1819, purposely refrained from using the term "college" for fear of ridicule.[14] This name was used by many southern schools for girls, however.

The pre-Civil War colleges for women, like those for men, were church and community sponsored institutions. The earliest were not equal to the best of the men's colleges, either in admission standards or requirements for degrees. But they probably compared favorably with many of the numerous institutions accepted as of collegiate status at the time, even though the Greek requirements, which were likely to be the weakest point of the women's institutions, were lower.

To begin to name those with good claims to college status is to open oneself to argument. But those that developed from earlier lower schools to a full four-year college course leading to an A.B. degree in the period before the Civil War were Oxford Female College, chartered in 1852, Illinois Conference Female College, chartered in 1854, and Ingham University, chartered in 1857.[15] Those founded as colleges were Georgia Female College, chartered in 1836 and conferring degrees as early as 1840, Mary Sharp College, organized in 1850, Elmira College, chartered in 1855, and Vassar College, charted in 1861.[16] Georgia Female College is accepted by some authorities as having been of college grade and thus the first women's college in the country.[17] Woody, on the contrary, regards Mary Sharp College, which required both Latin and Greek in a four-year course leading to an A.B. degree, as the first women's college comparable to men's. Accepting either evaluation, the honors go to the South. However, very few of the more than fifty women's "colleges" listed by Blandin[18] offered a four-year course and an A.B. degree.

Higher education for women was not limited to women's institutions. Oberlin accepted women in its collegiate department in 1837. Two other Ohio colleges admitted women when they opened—Hillsdale in 1844, and Antioch in 1853. Two state universities also admitted women when they opened before the Civil War. One of these, the University of Deseret (now the University of Utah), began instruction at the end of 1850 and a few women enrolled in the second term early in 1851. But the following year instruction was suspended owing to lack of funds, and was not resumed until after the Civil War.[19] The University of Iowa began instruction in 1855 with 89 students in the collegiate department, four of them women.[20] This appears to be the only state university which has a continuous record of co-education for over one hundred years.

Other state universities promised to admit women before the Civil War, but failed to do so. It was the decline in student enrollments that came with the war that weakened resistance and led to the opening of instruction to women in a number of universities during or immediately following the war. The University of Wisconsin, for example, admitted women to a newly established normal department in 1863 and allowed them to take regular college courses if they chose. By the end of the year there were approximately as many women enrolled as men.[21] But President Chadbourne never reconciled himself to coeducation, and in 1867 he established a separate women's college with more limited and more elementary course offerings than those available to men. The state legislature, pressured by taxpayers, had specified in 1866 that all departments of the university should be open to women, and individual members of the faculty continued to admit women to their classes at their own discretion; but some could not find room for them. When six women had completed the requirements for the bachelor's degree in 1869 the degree was granted. President Chadbourne at first protested that he would never "be guilty of the absurdity of calling young women bachelors," but he capitulated when someone pointed out that Webster's dictionary defined "bachelor" as (among other things) "a young unmarried woman." And the extra time and cost of repeating courses for women students led Chadbourne's successor, an outspoken champion of coeducation, to the abolition of the coordinate college and complete coeducation in 1871.[22]

This was about the extent of degree-granting institutions to which women might go until after the Civil War; but there were increasing opportunities for some college work in two and three year courses offered by some of the seminaries and by the public normal schools that began to appear in the second quarter of the century. And after the Civil War the state universities opened up rapidly.

In 1870 eight state universities were accepting women, although not without reservations. At Michigan, for example, a "female department" had been provided for in the original university charter in 1837, but the regents had failed to appropriate money for it. Continuing demands for the admission of women were successful only in 1870 after President Tappan, who was unalterably opposed to coeducation, had resigned; and after the women had raised $100,000 for the purpose. The University of Missouri also opened its doors, at least part way, to women in 1870. President Read appeared to favor the "experiment" but he had misgivings. Women were first admitted only to the normal department, but, quoting President Read: "Finding . . . that the young women at 'the Normal' did no manner of harm, we very cautiously admitted them to some of the recitations and lectures in the University building itself, providing always they were to be marched in good order, with at least two teachers, one in front and the other in the rear of the column as guards."[23] When this caused no great stir they were admitted to chapel, and were finally permitted to "lift their voices in prayer" with the men. Thus, gradually, and without any unfortunate consequences, they were granted all the privileges of the university. The eight state universities open to women in 1870 were, in the order of accepting women: Iowa, Wisconsin, Kansas, Indiana, Minnesota, Missouri, Michigan, and California. Utah did not reestablish a degree-granting institution until later. Iowa, Kansas, and Minnesota alone admitted women in the first year of instruction.

There is still some dispute over "firsts" but it is hardly necessary to quibble over this today. The important point is that women were getting at least the beginnings of a college education in the years just prior to the Civil War. The reasons for this development are many, but the growth of the public school system, as already indicated, was probably the most important single factor. Public schools, including many that offered secondary education, were multiplying. Most of the public schools were not yet free, but they were subsidized from public funds so that the cost was not excessive. Thus some girls whose parents could not afford to send them to the private academies were able to obtain an education that prepared them for college even though they might not have this end in view. More than this, the spread of education at the lower levels created a demand for teachers that the men failed to meet. Women had always taught in the dame schools. It was not too great a step from these to the public elementary schools. And women were cheaper. A "female teacher" could be had in Pennsylvania in 1835 for $9 a month.[24] No male teacher could be found at that price. The salaries of the men teachers were quite commonly from two to four times those paid to women.

Women teachers were also better than men, on the whole. It is not necessary to agree with Francis Wayland, president of Brown University, who wrote in 1854 that "women have a much greater natural adaptation to the work of instruction than men."[25] It seems more probable that the limited opportunities open to women for paid employment brought larger numbers of able women than able men into teaching. But whatever the reason, all the evidence points to Wayland's conclusion that "much of the improvement in education in New England is . . . to be ascribed to the employment of women, in place of men, in a large number of our schools." The employment of women teachers in the public school system began early in the nineteenth century. The scarcity of men during the Civil War further stimulated the trend; and by 1870 three out of five teachers in this country were women.

Those who still believed that education was for men were faced with a real dilemma. One of the principal reasons urged for the spread of the public school system was that a democracy can function successfully only with an educated electorate. At that time there was even less support for giving women the vote than for admitting them to college; but it was becoming increasingly apparent that the only way to get even a minimum universal education for male voters was to employ women teachers; and since the teachers must know at least as much as their pupils, and preferably more, it was necessary to concede that a very substantial number of the female population must be educated too.

The need for an educated clergy had been the principal impetus responsible for the early founding of Harvard College and the multiplication of denominational colleges in the ensuing years. As noted earlier, the students often had other ends in view. But the other ends were usually other professions—medicine, the law, and statesmanship. And when women began to press for admission to institutions of higher learning they too were motivated by professional aims.

For them the profession was teaching.

In emphasizing the importance of the opening of the teaching profession to women as a stimulus to higher education, other factors should not be overlooked. Women had begun to read. Papashvily, in *All the Happy Endings*, notes that sixty-four ladies' magazines began publication between 1830 and 1850.[26] *Godey's Lady's Book* claimed a circulation of 150,000 at its peak just before the Civil War. And while it was perhaps best known for its fashion plates, it was largely taken up with fiction, poetry, and serious discussions, including Mrs. Hale's pleas for better education of women and her careful recording of progress in this area.

Papashvily also records 1150 works of fiction published by native authors between 1830 and 1850—more than five times as many as had appeared in the years preceding.[27] Not all of these were written by women, but most of the best sellers of the nineteenth century were novels written by women, and largely for women. A college education was not essential in order to appreciate them, or even to write them. On the contrary, a check of the educational background of some thirty-five authors that Papashvily cites reveals the fact that none of them except Kathleen Norris had any college education. She attended the University of California "for a few months," and did not actually begin to publish until after the turn of the century.

This was not great literature; but it was a step ahead. It was something new for large numbers of women to be able to read and to have enough leisure for it—leisure they were beginning to enjoy, thanks to industrial progress. Spinning and weaving were no longer household tasks. And the invention of such labor-saving devices as the cook stove, the sewing machine, and even the match, were freeing women from much household drudgery. Moreover, gas light and improved oil lamps were making it possible to use the evening hours for reading. And so the housewife read; and the mill girls of Lowell were noted for their literary clubs. New vistas were opening up. Intellectual curiosity was aroused. And knowledge for its own sake was frequently the only aim of women seeking admission to college.

Another factor which promoted the cause of women's education was the growing number of women working outside of the home. Harriet Martineau, writing of the position of women in America as she observed it in her travels in the 1830's, said that she had found only seven occupations open to women.[28] Actually there were more, but the range of possibilities was small. Mrs. Hale, when faced with the necessity of supporting her family after the death of her husband, attempted millinery. Failing at this she took up writing. Her novel, *Northwood,* was only moderately successful, but her achievements as editor of the *Ladies' Magazine* and then of *Godey's Lady's Book* brought her fame. This was before the Civil War.

The Civil War opened many new opportunities to women. With large numbers of men in the armies, women took over work hitherto regarded as wholly unsuitable for the weaker sex, and many not only demonstrated their competence, but failed to return to the home when the war was over. The 1870 census of occupations listed at least one woman in every one of the 338 occupations in its classification, and the nearly two million women found in paid occupations accounted for one woman in eight of those over ten years of age. However, the effect of the Civil War must not be overrated. The occupations in which women were freely accepted were still few. Seven occupations— domestic service, agricultural laborers, seamstresses, milliners, teachers, textile mill workers, and laundresses, listed in order of the number of workers, accounted for 93 per cent of all women workers. The first two accounted for nearly half. And of these seven occupations, only teaching required any considerable education. The second profession for women was nursing, but this accounted for only .5 per cent of women workers.

Nevertheless, precedents were being established. Women physicians totaled 525. Elizabeth Blackwell, the first woman to be admitted to a medical school in this country, had graduated from Geneva University in 1849. There were 67 women among the clergy. Antoinette Brown graduated from Oberlin Theological School in 1850 and was ordained in 1853. Women lawyers were only five. Arabella Mansfield was the first woman to be admitted to the bar, in 1869.

Another factor favorable to the spread of higher education for women was the movement for equal political and legal rights. In the long debate over slavery it was inevitable that some should compare the position of women with the position of the slaves. Early in the debate, women delegates to the World's Antislavery Convention in London, in 1840, were outraged to find themselves excluded from the discussion. Were these human rights that were under consideration, or only rights of the male sex? The women's rights movement was well launched before the Civil War, thanks to such able and active advocates as Susan B. Anthony, Elizabeth Cady Stanton, and Lucretia Mott.

While the struggle for equal political and legal rights and the struggle for equal education supplemented each other, the early advocates of women's education were not wholehearted supporters of the suffrage movement. Many of them believed that once education was achieved the other problems would take care of themselves. And they feared that advocacy of other rights would retard the advance of women's education. Some, including Almira Phelps, even opposed woman suffrage. This doubt on the part of many of the leaders in women's education persisted until the equal suffrage movement ended in victory. When Elizabeth Cady Stanton's daughters were attending Vassar in the 1870's she was never invited to address the students. And thirty years later, Inez Milholland was refused permission to hold a suffrage meeting on the Vassar campus. The participation of Professors Salmon and Whitney in such a meeting in Poughkeepsie even later obviously embarrassed the trustees. And when I, as a brash young instructor, chaperoned some Vassar students to a suffrage rally the night before the New York voters approved the suffrage amendment in 1917, I was reproved by the head of my hall, herself a classmate of Harriot Stanton Blatch. Women's education was still on trial and must not be confused with other doubtful causes.[29]

The extent to which women took advantage of the early opportunities for higher education is revealed by the enrollment figures.

By 1870, when the United States Commissioner of Education first published fairly comprehensive statistics, the official estimate of women students in institutions of higher learning is some 11,000, or approximately one woman for every four men.[30] The proportion of A.B. degrees going to women was smaller—only one in seven. Even this is more than might be expected in view of the fact that the number of degree-granting institutions open to women was still very small, and to the further fact that degrees were not at that time necessary to secure a teaching position. On the contrary, a single year of normal school training gave an applicant high priority.

The incompleteness of the records makes an accurate breakdown of the figures impossible, but using the data found in the earliest published reports of the United States Commissioner of Education, a rough estimate of the number of women in different kinds of institutions is possible. The majority were in institutions that did not grant the bachelor's degree—something like 5000 in normal schools, and about 3000 in private seminaries and academies offering some work beyond the secondary school level. These, and also the four-year colleges, commonly had students below the college level, but such students have been excluded in making these estimates. This leaves something like 3000 women students attending the collegiate departments of institutions that were offering an A.B. degree. The great majority of these, approximately 2200, were attending women's colleges. While private coeducational colleges had given women their first opportunity, and about forty such institutions were open to women in 1870, the actual number of women students in their collegiate departments was small, apparently not over 600 in all. The number of women in the eight state universities open to them in 1870 was only about 200.

The greatest growth in women's education at college levels prior to 1870 had been in institutions for women. Excluding the normal schools —and many of these, too, were exclusively for women—only about one woman in six was in a coeducational institution. Coeducation was almost unknown in the east, although Swarthmore admitted women when it opened in 1870, and Cornell opened its doors to women two years later.

There were between thirty and forty women's colleges offering degrees, but the majority had less than fifty students in the collegiate department. Nine appear to have had between one and two hundred students each, and one—Vassar College—had more than two hundred, or more than the eight state universities combined. Vassar was the largest of the early women's colleges. It is true that a large proportion of her students in the first years were special students or in the preparatory department, but the Commissioner of Education reports 125 students taking regular or special college courses. Even the men's colleges were rarely as large as this. Before the Civil War reduced their enrollment only Harvard, the University of Virginia, the University of North Carolina, Yale, Princeton, Dartmouth, and the University of Michigan appear to have had more students than Vassar's Main Building was designed to accommodate.

The early women's colleges were plagued by many problems. Such is the fate of innovators. Some of their worries now seem trivial. One of these was the appropriateness of the word "freshman" for the female sex. Elmira avoided it by using the term "protomathian." Ingham University and Rutgers Female College adopted "novian." Vassar referred simply to the "first year students" in its earliest catalogues, and then boldly used the word "freshman" in the third issue. President Raymond, meanwhile, had argued with his trustees that the questionable word "man" is accepted, after all, in "human" and even "woman."[31]

The use of the word "female" in the names of women's institutions was standard until Sarah Hale took up the cause in *Godey's Lady's Book* and in private correspondence. In a letter to Matthew Vassar she asked: "What female do you mean? Not a female donkey? . . . Why degrade the feminine sex to the level of animals?" Mr. Vassar was impressed. When corresponding with her he carefully crossed out the offending word on his letter head, and it was officially removed from the name of the college in 1867.[32]

But there were more serious problems. The women's colleges were faced with the problems that confronted most of the colleges of the period. And for these new and unproved institutions the problems appeared in more acute form. The most serious of these were the inadequacy of the preparatory education and the inadequacy of college financing.

The inadequacy of the preparation was due both to the lack of well-defined standards of admission and the low level of many of the schools. Students often came long distances, sometimes without previous correspondence, and it was hard to turn them away. They frequently arrived in the middle of a term. Even when they came from nearby places it was often useless to return them to schools whose inadequate educational resources they had already exhausted. The colleges were forced to fill the gap by providing preparatory education. Only a few of the older institutions in well-settled areas could afford to devote themselves exclusively to collegiate education. Of the 140 institutions reporting the distribution of their students in different departments to the Commissioner of Education in 1870, 114 were operating preparatory departments.

The women's colleges, therefore, were in no way exceptional in establishing preparatory departments. But they were more often overshadowed by these appendages than the men's colleges, since they were able to recruit even fewer adequately prepared students. Of the 242 students enrolled in Elmira in its first year, only 37 were of college grade.[33] It took Vassar three weeks of testing, after it opened, to classify the students that appeared on its doorstep; and President Raymond reported to the trustees at the end of the year that 136 were eventually classified as of collegiate grade, including 66 "conditional" freshmen. He added: "The consequence of the liberal principle of admission which it seemed expedient to adopt last fall was . . . every grade of educational advancement from that of a respectable college Junior down to a point lower than I have any convenient way of indicating or should take pride in mentioning."[34] Wellesley, starting ten years later, found only 30 of its 314 students of college grade in its first year.³⁵ And Smith, which had the distinction of opening without a preparatory department, and which from the beginning adopted the same requirements as the best men's colleges, *including Greek*, had only 14 students in its initial year, 1875, to the great disappointment of local residents who had hoped for a prompt return on their investment in this new enterprise.³⁶ Vassar had two hundred students with collegiate status by 1875, and had been able to raise its entrance requirements to be "in line with Harvard, Yale, and Princeton," although still with the exception of Greek.³⁷

President Raymond made it clear to the trustees at this time that even with these gains he regarded the preparatory department as a detriment to the success of the college. But it was not until 1888 that Vassar was able to abandon it. Wellesley transferred her preparatory department to another location and made it independent of the college in 1880.

The difficulties of combining the two levels of study in a small residence institution were very great. They were particularly serious for the women's colleges because of the close supervision of the students that was believed to be necessary at that time. The existence of the lower school not only led outsiders to question the quality of the course; it also resulted in regulations which were an annoyance to mature students and a hindrance to serious study. In a period when the higher education of women was on trial it was particularly important, both for the morale of the students and for public relations, to avoid a boarding school atmosphere. Some of the women's colleges succumbed, reverting to junior college status or even abandoning all pretensions of college work, if they did not close down completely. The better women's colleges, however, gave up their preparatory departments earlier than the majority of other colleges. The number of preparatory students in all colleges, as reported by the Commissioner of Education in 1890, was almost as great as the number of college students. But in the fourteen "Division A" women's colleges, the college students outnumbered the preparatory and academic students by more than two to one. Seven of these fourteen colleges had no preparatory students at all.

The financial problem haunted all the colleges. Even the better and older men's colleges were inadequately financed. Many of the new colleges failed completely. More colleges were founded than the number of available students could support, just prior to the Civil War. This was due in part to the competition of the churches, and to a lesser extent to the competition of communities. The different denominations were concerned both with the quality of their clergy and the number of their members. The communities regarded a college in their midst as something of a distinction, and perhaps an economic asset, and many founders took advantage of this attitude to shop around and find the highest bidder. Elmira College considered offers from two other communities before settling in Elmira. And Sophia Smith made it a condition of locating Smith College in Northampton that the town should contribute $25,000. Such negotiations were by no means exceptional. Some colleges moved after they had been established because of financial inducements.

Even so, neither the churches nor the communities were prepared to provide adequate funds to make the new colleges going concerns. When the University of Vermont opened in 1799 it consisted of the president and a single student of college grade. President Sanders writes that "there were so few to attend at first it was little more than a common school, where even females were permitted to attend."[38] To teach girls was the final humiliation! In the period between 1790 and 1860 over five hundred colleges were established; but four out of five came to an untimely end. Under these conditions the preparatory departments served a double purpose. They not only prepared the students adequately. They also employed excess capacity and made survival possible.

Then, as now, there was less support for the women's colleges than for the men's. Mary Sharp College was named for a donor in return for a gift of $5,000. The founders had originally offered to name the college for the first donor who would give $10,000, but settled for the smaller sum and were rewarded later by some further contributions from the same source.[39] But this college never succeeded in mustering enough resources to maintain its position and closed in 1896. Elmira started with assets totalling $60,000, two-thirds of which had been borrowed.

In view of sums like these it is no wonder that Matthew Vassar's initial gift of nearly $400,000, with substantial later additions, caught the public interest. This was not only larger than any previous gift for women's education; it was larger than Sophia Smith's gift to Smith College some years later. Henry Durant's gifts to Wellesley in the 1870's are estimated at about one million dollars, and Vassar's assets in 1875 had increased to approximately the same figure.

Yet Vassar's large initial endowment proved inadequate even before it opened. The Civil War increased building costs to the point where practically the entire sum was spent for buildings and equipment. The equipment was exceptional for the period, but there was almost nothing left for operating expenses. Matthew Vassar himself assumed that the students should be charged enough to cover the operating costs for their education. Unlike many of the founders of the period, he was not committed to educating the poor. "It is not my purpose," he advised the trustees at their first meeting, "to make Vassar Female College a charity school."[40]

President Raymond, however, had real misgivings about the financial arrangements. In fact, he at first refused the invitation to become president, giving as one reason, in his letter to Vassar, that he "heartily regretted . . . that the munificent sum consecrated . . . to this sacred cause should, to so large an extent, have been absorbed in mere material provisions, compelling us to begin the ungracious work of retrenchment and enforced economy just as we reach the vital part . . . compelling us after the old fashion *to pinch the College at its heart.*"[41] President Raymond was persuaded to reconsider, but the shortage of funds was what made it necessary to fill the great Main Building from the beginning and was largely responsible, in consequence, for the struggle to maintain standards in the early years. There simply were not that many young ladies with the necessary preparation, the ambition, the willingness to flout public opinion, and the broad-minded parents who were able and willing to meet the costs.

Colleges continued to be established in excess of demand. Elmira's enrollment dropped from 242 in the first year to 134 in 1866, and "the increased competition of the widely publicized Vassar College" was given as the reason.[42] Vassar, in turn, suffered a decline in the number of its collegiate students in the late 1870's, making it necessary to take more, rather than fewer, students in the preparatory department. The decline was attributed to the opening of Smith and Wellesley in 1875; but the opening of the universities to women was also having its effect. Michigan admitted women in 1870, and Cornell in 1872. The first woman to apply at Cornell was a Vassar student, Emma Eastman, who had just completed her sophomore year at Vassar.[43] It is also worth noting that M. Carey Thomas chose Cornell, rather than Vassar, because "Vassar College could give her little more serious training than was obtainable at a young ladies' seminary."[44] And Harriot Stanton Blatch wanted to go to Cornell because of the "University's excellent departments in history and economics." At the time no courses were offered at Vassar in these subjects. She went to Vassar because of the preference of the aunt who was paying for her education; and President Raymond, discovering her interests, arranged a course of readings in economics and politics for her.[45]

The fact that the problems of deficient educational preparation of entering students and slender college incomes were greater for the women's colleges than for the men's was due primarily to the prejudices against higher education for women. It is important to consider these in some detail before tracing further the growing opportunities for women to get a college education, since the long and heated debate not only held the movement back, but had much to do with the direction that it took. The proponents had to prove that the critics were wrong before they could do what seemed to them perhaps most desirable.

First and foremost, of course, it was contended that women were mentally inferior to men and would be quite unable to meet the standards set for the men's higher education. This point of view was simply stated in an article in the *Saturday Review* in 1860: "The great argument against the existence of this equality of intellect in women is, that it does not exist. If that does not satisfy a female philosopher, we have no better to give."[46] Even some of those advocating higher education of women were ready to concede that women might not be of equal intellectual ability and should, in consequence, be educated in their own institutions.

This conviction has been modified as the result of experience, but it is not completely dead. A university professor of my acquaintance once told a friend of mine that she should not take his courses because the subject was beyond the comprehension of the female mind. When this did not deter her, and she proved to be the best student in his classes, he was able to recognize and acknowledge the quality of her work, but his conviction remained unshaken. He explained her achievement by the fact that she had a "man's brain." He is still of this opinion. And the *Congressional Record* for September 20, 1945, reports Representative Knutson as saying of Representative Claire Booth Luce: "I am in full accord with what the gentlewoman from Connecticut is saying. I want to pay her the compliment of saying that she has a masculine mind.[47]

The proponents of women's education argued first that women should at least be allowed to try. But they were met with the objection that to admit women to classes with men would only pull down the standards and impair the quality of the men's education. President Tappan of Michigan, for example, was convinced that the admission of women would be the end of progress at his university. This debate not only resulted in separate women's colleges, but was partly responsible for the fact that the women's colleges tended to set standards for admission and graduation which were the same as those prevailing in the men's colleges. They tended to duplicate the men's curriculums. In the coordinate colleges, in addition to being instructed by the same professors, they insisted on taking the same examinations. They had to prove that women could do exactly what the men were doing.

For those who take scientific evidence seriously the findings of the psychologists have considerably narrowed the field of debate. Some of the tests indicate that men and women have somewhat different aptitudes, on the average, in different fields. But while there is not complete agreement as to the significance of such differences as the tests indicate, there does appear to be complete agreement that variations among the members of each sex are so great that any measurable difference in the average performance between the sexes is of negligible importance. In other words, any differences in mental capacities that may exist are not in themselves reasons for differentiating the education of the two sexes. This was suspected by some acute observers long before the tests were made. When Samuel Johnson was asked, "Which is more intelligent, man or woman?" he replied, "Which man and which woman?"[48]

The actual performance of the women who have attended college over one hundred years has answered this question for most doubters. Women continue to go to college and to graduate. An Oxford professor once objected to the admission of women to Oxford degrees because of the "fatal facility of women in passing examinations."[49] Woody cites studies that have shown that women get more than their proportionate share of doctorates *cum laude* and more than their proportionate share of elections to Phi Beta Kappa.[50] Some Phi Beta Kappa chapters have been known to ration the number of women elected in order to make this honor acceptable to men. And in the University of Michigan in 1956-1957, 45 per cent of the academic honors conferred went to women, although they constituted only 32 per cent of the enrollment.[51]

This type of evidence does not, of course, prove that women are abler than men. But whether the better record is due to passive acceptance of "what the professor says" or—more probably, in my judgment—to the fact that being a smaller group they are more highly selected, it does offer some evidence that substantial numbers of women are able to profit by a college education.

A second argument that was advanced against college study for women was that they could not stand the physical strain of higher learning. Women were thought to be frail—and often were, in the days of wasp waists and no exercise. Overstudy would surely give them brain fever! And should they manage to survive college, their children would be sickly, if they were able to have children at all.

The women's colleges endeavored to protect themselves from such charges by introducing hygiene, physiology, and physical education into their curriculums to a greater extent than had the men's colleges. Vassar, for instance, required physiology and hygiene in the freshman year. No such courses appear in the curriculums of Yale, Harvard, or Columbia at this time, although Harvard and Yale, as well as Vassar, offered physiology and anatomy in the senior year. Columbia offered neither at any point in its curriculum.[52] Harvard offered a course in physiology and hygiene a little later, in 1879, but it was not required and was dropped after three years.

One of Vassar's three original buildings was a gymnasium containing rooms for a riding school, calisthenics, and a bowling alley. The Main Building was provided with spacious corridors with windows overlooking the campus (at the expense of a tier of inside bedrooms in the center of the building) to provide "room for exercise in inclement weather."[53] And walks and drives "full three miles in extent" were laid out on the campus to tempt the students outdoors when the weather favored.[54] Even today the students are required to take physical education courses in their first two years, and they must pass a swimming test before graduation. The outdoor swimming pool that Matthew Vassar planned was never provided, but an indoor pool was incorporated in the second gymnasium, built in 1889. Harvard and Yale had gymnasiums at the time that Vassar was opened, but no required physical education. And the original Harvard gymnasium was introduced to give the young men opportunity to work off excess energy, in the hope that this would reduce student pranks, rather than as a health measure.[55] Yale had made some provision for physical exercise and medical examinations, but required neither.

The University of Wisconsin provided medical care for women ten years before it was provided for men.[56] The women's college doctors, who were likely to be determined pioneers of the women's medical profession, enforced physical examinations and a variety of health measures beyond those practiced in most of the students' homes. In consequence, it was possible to demonstrate, after there were enough guinea pigs, that the college graduates were healthier than noncollege women of that time.

The early evidence that women survived very nicely did not deter Dr. E. H. Clarke, a prominent Boston physician, from writing a small book in 1873, to prove that while women might be exposed to some higher education without serious harm, it must be administered in small doses.[57] This pointed both toward separate women's colleges and toward lower academic requirments. Dr. Clarke's statistical evidence was limited to six cases that had come to his attention. One was not a college woman at all; three were from unnamed institutions; and two were from Vassar College. The facts with regard to the Vassar students were quite inaccurate, as the Vassar authorities were quick to point out. Even had all six cases been valid, however, they would hardly have proved his point. But the book confirmed prejudices; and the obvious fact that the great majority of women students enjoyed better than average health had to be bolstered up with special studies.

The Association of Collegiate Alumnae accepted this challenge and gathered data from their members which were submitted to Carroll Wright, the able State Labor Commissioner of Massachusetts at that time. He concluded that "The facts which we have presented would seem to warrant the assertion . . . that the seeking of a college education on the part of women does not in itself necessarily entail a loss of health or serious impairment of the vital forces. Indeed, the tables show this so conclusively that there is little need, were it within our province, for extended discussion of the subject.[58] It should be added that the proportions of those who considered their health good were 78 per cent for the college women and 50 per cent for the noncollege women. This was published in 1885. A still later study found that proportionately more Amherst students than college women dropped out of college for reasons of health.[59] And an editorial in the *Medical News* for December 14, 1889, finds "nothing in thorough training, properly conducted, that is of itself adverse to the highest physical well-being of either sex."[60]

The fact that the college graduates turned out to be healthier than other women may have been due to the selective factor. Only the comparatively well-to-do and well-educated parents were sending their daughters to college. But the regimen of exercise and other health measures enforced by the women physicians of the colleges, in addition to courses in physiology and hygiene, may well have made some contribution to the outcome.

Proving that college did not undermine the women's health was not too difficult; and if it put additional emphasis on the study of biological sciences, this can hardly be regarded as a shortcoming of women's education. The argument that education would reduce the number of marriages and the size of families was not as easily answered. President Jordan of Stanford University, who favored the education of women, argued that there was not the slightest evidence that it unfitted them for marriage and children. And if it delayed marriage, what of it? They would take better care of their children, and mere numbers were not important.[61] He also commented: "There is no occasion for such warmth. What you and I may think about it is of no consequence. If the college woman is a mistake, nature will eliminate her."[62] He believed in the survival of the fittest; but few on either side could view the subject with this degree of detachment.

The statistics could be variously interpreted. Vassar College statistics, which cover a longer period of time than most records of college women, show a declining average number of children per Vassar graduate from the early years until the middle 1890's. From that point they show an increase, and in the early years of this century they approached the national average, which continued to decline for some years after the Vassar figures began to increase. However, at the end of the nineteenth century the average number of children per married

Vassar alumna was only 2.0, compared with 2.7 for the women of the country as a whole.[63]

To state the facts is not to explain them. Those who married young never got to college; nor did many of those whose only ambition was early marriage. More than this, the period during which college education of women was on trial was a period of late marriages and a declining birth rate—for the less educated as well as for college women. And the birth rate was lowest for the upper classes from which the students mostly came. It could be proved that college women had almost as many children as college men; that if the birth rate was low for college women, the infant death rate was also low; that their sisters and cousins who did not go to college had very few more children than they. Some of the studies showed an appreciable difference; others did not. Nevertheless, it could not be proved that the birth rate was going anywhere but down; or that it was as high for college women as for all women of their age group; or that it was high enough to replace their group. But this has ceased to be a matter of concern. Today the college students marry so young and have so many children so fast that the problem is how to get them educated first.

Thus all three of the most persistent arguments against higher education of women have been settled by events. There were, however, other objections that should at least be mentioned. Some concerned only coeducation—namely that women in classes would distract the men; that the male students would not like having women around; that the founders had intended the colleges in question for men only; that there was not enough money for both; that, women being thought to be mentally inferior, their admission would lower the esteem in which the institution was held even though they might not be inferior in fact. There were the fears that education would destroy religious beliefs, even though the colleges were largely church controlled; that college women would make inferior housekeepers. All these, and many more. Most of the opposition was less concerned with whether education was good for women than whether educated women were acceptable to men. Much of the debate is being repeated today, in a somewhat different context, in the efforts to abolish segregated schools for white and Negro students.

The principal argument *for* higher education of women was a matter of human rights. But the social good was also strongly emphasized, as it was by those arguing for universal education of men. This was an old debate. Plato had argued that if women are to have the same duties as men, they must have the same education.[64] Aristotle criticized the Spartans for neglecting the women in their educational system—half of the city would be unaffected.[65] Daniel DeFoe wrote:

I have often thought of it as one of the most barbarous customs in the world, considering us a civilized and a Christian country, that we deny the advantages of learning to women. We reproach the sex every day for their folly and impertinence, while I am confident, had they the advantages of education equal to us, they would be guilty of less than ourselves.[66]

And a pamphlet on Queens College, the first women's college in England, established in London in 1849, says: "educate women and you educate the teachers of men."[67] Charles McIver put it a little differently: "Educate a man and you have educated one person; educate a mother and you have educated the whole family."[68] It was probably this argument that was the most persuasive. Women were needed as teachers, whether at home or in the schools.

NOTES

[1] S. E. Morison, *The Founding of Harvard College* (Cambridge, 1935), p. 247.
[2] G. P. Schmidt, *The Liberal Arts College* (New Brunswick, 1957), pp. 24-25.
[3] *Ibid.*, p. 268.
[4] W. H. Small, *Early New England Schools* (Boston, 1914), p. 162.
[5] H. S. Blatch and A. Lutz, *Challenging Years* (New York, 1940), p. 10.
[6] T. Woody, *A History of Women's Education in the United States* (New York, 1929), vol. 1, pp. 142-143.
[7] *Ibid.*, pp. 144-145.
[8] *Ibid.*, pp. 145-146.
[9] B. Rush, "Of the Mode of Education Proper in a Republic" (Philadelphia, 1786).
[10] Woody, *op. cit.*, vol. 1, pp. 392-395.
[11] *Ibid.*, pp. 519-520.
[12] S. Stow, *History of Mount Holyoke Seminary* (Springfield, 1887), p. 318.

[13] A. C. Cole, *A Hundred Years of Mount Holyoke College* (New Haven, 1940), p. 181.

[14] A. Lutz, *Emma Willard, Daughter of Democracy* (Boston, 1929), p. 60.

[15] Illinois Conference Female College is now McMurray College, a coeducational institution in Jacksonville. Oxford Female College, Oxford, Ohio, closed in the late 1920's; Ingham University, Leroy, New York, closed in the latter part of the nineteenth century.

[16] Georgia Female College is now Wesleyan College at Macon. Mary Sharp College closed late in the nineteenth century.

[17] Georgia Female College is listed, for instance, in the American Council on Education, *American Universities and Colleges* (1952, p. 17), as the first women's college. It is not included by the United States Commissioner of Education, however, in the list of universities and colleges in his early reports. It is grouped instead with "institutions for the superior instruction of women."

[18] I. M. E. Blandin, *History of Higher Education of Women in the South Prior to 1860* (New York, 1909), pp. 77 ff.

[19] University of Utah, *Centennial Commemoration Proceedings* (Salt Lake City, 1950), p. 26.

[20] J. L. Pickard, "Historical Sketch of the University of Iowa," *Annals of Iowa*, (Iowa City, 1899), p. 31.

[21] M. Curti and V. Cardensen, *The University of Wisconsin, A History, 1848-1925* (Madison, 1949), vol. 1, pp. 116-117.

[22] *Ibid.*, pp. 371-372.

[23] D. Read, "Historical Sketch of the University of Missouri," *Historical Sketches of State Universities* (United States Bureau of Education, 1883), p. 41.

[24] *Annual Report of the University of the State of New York, 1919* (Albany, 1921), vol. 1, p. 60.

[25] Francis and H. L. Wayland, *A Memoir of the Life and Labors of Francis Wayland, D.D., LL.D.* (New York, 1868), vol. 1, p. 24.

[26] H. W. Papashvily, *All the Happy Endings* (New York, 1956), p. 40.

[27] *Ibid.*, p. 35.

[28] H. Martineau, *Society in America* (New York, 1837), vol. 2, 257.

[29] President MacCracken, it should be noted, had publicly declared himself for woman suffrage in 1915.

[30] United States Office of Education, "Faculty, Students, and Degrees," *Statistics of Higher Education*, 1953-54, p. 6.

[31] *Report of the President to the Trustees of Vassar College, 1866-67* (unpublished).

[32] R. E. Finley, *The Lady of Godey's: Sarah Josepha Hale* (Philadelphia, 1931), pp. 205-206.

[33] G. Meltzer, *The Beginnings of Elmira* (Elmira, 1941), p. 38.

[34] *Report of the President to the Trustees of Vassar College, 1865-66* (unpublished).

[35] F. Converse, *Wellesley College, A Chronicle* (Wellesley, 1939), p. 21.

[36] L. C. Seelye, *The Early History of Smith College, 1871-1910* (Boston, 1923), pp. 34-35.

[37] J. M. Taylor and H. E. Haight, *Vassar* (New York, 1915), Ch. 4.

[38] J. I. Lindsay, *Tradition Looks Forward* (Burlington, 1954), p. 50.

[39] Woody, *op. cit.*, vol. 2, pp. 141-142.

[40] M. Vassar, *Communications to the Board of Trustees of Vassar College* (New York, 1886), p. 7.

[41] H. R. Lloyd, ed., *Life and Letters of John Howard Raymond* (New York, 1881), p. 511.

[42] Meltzer, *op. cit.*, p. 106.

[43] W. T. Hewitt, *Cornell University: A History* (New York, 1905), vol. 1, p. 261.

[44] E. Finch, *Carey Thomas of Bryn Mawr* (New York, 1947), p. 53.

[45] Blatch and Lutz, *op. cit.*, pp. 36-39.

[46] Quoted in *Littell's Living Age*, January 1860, p. 184.

[47] P. 8871.

[48] Quoted in G. D. Stoddard, *On the Education of Women* (New York, 1950), pp. 94-95.

[49] M. C. Thomas, "Future of Women in Independent Study and Research," *Association of Collegiate Alumnae Publications*, February 1903, p. 13.

[50] Woody, *op. cit.*, vol. 2, pp. 158-159.

[51] University of Michigan, *President's Report*, 1956-57.

[52] M. MacLear, *History of the Education of Girls in New York and New England, 1800-1870* (Washington, 1926), pp. 84-86.

[53] B. J. Lossing, *Vassar College and Its Founder* (New York, 1867), p. 114.

[54] *Ibid.*, p. 167.

[55] S. E. Morison, *Three Centuries of Harvard, 1636-1936* (Cambridge, 1936), p. 207.

[56] Curti and Cardensen, *op. cit.*, vol. 1, p. 686.

[57] E. H. Clarke, *Sex in Education* (Boston, 1873).

[58] C. D. Wright, "Health Statistics of Female College Graduates," *Annual Report of the Massachusetts State Bureau of Statistics of Labor* (Boston, 1885), p. 77.

[59] G. Stanley Hall, *Adolescence* (New York, 1904), p. 584.

[60] Page 667.

[61] D. S. Jordan, "Question of Coeducation," *Munsey's Magazine*, v. 34 (March 1906).

[62] Quoted in M. S. Cheney, "Will Nature Eliminate the College Woman?" *Publications of Collegiate Alumnae Magazine*, January 1905.

[63] M. Newcomer and E. S. Gibson, "Vital Statistics from Vassar College," *American Journal of Sociology*, January 1924, p. 437.

[64] *Republic*, Bk. V.

[65] *Politics*, Bk. II, ch. 9.

[66] "An Academy for Women," *Essays on Projects*.

[67] C. G. N., "Queens College, London, for Female Education. Its Origin and Progress." *English Journal of Education*, 1849, p. 4.

[68] North Carolina educator, quoted in United States Commissioner of Education, *Report*, 1907, vol. 1, p. 336.

IT IS NOT ALTOGETHER IMPOSSIBLE THAT SOME OF THE OLD
LINE CLASSICAL WOMEN'S COLLEGES WILL HAVE TO MOVE
TOWARD COEDUCATION.

C. W. DE KIEWIET—PRESIDENT, ROCHESTER UNIVERSITY*

3. Women's Colleges
vs. Coeducation

ALL THE TIME that the debate concerning higher education for women was raging, the women were going to college in increasing numbers. The battle for admission to secondary schools had been won. In 1870, when the statistics begin, only 2 per cent of all seventeen-year-olds were graduating from secondary schools; but even at that early date the number of girls exceeded the number of boys. And since many of these schools were preparing their students for college, a good many girls were meeting the requirements for admission. However, the private schools for girls, unlike those for boys, were rarely giving their students adequate college preparation. And when public high schools segregated boys and girls, the girl's schools were likely to be inferior. A Goucher student notes that before 1888 only Negro girls in Baltimore could have passed college entrance examinations, since only the Negro high schools were coeducational.[1]

The number of universities and colleges open to women increased rapidly in the years following the Civil War. New women's colleges were founded, and in the Middle West, coeducation became the rule rather than the exception. If too many colleges were being founded,

* In the *New York Times*, April 30, 1952.

at least this worked in favor of the women—it was sometimes necessary to tolerate them in order to make ends meet. But there were other factors working toward this end. Industrialization was gradually releasing women from domestic duties. At the same time the growth of the public school systems was creating a demand for teachers. And teaching was one of the few occupations open to women that was acceptable by middle class standards. It is true that a college degree was not regarded as essential for a teacher, even in the late nineteenth century. But teaching did require a level of education far above that offered to women earlier; and those who achieved it were apt to find that they had achieved the admissions requirements for higher education at the same time. Many women wanted to go to the top, and did so. Also, the Morrill Act of 1862 stimulated the growth of state universities, and as these developed the taxpayers demanded admittance of their daughters as well as their sons. The women themselves were organizing. When they were told that a particular institution could not afford to take in women they raised the money and bought their way in. Finally, the emphasis of the Civil War on the rights of Negroes had raised the question of the rights of women in many minds. The arguments appeared to be much the same.

The trend in the proportion of institutions open to women is shown in Table 1. These figures include all institutions of higher education listed by the United States Office of Education. The figures from decade to decade are not entirely comparable because of changes in classification, but there is no question with regard to the trend.

Fourteen of the private, independent, four-year colleges for women, other than the Roman Catholic colleges, that were in existence in 1930 were founded prior to 1860. Most of these began as seminaries rather than four-year colleges, but they presumably offered some work beyond the secondary school level.[2] Fifteen more were founded in the next twenty years—1861 to 1880—and 27 opened in the last twenty years of the century. This represented the peak. In the twentieth century, 20 were founded between 1900 and 1920, and five between 1920 and 1930. None has been founded since 1930, although Benning-

Table 1.

COLLEGES OPEN TO MEN AND WOMEN, RESPECTIVELY
1870–1957[a]

Year	Number of Institutions	Percentage Distribution			
		Total	Men Only	Women Only	Coeducational
1870	582	100	59	12	29
1890	1082	100	37	20	43
1910	1083	100	27	15	58
1930	1322	100	15	16	69
1957[b]	1326	100	13	13	74

[a] These data are from the *Statistical Reports of the United States Office of Education*. They include all institutions of higher education and are not limited to the four-year degree-granting universities and colleges, except in 1957. The decline in men's institutions is partly due to the fact that professional schools, such as those for law and medicine, have in many instances become attached to coeducational institutions and are no longer included among independent institutions although in a few instances they continue to exclude women. Approximately half of the women's institutions in the latest year are Catholic colleges. The men's institutions are largely Catholic colleges or technical institutes.

[b] Four-year degree-granting institutions.

ton, chartered in 1925, did not open until 1932, and Sarah Lawrence and Finch, formerly junior colleges, introduced four-year courses in 1931 and 1952, respectively.

The Catholic women's colleges came much later. The founding of new colleges in this group reached its peak in the twenty-year period from 1921 to 1940. In that period new institutions averaged about two a year, but in the past ten years only one such new institution has been noted. At the present time the Catholic women's colleges account for approximately half of the women's institutions.

The number of private, independent, four-year liberal arts colleges for women, other than the Roman Catholic institutions, has declined since 1930. In that year there were 78 such colleges in operation.

Three, Bennington, Sarah Lawrence, and Finch, have been added to the number since. Meanwhile, however, 21 of the former women's colleges have converted to coeducational or coordinate colleges, two have reverted to junior college status, and five have closed. This leaves only 53 women's colleges of this class, and at least one-fourth of these are admitting local men students to their classes in considerable numbers. Several are granting degrees to men.

The men's colleges of this class (i.e., four-year, independent, non-Catholic, liberal arts institutions) show a similar trend. Sixteen of the 44 in existence in 1930 have shifted to coeducational institutions, and only one, Claremont Men's College, has been added. The change to coeducation is not, like the earlier trend in this direction, due primarily to the fact that very few institutions were open to women. Most of the men's colleges opening to women since 1930 made this change in the depression years. In many cases their enrollments declined sharply at this time. And local women who could not afford to go away from home to college were eager to attend the college at their doorstep. A few of the women's colleges shifted to coeducation in these years for the same reasons. During World War II some of the men's colleges opened their doors to women when they again experienced a decline in enrollment. And after the war the women's colleges opened to the great flood of veterans who were having difficulty in gaining admission to men's or coeducational institutions. Some of these colleges shifted permanently to a coeducational basis, and this trend continued after the greatest need had passed. In fact, half of the women's colleges that have admitted men in the past quarter of a century have done so since 1950.

The principal reason given by both men's and women's institutions for making the change is declining enrollment. A second important consideration has been pressure from local residents of the excluded sex who cannot afford to go away from home for their college course. A third reason, mentioned by the presidents of both former men's and women's colleges in a few instances, is that they wished to go on record as being opposed to "segregation."[3]

The public universities and colleges are almost entirely coeducational at the present time. Some of the public women's colleges suffered declining enrollment before they changed. But the pressure of local residents, who are both voters and taxpayers, for the admission of both sons and daughters has been a more important factor for this group than declining enrollment. Only the University of Virginia, among the state universities, has withstood the trend.[4] It has adopted Mary Washington College as a "coordinate" college instead. But while the latter is administered by the university, its location in Fredericksburg is too remote from Charlottesville to give it a status comparable to other coordinate colleges, all of which are located in close proximity to the parent institution. The public women's colleges have withstood the pressure better than the men's, but of the ten liberal arts institutions of this class in 1930 (excluding teachers colleges and normal schools) only six remain, and four of these have suffered a serious decline in enrollment. The teachers colleges, too, are rapidly being converted to coeducational institutions.

New liberal arts colleges, public and private, which have appeared at the rate of about one a year over the past twenty-five years, have all been coeducational with the single exception of Claremont Men's College, a coordinate institution. Even among the Catholic colleges a trend toward coeducation is perceptible.[5]

There appear to be two basic reasons for the shift to coeducational institutions. The first is the increasing insistence of students on attending the institution within reach of home. This is primarily a financial matter, and its growing importance seems to result from the fact that with the increasing numbers of young people who go to college, a larger proportion is coming from the lower income groups. Another factor limiting students to institutions in a particular area is the growing tendency to marry before graduation from college. This, particularly for women, but also to some extent for men, limits the range of choice. The woman can complete her education only if she can attend her husband's college, or the only institution within reach of his job. And sometimes the husband is similarly restricted to the place where his wife can find employment.

The second reason, related to the earlier age of marriage, is a strong preference on the part of students for coeducation. This is particularly apparent for the women, but it seems to be operating also for the men. The remaining men's colleges do not show the decreases in enrollment apparent in many of the women's colleges, but this happens to be a period of very rapid growth in the number of men attending college. The number of women students is increasing much more slowly.

The coordinate colleges have been left for separate consideration.[6] The older coordinate colleges in this country were established as a compromise between those who favored admitting women to established men's colleges and those who were opposed. This was the reason for the short-lived Female College at the University of Wisconsin in the 1860's. They developed as a result of the demands of women for admittance to men's institutions. The women would have been satisfied with coeducation. In fact, they probably would have preferred it since the provisions made for women's instruction in the coordinate colleges in the early years were far more limited than those for men. This was an inevitable result of the separate college in view of the small number of women students in the first years and the very inadequate resources that women were able to muster. The first budget proposed for Barnard College, for example, was $7,500 for a year. They were unable to hold it to this figure, but financing was tenuous, at best, for many years.[7]

Some of the members of the faculties and administrations concerned favored coeducation. President Barnard of Columbia, for instance, urged coeducation in his report to the trustees on this subject in 1879. He believed it to be more economical than a separate institution, and he also stated that: "It is unjust to young women, when admitting their right to liberal education, to deny them access to the best."[8] He did not believe that the women's colleges were likely to provide the best, but in the end he accepted the only compromise that he could get.[9]

Precedent for the coordinate college was found in England, where coeducation did not exist. Queens College, London, established in 1848 and offering a real college education in 1853, followed Kings College in its curriculum and requirements, and was staffed by Kings College faculty.[10] Hitchin—now Girton—founded in 1869, depended on the faculty of Cambridge University. These were well established when Harvard first took some responsibility for the higher education of women. The Harvard project appears to have started in the late 1870's when Abby Leach, later a professor of Classics at Vassar College, persuaded three Harvard professors to tutor her in Greek, Latin, and English. The first formal arrangements were made in 1879. It was then agreed that Harvard would provide the faculty, and that whatever courses were offered would be the same as those offered at Harvard. But Harvard would not grant the degree or finance the project. Under this arrangement, 27 women enrolled in 1879. The Society for the Collegiate Instruction of Women was established in 1882 to formalize arrangements and obtain financial assistance. A few years later it obtained authority to grant degrees. Previously, students had only received a certificate. In 1894 it was incorporated as Radcliffe College. Harvard continued to supply the faculty but Radcliffe had its own trustees and administrative officers, and separate financing. Radcliffe granted its first A. M. degree in 1890, and its first Ph.D. in 1902.

The bargain that launched Barnard College was different. As noted above, President Barnard first raised the issue in 1879. A few women, including a trustee's daughter, had been permitted to visit classes earlier, but this was found to be contrary to college regulations, which the trustees refused to rescind.[11] In 1886 the trustees finally agreed that women could be given the Columbia degree if they could pass the examinations, but that no provision would be made for their instruction. Since it was difficult to pass examinations without instruction, it became necessary to set up a curriculum and faculty. It was agreed that the faculty might be members of the Columbia faculty or others approved by the president of Columbia. The original faculty members were, in fact, all from Columbia, and the result was thus not very different from Radcliffe. Barnard did have one advantage, however, in that from the first the students had access to most of the university libraries. Also, the university faculties soon began, one by one, to open their courses to Barnard seniors.

Among the early coordinate colleges, Newcomb and Pembroke had similar histories. Flora Mather was a little different, since it was created in order to permit Adelbert College—the undergraduate liberal arts college of Western Reserve—to limit its instruction to men. The decision was made by the administration, not the students, and was defended by President Haydn on the ground that while coeducation was inevitable under frontier conditions, the "demand for separate education is one of the later growths of civilization and the advance of wealth."[12] Jackson College at Tufts and the Women's College of Rochester University are further instances of previously coeducational colleges establishing coordinate institutions. In these instances the decision was made, after experimenting with coeducation, in the belief that separate colleges were better. But it appears to have been the men's decision, not the women's. Rochester has since returned to coeducation, and Jackson has no segregated classes.

The majority of coordinate colleges now in existence were launched by universities which had no provision at the time for undergraduate instruction of women. Three of the present coordinate colleges, however, started as independent women's colleges and joined with men's colleges in the same area to the extent of having the same course offerings, and teaching men and women in the same classes. And quite recently two women's colleges which had no men's institutions within easy reach have established new coordinate institutions for men. These are Rockford, beginning in 1955, and McMurray, beginning in 1957.

The present trend is in the direction of coeducation. The new coordinate colleges provide a certain amount of joint instruction for men and women where previously there was a men's or a women's college, or separate men's and women's colleges in the same neighborhood. Rochester returned to coeducation in 1952, giving as the reason that separate campuses and separate classes were too expensive both in money and the time of faculty and students. An increasing number of courses open to both men and women had made it necessary to transport students, as well as faculty, from one campus to the other, four miles distant. And in those colleges where separation is still maintained, at least in name, the degree of separation is diminishing in fact.

Harvard and Radcliffe abandoned separate classes as a permanent policy in 1947. Even earlier, and particularly during the war, undergraduates as well as graduates had been attending an increasing number of mixed classes. From the point of view of the present educational program the two schools constitute a coeducational institution—or almost. The men still have exclusive use of an independent library which is superior to that available to the women; and the women get Radcliffe—not Harvard—degrees conferred in separate commencement ceremonies. Also, there is still some separation of administration and finances. President Pusey, when questioned about their status on a television interview in October 1957, stated that there was no difference between the program as conducted and coeducation, and that the coordinate administration had been retained largely out of deference to tradition. The *Radcliffe Catalogue* continues to announce that they have the advantages of both coeducation and the women's colleges. But the residual advantage usually cited under these conditions is that women can run their own extracurricular activities, holding all the more responsible positions. Without questioning the virtue of this, it seems safe to predict that the students will be less and less interested in the segregation of such activities. Dramatic productions, by their very nature, need the cooperation of both sexes. Women's colleges regularly import men for these events. And there is very little news of exclusive interest to one sex when all important activities are participated in by both. In fact, Harvard and Radcliffe students are already showing interest in further fusion of activities. The *New York Times* of November 22, 1957 reports that "Harvard and Radcliffe authorities approved this week student council requests for joint social and cultural organizations."

Barnard College still retains independent classes, particularly in the first two years, since Barnard is unwilling to accept the two-year general education program of Columbia College. But the students go back and forth freely in the junior and senior years, and there are five joint departments—Music, Physics, Religion, Mathematics, and the Classics. The *Report of the President's Committee of Columbia University on the Educational Future of the University* (1957) urges further integration of the curriculum of the two undergraduate colleges in the junior and senior years. And while it states that the majority of the committee does not favor complete integration at the freshman and sophomore levels, the majority does agree that "changing conditions and future experience may justify a revision of this judgment."[13]

Most of the sixteen coordinate colleges reviewed here have a completely joint curriculum like that of Harvard and Radcliffe. Both considerations of economy and the obvious fact that the "separate" has never quite been "equal" have been factors in the trend. Moreover, the men as well as the women of the younger generation appear to prefer coeducation.

President McBride of Bryn Mawr has recently stated that she regards the coordinate college as the best kind of undergraduate institution,[14] and Bryn Mawr's increasing cooperation with Haverford and Swarthmore, and Smith's and Mount Holyoke's growing provision of joint facilities with Amherst and Massachusetts State University, are trends in this direction.

Throughout these shifts the colleges have tended to defend their status as of the moment. This is, of course, because they introduced the system they are acclaiming as a matter of conviction; and also because most of us tend to like the system with which we are most familiar. Thus we find Rochester stating in 1930: "For the best interests of both men and women separate organizations were subsequently developed, and in 1912 the trustees created a College for Women. . . . The removal of the College for Men to its new River Campus now completes this segregation for undergraduate work, to the mutual advantage of both colleges alike."[15] And in the University of Rochester *Catalogue* for 1955-1956 the statement appears that "coordination and efficiency" dictated the 1952 decision to merge the two colleges. The President also mentions the demands of women for more complete access to the whole range of education as a reason.[16]

A number of the catalogues of the coordinate colleges claim that they have the best of both systems, and while they are not very specific about what the advantages are, they appear to be joint classes on the one side and the opportunity for women to hold top positions in extracurricular activities on the other.

The foregoing discussion makes it clear that the coeducational institutions have multiplied in recent years, whereas the women's institutions constitute a declining proportion of the total in spite of the recent growth of Catholic women's colleges. Now that the great majority of colleges and universities admit women, the women's colleges have lost some of their attraction. Not only the liberal arts colleges, but also the graduate schools, including medicine, law, theology, and engineering, are now freely accessible to women who wish to study in these fields. Some schools still admit women grudgingly; a few do not accept them at all; but there are enough high ranking schools that accept women freely to leave little cause for complaint.

The next question concerns the extent to which women are taking advantage of these opportunities. Beginning with the total figures, the number of women enrolled has multiplied nearly one hundred times since 1870, and in 1870 the movement was already well started. There are today more than one million women in our universities and colleges, and the proportion of women of college age that are enrolled in college has increased from .7 per cent to 23 per cent. These figures are given in Table 2.

The proportion of women among total college students shows a different trend. This increased from 21 per cent in 1870 to 47 per cent in 1920. It looked for a time as though higher education would become as much a matter of course for women as for men, particularly in view of the fact that there were three girls graduating from high school for

Table 2.

WOMEN ENROLLED IN INSTITUTIONS OF HIGHER LEARNING, REGULAR SESSION 1870–1958[a]

Year	Number of Women Enrolled (thousands)	Percentage of All Women 18 to 21 Years of Age	Percentage of All Students Enrolled
1870	11	0.7	21.0
1880	40	1.9	33.4
1890	56	2.2	35.9
1900	85	2.8	36.8
1910	140	3.8	39.6
1920	283	7.6	47.3
1930	481	10.5	43.7
1940	601	12.2	40.2
1950	806	17.9	30.2
1956	1,019	21.0	34.6
1958	1,148	23.0	35.2

[a] Data from *Reports of the Commissioner of Education* and the *Decennial Census*.

every two boys. But high school is still the end of formal schooling for the great majority of girls in spite of the great gains in the higher education of women over the past century.

The fact that a larger proportion of girls than boys finish high school is more closely related to job opportunities than college plans. The boys have ordinarily had the alternative of a paid job. In the earlier period the job opportunities were not greatly improved by a high school diploma. For the girls, on the contrary, the alternative was likely to be staying at home. Unless the family need was great, a girl was not apt to be allowed to take a paid position until she was older; and even then the respectable positions to which she might aspire were largely in teaching for which a high school diploma was useful, if not required. Today the teacher is expected to go farther in her schooling, but the office job, which has more appeal to most girls of this age than teaching, is available to high school graduates.

As the state laws have increased the age of school leaving, and a high school education has become more important for the boy's job advancement, too, the proportion of girls among students completing high school has declined from 60 to 52 per cent—approximately their proportion of the total seventeen-year-old population. The percentage of all seventeen-year-olds graduating from high school has increased meanwhile to about 60 per cent. Among adults, women still have a higher average number of years of formal schooling to their credit than men, because of their persistence through high school in the past. The 1950 Census reports the average years of schooling for the population 25 years of age and over as 9.0 for men and 9.6 for women. And a Census study made as late as March 1957 found the average woman worker had completed 12.1 years of school where the average male worker had completed only 11.3.[17] But this higher average has come from the regular attendance of the girls in high school, not from the college record. And with the proportion of boys who complete high school overtaking the proportion of girls, the men of the future will average more years of formal schooling than the women. Although the proportion of women of college age that are enrolled in some institution of higher learning continues to increase, it has not kept pace with the increase in the men enrolled. There are now nearly two men in college for every woman.

Women not only enter college in smaller numbers than the men; those that do enroll are less likely to continue through the entire course. The graduates of 1956 constituted 62 per cent of the "first-time enrollment" of four years earlier for men and 52 per cent for women.[18]

The decline in the proportion of women among the recipients of bachelor's degrees has been accompanied by a similar decline in the proportion of women among the recipients of master's degrees. This degree is increasingly a requirement for teaching positions, but only one-third of the recipients were women in 1956, as compared with 40 per cent in 1930.

The women are lagging most of all in obtaining doctor's degrees. Fewer than 900 achieved this goal in 1956. This was less than one in ten of the total doctor's degrees conferred, whereas in 1920 women received one in six of these degrees. It is true that the absolute number of women earning this degree has continued to grow. The number receiving it in the decade 1946 to 1955 was almost double the number receiving it in the decade 1926 to 1935. But the men received three times as many in the later as in the earlier decade. The doctor's degree in education accounted for one-third of the women's degrees in 1956. Sciences accounted for 185, and social sciences for 101. Medical degrees are not included in the above figures. Three hundred fifty-five of the M. D. degrees conferred in 1956 were received by women. This is a smaller proportion, as in the case of other advanced degrees, than women received in earlier periods.

To summarize, not only the number of women going to college, but the proportion of women of the appropriate age groups who go, has increased. It is only in relation to the number of men going to college that the women have lagged.

Before considering the reasons for the failure of the women to keep pace with men in college attendance, it is of interest to look at the trends in the number of women enrolled in different kinds of institutions. The figures are given in Table 3.

Women's education is often thought of in terms of the women's colleges. But it is obvious from the data in Table 3 that these have not been responsible for educating the majority of college women since the 1870's, and their role has steadily declined until today their enrollment is less than 10 per cent of the total number of women in college. The private non-Catholic four-year colleges, which in 1880 enrolled nearly three out of every ten college women, today enroll three out of every hundred. There were more women in this group of colleges thirty years ago than there are today.

The women's colleges gave women their opportunity for higher education in the days when established institutions were slow to open their doors, and the men students, partly because they saw educated

Table 3.

WOMEN ENROLLED IN INSTITUTIONS OF HIGHER LEARNING ACCORDING TO TYPE OF INSTITUTION 1869–1957[a]

Year	Total	Coeducational Institutions	Women's Colleges				Normal and Junior: Public and Private
			Total in Women's Colleges	Public Four Year	Private Four Year: Non-Catholic	Catholic	
Thousands of Students							
1869-70	11.1	4.6	6.5	—	2.2	0.1	4.2
1879-80	39.6	23.9	15.7	—	11.2	0.1	4.3
1889-90	56.3	39.5	16.8	—	11.9	0.2	4.7
1899-00	85.4	61.0	24.4	0.2	16.3	0.2	7.6
1909-10	140.6	106.5	34.1	0.1	20.8	0.4	12.8
1919-20	282.9	230.0	52.9	6.4	24.7	2.5	19.4
1929-30	480.8	398.7	82.1	18.3	36.5	10.1	17.2
1939-40	601.0	494.9	106.1	24.5	37.2	26.5	17.9
1949-50	806.0	709.1	96.9	9.2	30.8	35.2	21.7
1956-57	1019.0	920.7	98.3	11.1	30.9	42.9	13.4
Percentage Distribution							
1869-70	100.0	41.1	58.9	—	19.8	0.9	38.2
1879-80	100.0	60.4	39.6	—	28.3	0.4	10.9
1889-90	100.0	70.1	29.9	—	21.1	0.3	8.5
1899-00	100.0	71.4	28.6	0.3	19.1	0.2	8.9
1909-10	100.0	75.8	24.2	0.1	14.8	0.3	9.0
1919-20	100.0	81.3	18.7	2.3	8.1	0.9	7.5
1929-30	100.0	82.9	17.1	3.8	7.6	2.1	3.6
1939-40	100.0	82.3	17.7	4.2	6.2	4.4	3.0
1949-50	100.0	88.0	12.0	1.1	3.8	4.4	2.7
1956-57	100.0	90.4	9.6	1.1	3.0	4.2	1.3

[a] Data from *Biennial Statistics of Education,* Office of Education. The distribution of students among different types of institutions has been partly estimated for the earliest years. The coordinate colleges have been included with women's colleges if they have separate classes, at least in part, and with the coeducational group when all classes are coeducational.

women as a threat to masculine superiority, were reluctant to study with them. Now that women are freely admitted to the great majority of institutions, the original function of the women's colleges is not important. The public coeducational institutions are cheaper. And it is clear that the majority of students—men and women both—prefer coeducation today. There is no indication that the majority of women have ever preferred the separate institutions. This does not mean that women's colleges cannot still provide the best kind of education for some women students. Individuals vary greatly in the conditions under which they develop best; and the women's colleges have some unique qualities. Moreover, trends often reverse themselves.

Of greater concern, in my judgment, is the fact that the increase in the number of women going to college has failed to keep pace with the increase in the number of men. Now that women are free to go to college they are not so eager after all! And now that the majority of college men appear to prefer college women for wives there are only about half enough to go around. But before evaluating these trends further, the nature of the college education that women have received, the kind of women who have gone to college, and the uses to which they have put their training must be considered.

NOTES

[1] A. Comstock, *American College Girl* (Boston, 1930), p. 36.

[2] The addition of work beyond the secondary school level came so gradually in some of these, and the standards are so uncertain, that it is not always possible to be sure when college work was introduced.

[3] Statements in letters to the author.

[4] It should be noted that Rutgers has coordinate men's and women's colleges in New Brunswick, but coeducational institutions on its other campuses.

[5] While there is no reason to expect this trend to be reversed, there are some indications that it may be slowed down in the South in order to insure, as integration takes place, that white women students may have the opportunity to study in institutions from which Negro men students are barred.

[6] The arrangements made for coordinate women's colleges are so varied that it is difficult to distinguish coordinate from coeducational institutions at one extreme, and from independent colleges at the other. The coordinate college usually has its own charter, but shares some of the faculty, libraries, and even courses

of the sponsoring institution. But the extent and kind of cooperation varies greatly. The colleges discussed here include, in order of their founding or reorganization as coordinate institutions, Radcliffe, Sophie Newcomb, Flora Stone Mather, Barnard, Pembroke, Jackson, Douglass, Scripps, Spelman, Centre, Duke, College of Liberal Arts for Women of the University of Pennsylvania, William Smith, Clark, Rockford, and McMurray. Although Mary Washington at Fredericksburg is listed as a coordinate college of the University of Virginia it is excluded from the group here because the physical distance between the two institutions makes any significant sharing of faculty, libraries, or other educational features impossible. The fact that Mary Washington has been controlled by the Rector and Visitors of the University of Virginia since 1944 does not appear to change its essential character as an independent college. Scripps College, which is often regarded as an independent college, has been included because it has been a member of the Associated Colleges of Claremont from the beginning, and shares with them some of its officers and faculty, and certain library facilities. Also, students may take some courses at the other colleges. This kind of cooperation is now developing in the Philadelphia area, where Bryn Mawr, Haverford, and Swarthmore have some interchange of students and faculty; and in the Connecticut Valley, among Amherst, Massachusetts State, Mount Holyoke, and Smith. However, the long history of independent institutions in these instances, and the less formal nature of the cooperative arrangements, has led to their exclusion here.

[7] M. C. White, *History of Barnard College* (New York, 1954), p. 17.

[8] F. A. P. Barnard, "Higher Education of Women," *Barnard's American Journal of Education*, 1881, p. 385.

[9] White, *op. cit.*, p. 9.

[10] C. G. N., "Queens College, London, for Female Education. Its Origin and Progress," *English Journal of Education*, 1849, p. 14.

[11] White, *op. cit.*, p. 11.

[12] H. C. Haydn, *From Hudson to Cleveland, 1878-1890* (Cleveland, 1905), p. 103.

[13] Pp. 201-202.

[14] *Newsweek*, September 23, 1957, p. 65.

[15] H. A. Smith, *The University of Rochester* (Rochester, 1930), p. 28.

[16] *New York Times*, April 30, 1952, p. 29.

[17] *New York Times*, December 8, 1957, p. 54.

[18] Department of Health, Education, and Welfare, Office of Education, *Earned Degrees, 1955–56*. Circular 499, p. 3.

4. The Aims of the Women's Colleges and the Aims of Women Students

ONCE THE right of women to go to college was firmly established, and adequate opportunities had opened up, the question of whether a college education was worth the required time and cost could be left, it was believed, to individual decision. But now that our complacency about the quality of our entire educational system has been somewhat shaken by events, we are beginning to wonder how to make education worth while for larger numbers of young people. As we feverishly attempt to reevaluate our educational offerings, the question of whether women's education should differ from men's is being debated with renewed vigor. One indication of present interest in this problem is the establishment of the Commission on the Education of Women by the American Council on Education.[1]

To get perspective on this problem it is useful to review the aims of the educators who have been especially concerned with the education of women over the past century, and the extent to which the education offered women has differed, in fact, from that offered to men. It is even more important to review the women's reasons for going to college and the choices the women students themselves have made. These matters are discussed in the following chapters.

For a consideration of aims it is necessary to turn to the women's colleges, since the coeducational institutions have generally assumed that if differentiation between men's and women's training is desirable, this can safely be left to the students' own choice of courses of study. The state universities and colleges, particularly, have shown by their course offerings a real concern for women's special professional interests. One of their first obligations is the preparation of teachers for the state school systems, and provision is regularly made for departments of education with voluminous course offerings in the state universities, usually supplemented by state teachers colleges. Courses are also quite regularly provided in such "women's professions" as home economics, nursing, library training, and secretarial work. But this does not preclude the men from obtaining degrees in nursing or women from obtaining degrees in engineering.

The state institutions are less likely than the private colleges to make any elaborate statement of their aims. And if they have different aims for men and women no explicit statement to this effect can be found. The founders of the private women's colleges, on the contrary, have been for the most part fairly specific about their aims. Those who dedicate their fortunes, like Wellesley's Henry Durant, or their lives, like Mount Holyoke's Mary Lyon, to a cause that has not yet been accepted by the majority of people, are sure to have convictions. Consequently, the aims of the early women's colleges were clearly stated and widely discussed.

Mary Lyon did not found a four-year college, but she did establish an institution that offered some measure of college education. Her central purpose was teacher training, both because she regarded this as a desirable occupation for women and, even more, because she believed such training to be essential to raise the general level of education in the lower schools. The aim was frankly professional. Secondary objectives were religious education and health education. The domestic work which all students participated in during the earlier years was not an integral part of her educational plan. She repeatedly emphasized that it was merely an essential economy to bring costs within reach of those of limited means, and that it should be abandoned when adequate financing made this possible. She believed that educated women would make better wives and mothers but she was not training housekeepers. Housekeeping was an art that they should learn at home.[2]

Catherine Beecher, Mary Lyon's contemporary, was also concerned with the training of teachers first of all. She noted that a seven year apprenticeship was required to make a shoe, but none to teach.[3] She believed that no woman was qualified to be a homemaker unless she had had experience first as a teacher.[4] She also advocated health education. But unlike Mary Lyon, she believed that instruction in "scientific domestic economy" should be an essential part of women's formal education. Partly for this reason she regarded the suitable education of women as sufficiently different from that of men to require separate schools. She did not regard the women's institutions as necessary "second bests" as long as women were excluded from men's colleges.[5] Women's colleges were to offer an education equal to that of the men's colleges, but different. The remedy for woman's position was not to lead her into men's professions and business but to train her properly "for her own proper business."[6]

Among the early women's colleges in New York State, Ingham University made some concessions to the special interests of women. This was reflected in the early curriculum by the offering of physiology and modern history in the freshman year. Training in domestic economy was not provided. The president of Rutgers Female College, which attained collegiate status in 1867, stated in his inaugural address that the purposes of the college were two: "to elevate and improve the mental training of women" and "to open up new fields of employment." Elmira, on the contrary, emphasized from the beginning that it was designed to give women the same education as that offered to men. Some deviations from the unmodified classical curriculum appeared in the actual course offerings, but no more than were made by some of the men's colleges at that time in the alternative "scientific courses" that were beginning to compete with the classical course.

Vassar, like Elmira, was designed "to accomplish for young women what colleges of the first class accomplish for young men; that is, to furnish them the means of a thorough, well-proportioned, and liberal education but one adapted to their wants in life."[7] Some concessions were made in the first Vassar curriculum to women's special sphere, although domestic economy was never taught. President Raymond felt that the women's colleges should follow in the footsteps of the men's at least until they had established their worth. He was willing to make concessions to the claims of aesthetics, and he was practical enough to make other concessions as temporary measures. But he believed that the value of the women's college lay in the residential system rather than in a curriculum that differed from the men's.

By the time that Smith and Wellesley opened, there were more opportunities for women in coeducational institutions, but not sufficiently widespread to make unnecessary the establishment of more women's colleges in order to give women the same opportunities as men. Sophia Smith's will, providing for Smith College, states that it is "with the design to furnish my sex means and facilities for education equal to those which are afforded now in our Colleges for young men." And Smith opened with admission requirements that made no concessions to possible differences in women's interests and preparation. The early catalogue statements made it clear that Smith was not preparing women specifically for teaching or homemaking. "The college is not intended to fit women for a particular sphere or profession, but to perfect her intellect by the best methods which philosophy and experience suggest." This did not preclude some deviations in the curriculum from those typical of the men's institutions, especially in the arts. But the differentiations on account of sex appeared more in the social regulations and living arrangements than in the curriculum.[8]

Wellesley's founder, like Vassar's, established the college in his own lifetime, and actually directed the affairs of the college in its early years. President Jewett and President Raymond played a more important part in determining the character of Vassar College than its founder, interested though he was in its development. But Henry

Durant of Wellesley made all the important decisions concerning its development in its early years; the first president merely carried out his commands. He believed that women's education should be as thorough as men's but not the same. He stressed the importance of developing powers of thought and reason, but he wanted instruction in religion and health, and he regarded one hour of domestic work a day as an integral part of the educational program—not just a concession to economy. He was also concerned with the training of teachers.[9]

Bryn Mawr, opening ten years later, followed the then well-established formula. It was, according to the terms of Joseph Taylor's will, to give women "all the advantages of a College education which are so freely offered to young men."[10] By this time the necessity for a college that would give women the *same* education as men might have been questioned, since the number of colleges and universities open to women had increased to more than half of the total. But as results have shown there was room for another—at least a good one; and Bryn Mawr's standards were high. The college not only opened without a preparatory department; it provided the unique feature, for a women's college, of a graduate school. As Carey Thomas explaned later, they had been charged by the founder with preparing teachers, and how else could teachers be adequately prepared? At no point, apparently, was any thought given to the possible virtues of training in domestic economy, theoretical or practical.

These instances make it clear that there was no real agreement among the early advocates of higher education as to whether the nature of that education should differ from men's. Several stressed the importance of education in homemaking but none made specific provision for it in the curriculum. Provision was regularly made for health education, which was infrequent in the men's colleges, and more emphasis was placed on the arts than was to be found in the men's colleges. This last appears to have been a concession to student demands more than a conviction of the founders, although they never showed the same reluctance to providing it that they showed toward training in domestic economy. So far as the curriculum was concerned these were the differences urged by those who wanted education of women to be "equal but different." Those who believed that the education of women should be the same as the education of men supported their case for separate institutions in the early years on the ground that women were excluded from most colleges; and as this became less true they urged that men and women could study better in separate classes, and that the living arrangements and extracurricular activities were different and contributed much to their total education.

The aim of the early men's colleges was training students for professions. Insofar as the women's colleges were designed to train teachers, their aims differed from the men's only in the profession for which they trained. But by the end of the Civil War those responsible for the institutions of higher learning were emphasizing other objectives. One study of the aims of the universities and colleges in the immediate post-Civil War period finds that among twenty-seven of the leading institutions the aims most often mentioned were training in religion, morality, and character.[11] Second to these was the aim to provide a liberal education as an end in itself. Third was mental discipline and the development of powers of thought; and fourth was personal improvement, including such matters as health, manners, and speech. Training for professions or any occupation was fifth place on the list. These are the same ends that concerned the women's institutions, but the emphasis was different. Training for a profession came higher on the list of women's college objectives, and personal improvement, except for health, came lower.

What the women who went to college wanted is not so clearly recorded. But to judge from their later careers, as well as their written statements, they were concerned with preparation for teaching and with knowledge for its own sake. A college education was not something to be taken for granted, to be embarked on without serious thought or purpose. It brought little or no social prestige. Whatever the college authorities might say about its value as preparation for homemaking, the students and their parents did not regard a college education as useful for this purpose. On the contrary, they had some misgivings as to whether it might impair the girls' chances of marriage; homemaking was something to be learned at home. The early women students did in fact usually marry as well as teach, but the majority went to college because they had serious professional aims or a real desire for knowledge.

As conditions change, so also, it may be assumed, do the goals of the students and of those directing the course of these institutions. Home economics as a special field of college study for women grew rapidly in the first quarter of the twentieth century, partly as a result of the encouragement of the Smith Lever Act of 1914, but even more because it was being introduced into the lower schools and specially trained teachers were needed. In the lower schools home economics was preparation for homemaking, but in the colleges its primary purpose was vocational—to prepare teachers, dietitians, and other specialists in this field. A study of the catalogues of 54 women's colleges in the South in 1930 showed that 34 of these either mentioned homemaking specifically in their aims or gave it special emphasis in their offerings of home economics courses.[12] Another study of aims of the 74 private, Protestant, or nondenominational women's colleges in existence in the early 1940's finds only seven mentioning homemaking.[13] The number with a substantial course offering in this field is not given, but there is other evidence that interest in homemaking was declining.

This study states that 22 of these 74 colleges either made no mention of aims in their catalogues, or stated them in such general terms as to make them meaningless. The great majority were concerned with the special functions of women, but were not very realistic about them. Over half did not list any vocational aims, although all but two provided some vocational courses. One stated that while it offered no vocational or professional work per se, it was "intended to equip young women for modern life and . . . the problems which they must face in their professions and in their homes."[14] Although 30 listed religious objectives this did not include all of those that had been founded with religious aims. Only two were concerned with giving women equal opportunity with men. That battle had been won. And as a new objective, not found in the early period, five mentioned usefulness in the community.

I have examined the current catalogues of 34 of the women's colleges—a little better than half of the number now existing. The selection was made on the basis of catalogues easily available, and the smaller, denominational colleges are under-represented in the sample. Nevertheless, some trends are clear. Religious aims are less apparent, even after allowing for the bias of the sample. Civic and social responsibility appears with increased frequency—15 out of 34 colleges mention it, as compared with 5 out of 74 in the early 1940's. Twelve include vocational or professional training among their aims, and five include homemaking. Fourteen concern themselves with developing powers of independent thinking and judgment. Scholarship, in the sense of developing intellectual curiosity and love of knowledge for its own sake, is mentioned by only four. In contrast to this, 10 emphasize their concern with developing the "whole person" or preparation for "life's needs." This last objective is not peculiar to the women's colleges. The men's colleges frequently state as an objective the development of the "whole man."

Of the eight early women's colleges whose original aims have been listed above, six still exist. All are explicit about their aims, as are practically all the 81 institutions (men's, women's, and coeducational), whose catalogues I have checked. There has been more than the usual questioning in the postwar period as to what we want higher education to accomplish, and the colleges are no longer offering their wares without explaining their virtues.

President Blanding of Vassar states that the liberal arts education "offers young women a sound preparation for intelligent and creative living. . . . It is an instrument of growth, including responsible citizenship."[15] This represents a considerable shift of emphasis, although Matthew Vassar's education "adapted to their wants in life" offers room for such a statement of objectives.

President Clapp of Wellesley says: "All students should be told upon entering that a liberal arts education is not intended to train them in the techniques of scholars or mothers or business people. Its purpose is to help them in their search for self-knowledge, abiding principles, a broad cultural background, and honest, orderly processes of thought and methods of approaching situations."[16] Mount Holyoke's 1956 catalogue states that its "liberal education seeks to show the way for those whose growth in later years may bring ripeness of thought and wisdom of action." Bryn Mawr's catalogue speaks of mental discipline, education for civic and social responsibility and "intellectual enrichment." Smith's catalogue states simply that its aim is to provide a liberal education, and Elmira stresses the importance of adapting educational programs to individual needs. None of this group professes to offer vocational or pre-professional training. Some specifically deny such offerings. And none mentions homemaking, as such, as an objective.

The older colleges are likely to become bogged down by tradition and vested interests. It takes uncommon leadership, or the threat of sharply declining enrollments, to get any radical change. A new college, on the contrary, can start with fresh objectives and recruit a faculty and a student body in sympathy with these aims. It is, therefore, of some interest to look at the aims of the newer colleges.

Unfortunately new women's colleges of the private, liberal arts, nondenominational, residential persuasion are very rare. None has been established in the last quarter-century and only three were chartered in the 1920's—Scripps, Sarah Lawrence, and Bennington. Scripps differs from the other two in that it forms one of a group of cooperating colleges. But it has been free to shape its own program, and it has chosen to emphasize the importance of a common body of knowledge for all students, and more particularly the "great tradition." Students are required to take a double course—two-fifths of their total program—in the humanities for the first three years. In addition, sophomores take a course in "Man as a Biological Organism." In Scripps' statement of aims, emphasis is put on the development of the whole personality. There is no statement that the education of women should differ from that of men. In fact, it appears to be accidental, in this instance, that the students are all women. The one concession to feminine interests appears to be special emphasis on the creative arts.

Bennington and Sarah Lawrence have approached the education of women as something a little special, although it appears to have been a matter of political expediency rather than conviction that dictated the establishment of a women's college at Bennington in the first place.[17] These colleges take the position that education should begin by taking into account individual student interests and aptitudes, and programs of study should differ with these individual differences. This is in sharp contrast to Scripp's conviction that all students should share a common store of knowledge. They also represent the opposite of Scripp's position in concerning themselves with today's world rather than the "great tradition." Both stress the importance of field work as a method of study and Bennington devotes a winter nonresident term to this activity. In its early history Bennington had a special program centering around the homemaker, but abandoned it because it failed to attract the better students and was regarded by these as suitable only for mediocre minds.[18] Nevertheless, most of the courses which it comprised were retained, together with the nursery school.

These two colleges, like Scripps, feature the creative arts as an important ingredient of a liberal arts education and as of particular interest to women. Otherwise their curriculum offerings differ little from those in the men's colleges. In fact, President Taylor of Sarah Lawrence stresses the fact that the difference is one of emphasis only. He takes the position that training women students to be wives and mothers is to assign them to a fixed and subservient role "in terms of the needs and wishes of men, and not in terms of their own fulfillment. . . . The most that can be done in college to prepare for the consequences of living for long periods with children and husbands is to become as intellectually and emotionally mature as the curriculum of the college will allow, and to become more and more resourceful about organizing one's own life. . . . Nothing very helpful can happen until the individual woman student learns to see life as something which extends beyond the circle of her own private interests."[19] He suggests that one of the virtues of a women's college is that experimentation is possible because it is not committed to specific professional training. None of these colleges has accepted Lynn White's position that the education of women should be oriented toward their homemaking concerns.

It is difficult to reach any clear conclusions concerning the aims of the colleges, either with regard to changes in objectives over a long period of time or with regard to differences between men's and women's colleges. Official statements are often vague because there is no agreement within the college as to the direction education should take, or because it is felt that it must appeal to a wider clientele than the college would like to attract if enough applicants could be found in the more select circle.

Most presidents and deans are probably clear in their own minds as to the direction in which they would like to see their institutions go, but comparatively few have given evidence, either in writing or action, of positive leadership toward a clearcut goal. They are distracted by the details of a large business operation; and they are handicapped even more by resistant faculties protecting their vested interests, and equally resistant alumni who, just because they are reasonably content with their own education, want things to stay exactly as they were. The trustees, in turn, are ready to go in any direction that appears to interest a prospective donor. All these varied pressures must be taken into account not only in formulating the actual educational program but in making a simple statement of the institution's purposes in official documents. In addition, the statement must have some appeal to prospective students and their parents.

Even a clear and positive statement of direction—and these can be found occasionally—may not be sufficiently understood or accepted by those administering it to insure its being carried out in practice. I sometimes wonder how many members of the faculty could state the official educational aims of their institution. Do they ever read that part of the catalogue? They may be gifted teachers of their particular art or science. But beyond the conviction that their own field is important for every student—a conviction that is almost inevitable for effective teaching—and a belief that one or another teaching device is more effective than most, what are their educational philosophies? I can still recall my own astonishment when, early in my teaching career, I was asked to write a statement of the aims of our department. My only aim had been to teach the students economics as best I could!

With all these reservations I still believe that the official statements of objectives represent genuine shifts in points of view. One marked difference between the aims of the colleges today and one hundred years ago is that social responsibility has replaced personal improvement. In spite of the stress now laid by many colleges on adjusting programs to individual differences, the ultimate aim appears to be social welfare rather than personal satisfaction. The early argument for free public schools was that in a democracy every citizen should at least be able to read and write. Today he is expected to be able to think, reach independent conclusions, and act upon them. It is no longer enough to educate the clergy. And it is not enough for the college graduates to use their education for their own advancement. Men and women, more particularly women, are being trained for civic and social responsibilities. Leadership, which was a common aim in the 1920's has gone out of fashion. Eleven of the 40 colleges cited by Koos and Crawford emphasized leadership in 1918. I found it mentioned in only three of the 81 catalogues that I examined. With such a large proportion of our youth now going to college it is clear that so many leaders could hardly be absorbed in our society. Besides, "Der Fuehrer" has somewhat discredited leadership in the more recent period.

Some comment should be made concerning the development of

the "whole person" as an objective. This has arisen from the recognition of the fact that while the primary business of the college is intellectual development, this cannot be isolated from other interests and concerns, and the student who is healthy, happy, and interested in a variety of things will usually learn faster and put his education to better use than a maladjusted individual. It has sometimes been carried to a point, however, where the college appears to belittle intellectual achievements. Some colleges have even favored, in their admissions policies, the student who has engaged in a wide variety of extracurricular activities as compared with a "grind." Onesidedness, even though it be intellectual onesidedness, has been deplored. The students themselves have received the impression that preoccupation with studies is to be avoided. This attitude was more common a generation or so ago, when so much emphasis was put on leadership, than it is today. Most of the colleges that still emphasize the "whole person" are careful to make it clear that intellectual pursuits are the primary purpose of their educational program. But many leave this reader, at least, in doubt as to their position on this score.

In spite of other changes, faith in the liberal arts education rather than specialized preparation for professions at the undergraduate level has remained unchanged—possibly even strengthened—although the content of such an education is both more varied and different in emphasis than that of a century ago.

But these factors are common to men's and women's education alike. It is not that the women's colleges have ignored the special concerns of women. It is, rather, that a liberal arts education is accepted as the best preparation for homemaking, as well as for the professions. In the stated aims of the liberal arts colleges as a group —women's, men's, and coeducational—occupational training lags behind both social responsibility and knowledge for its own sake, or the development of powers of independent thinking. But the fact remains that these colleges appear to be doing more about professional training than their printed objectives indicate.

To stop with official statements of aims would be misleading, even if these reflected the clear purpose of those responsible for the educational program. The aims of the students are of at least equal significance. Over the years the students have shaped the educational programs to meet their needs and desires more than is sometimes recognized. They cannot prescribe the curriculum, but they can select their college, and they can select the particular courses that suit their interests. Also, they can petition for new courses with a good chance of success. It was student approval of the free elective system that made it spread so rapidly once a few colleges had accepted it. And it has been student preferences that have multiplied offerings, particularly in the arts and social sciences.

Unfortunately, the aims of the students do not appear in the official publications. They are rarely set down in print at all. Also, the students, like the faculty, are probably not accustomed to analysing their motives. They may have to state their reasons for wanting to go to a particular college, or for wanting to go to college at all, in letters accompanying an application for admission. But these, like the catalogue statements, are likely to be written with an eye to the effect. When confronted by a questionnaire on the subject they often fill it out without much thought or conviction. Their motives are apt to be complex and they may not know themselves what the deciding factors have been. The majority of today's students have, in all probability, taken it for granted for as long as they can remember that they would go to college.

A recent study has been made, by the United States Office of Education, of students' reasons for attending college, which includes returns from nearly 13,000 students in all types of institutions of higher learning. This is the most comprehensive study of this question that I have found. The reasons have been grouped in five categories: (1) academic (including such factors as intellectual curiosity and enjoyment of study); (2) occupational (including importance of a college degree for a better paying job or a particular kind of work, and college acquaintances as a help in job advancement);

(3) personal (friendships for their own sake, the hope that college will be a good place to find a congenial husband or wife, or that it will make them better husbands or wives, or simply that they have no interesting alternative); (4) social service (help toward participation in civic affairs); (5) traditional (influence of family, friends, or teacher, or tacit assumption of family and friends that young people of one's group always go to college).[20]

The results show few differences between the women and the men students. The women, however, place academic reasons first and occupational reasons second. The men reverse this order. Both place social service third, personal reasons fourth, and traditional reasons fifth. The one difference between the reasons for going to college as the students saw them after attending college, and as they recalled their reasons for deciding to go in the first place, is in the importance attached to social service, which ranked fourth for the men and fifth for the women in their original decision to go to college. This suggests that the educators who state this as an important aim have, in some measure, been successful in achieving it. The third place, in the aims of the precollege students, was given to tradition for the men and personal reasons for the women.

The fact that women put less emphasis on occupational reasons than men is not surprising, but the fact that they put academic reasons ahead of occupational reasons is surprising in the light of other evidence. A *Fortune* survey made in 1949[21] showed that 48 per cent of the parents wanted their daughters to go to college for occupational reasons, and 16 per cent for academic reasons. And a recent study made by the Michigan Survey Research Center[22] reports that half of the girls from eleven to eighteen years of age who were interviewed and who wanted to go to college gave professional training as their objective—social work, teaching, and nursing being the principal professions named. Only 13 per cent were primarily concerned with intellectual training; 37 per cent had no specific purpose. The small proportion concerned with intellectual training is probably due in some measure to the age of the respondents. It is hardly to be expected that girls of eleven to eighteen will be much preoccupied with scholarly interests that have no concrete goal. There is other evidence, however, that occupational training is a dominating motive on the part of students as a whole.

The most convincing evidence of the emphasis placed on occupational training is the record of the students' major fields. This is discussed at length later.[23] It is sufficient to note here that among the graduates of 1956 more than three-fifths of the women had specialized in education, secretarial courses, nursing, and home economics.

All of the evidence shows that the personal, or social, reasons weigh more heavily with the women than the men. A wife with some college education, although not necessarily a degree, has come to be regarded as a social asset. The students themselves are aware of this. One applicant to Vassar writes as a reason for wanting a college education: "I want to be a real partner to the man I marry." Another says, "When I marry, I would like to converse with my husband's friends and business acquaintances with a mature and confident manner that can only come from a thorough education." Also, if one goes to the "right" college one will meet the "right" people. Announcements in the newspapers of engagements and marriages now regularly list the girl's college as part of her social background. It appears to have the same prestige as an important ancestor. Students making out their course programs are careful to include the appropriate proportion of "cultural" subjects, and only if their major field is not so rated do they worry about overspecialization. Fortunately, a year or two of college suffices for purely social purposes, and it is safe to assume that the student who continues for the degree has other ends in view.

For the majority of women students who graduate, and many who do not, the important factors are academic interest and the conviction that the college training will make them better wives and mothers and widen their job opportunities. Not many students are as wholehearted about the pursuit of knowledge as the recent Vassar applicant quoted at the beginning of this chapter, but many of those who stay on develop intellectual curiosity as they go. It is not uncommon for a student to admit that she has become interested in a subject "in spite of herself." The fact that the majority of the students in the private two-year accredited colleges transfer to four-year institutions is evidence of this.[24] Few who plan in the beginning to go through a four-year course will choose to go to a residential junior college in the first place. In the end it becomes difficult to distinguish between academic and occupational motives for large numbers of students. Social service is more rarely a motive. Concern for those beyond their immediate circle comes a little later in most students' lives. But there is no necessary conflict among the motives listed above, and several may be important for a single individual.

The reasons for selecting a specific college are somewhat different. A student may be primarily concerned either with knowledge for its own sake or professional training. And she may be convinced that the liberal arts training is the best for either end. But how does she decide on the specific college? Reading through a large number of letters from applicants for admission to college, it becomes clear that they are fairly definite about the type of college they want to go to, and why, but that they are very uncertain as to which college of this type will best fit their needs. Many have not yet selected the subject in which they wish to specialize, and even when they have they rarely know which of the colleges under consideration is strongest in this field. Beyond the course descriptions, the college catalogues give them no clue. Even when the applicants mention the superior quality of the educational offering in the fields of their special interest they have no sound basis for judgment. They have to assume that a college with a high academic rating that offers an adequate number of courses in the field of their interest will give them the best possible training in this area.

Surveys of reasons why students selected Vassar College were made by the statistics class of the college in 1938 and 1957. Since the returns were anonymous and not used for any official purpose, it can be assumed that they represented the honest judgment of the students as they attempted to evaluate their own motives. It cannot be assumed that these reasons are representative for all colleges, but they are of more than local interest.

In the 1957 survey the academic reputation of the college was listed first. Thus, whether their motive for getting a college education was professional advancement or intellectual curiosity, the students appear to have made an honest effort to select a college that would provide a good education. The influence of other people ranked second, although in the earlier period it had ranked first. This relates, of course, to the choice of a specific college, not to the original decision to go to college. When the advice comes from their preparatory school teachers, it may be assumed that it is based on academic reasons. When it is their contemporaries who persuade them, social reasons presumably dominate. But most frequently those whose advice was taken were members of the immediate family. And whether the family decision was based on what they believed to be academic advantages, social reasons, or proximity to home cannot be known. It is worth noting, however, that influence of others was much more important in the earlier period than the later one. This seems to belie the frequent complaint that the younger generation of today is not as independent as yesterday's.

The geographic location of the college ranked third in importance in the later period—almost equal to the influence of others. Whether the selection was made because of proximity to home, or for other reasons, is not stated. But for Vassar, in particular, it is not nearness to a men's college. Social prestige not only came last, but it appears to be of little importance—of less importance in 1957 than in 1938.

It seems probable that even serious students sometimes select their college on the basis of the advice of friends or geographic location simply because their knowledge with regard to its rating in the field of their special interest is inadequate. I talked recently with a high school junior who was making a tour of colleges during her spring vacation. She commented about a specific college that she had just visited that she had crossed it off of her list after her interview with the admissions officer, but that some of the undergraduates with whom she subsequently talked told her "not to pay any attention to her," and persuaded her that she would like the college after all. When I commented that the college in question was particularly strong in the field of her chosen interest, about which she had a real conviction, she said: "Is it? Nobody told me that."

Few colleges are prepared to emphasize one field of study rather than another. And no college officer is likely to be frank about the strengths and weaknesses of the school's offerings when talking with a candidate. Advice from relatives on this score is likely to be outdated. Consequently, it is not surprising that even the students who have chosen their special field of interest give undue weight to less important, and sometimes quite irrelevant, factors. Geographical location becomes important. Is the college "far enough away from home, but not too far?" Is it (if a women's college) within reach of a men's college? Or within easy reach of a large city? These are tangible factors that can be judged. No matter how great one's concern with the quality of the educational offering may be, if all are equally good, as far as the prospective student can learn, one may as well go with one's friends. Or please one's mother by going to her college. Even the degree of friendliness of the officer interviewed, or whether the sun was shining that day or it was raining, may be decisive. This does not indicate lack of serious interest as much as lack of dependable information and guidance of the kind that is important.

If instead of attempting to excel in everything, the colleges would make up their minds to specialize a little, either in subject matter or methods of study, it would probably help them and the students in matching college offerings with student interest and abilities. A few colleges, of course, have done this. Scripps with its emphasis on the great tradition, Bennington and Sarah Lawrence with their emphasis on the creative arts, and the colleges with honors programs or required field work programs, are instances of this, as are the colleges, like Simmons, that feature occupational training.

It would also help if the colleges were more specific in their official aims, and particularly in the ways, if any, a student's professional interests can be furthered by their course offerings. And it would help if they would decide whether intellectual curiosity or well-roundedness was their chief concern either in selecting students in the first place or in turning them out in the end.

NOTES

[1] This was established in 1953, and while it was comparatively inactive from 1955 to 1957 it has been making an active study of the problems since that date.

[2] A. C. Cole, *A Hundred Years of Mount Holyoke College* (New Haven, 1940), p. 39.

[3] C. E. Beecher, *Suggestions Respecting Improvements in Female Education* (Hartford, 1829), pp. 5-6.

[4] C. E. Beecher, *True Remedy for the Wrongs of Women*, (Boston, 1851), quoted in T. Woody, *History of Women's Education in the United States* (New York, 1929), vol. 1, p. 109.

[5] C. E. Beecher, *Treatise on Domestic Economy for the Use of Young Ladies at Home and at School* (Boston, 1842), Quoted in Woody, *op. cit.*, vol. 1, p. 400.

[6] C. E. Beecher, "How to Redeem Woman's Profession from Dishonor," *Harper's New Monthly Magazine*, November 1865, p. 710.

[7] *Vassar College Catalogue, 1865-66*, p. 16.

[8] L. C. Seelye, *Smith College Quarter Centennial Anniversary, 1875-1900* (Cambridge, 1900), p. 103.

[9] F. Converse, *Wellesley College, A Chronicle of the Years 1875-1938* (Wellesley, 1939), ch. 1.

[10] Margaret C. MacIntosh, *Joseph Wright Taylor* (Haverford, 1936), p. 209.

[11] L. V. Koos and C. C. Crawford, "College Aims, Past and Present," *School and Society*, December 3, 1921, pp. 499 ff.

[12] D. S. Campbell, "Problems in the Education of Women," George Peabody College for Teachers, *Field Study no. 6* (Nashville, 1933), p. 18.

[13] E. A. Leonard, "Aims of Higher Education for Women in the United States," *School and Society*, October 16, 1943, p. 297.

[14] *Ibid.*

[15] S. G. Blanding, "The Vassar Education," *Bulletin of Vassar College*, 1951.

[16] M. Clapp, "Realistic Education for Women," *Journal of the American Association of University Women*, Summer 1950, p. 202.

[17] R. L. Duffus, *Democracy Enters the College* (New York, 1936), p. 205.

[18] B. Jones, *Bennington College* (New York, 1946), p. 39.

[19] H. Taylor, *On Education and Freedom* (New York, 1954), pp. 165-167.

[20] R. E. Iffert, "Retention and Withdrawal of College Students," *Office of Education Bulletin (1958), no. 1*, pp. 22-24.

[21] E. Roper, "The Public Looks at Higher Education," *Fortune Magazine Supplement*, June 1949, p. 259.

[22] Cited in *Higher Education*, December 1957, p. 62.

[23] See page 92 ff. below.

[24] Ordway Tead, "Junior Colleges: Their Role in Liberal Arts Education" (1956, mimeographed).

WE FIND IT TAKEN FOR GRANTED THAT GIRLS ARE NOT TO
LEARN THE DEAD LANGUAGES AND MATHEMATICS, BECAUSE
THEY ARE NOT TO EXERCISE PROFESSIONS WHERE THESE
ATTAINMENTS ARE WANTED; AND A LITTLE FURTHER ON WE
FIND IT SAID THAT THE CHIEF REASON FOR BOYS AND YOUNG
MEN STUDYING THESE THINGS IS TO IMPROVE THE QUALITY
OF THEIR MINDS.

HARRIET MARTINEAU*

5. The Course of Study

In MID-NINETEENTH century when the higher education of women
began to receive serious consideration, the classical tradition still dominated the colleges. Harvard had patterned its curriculum after Em-
manuel College at Cambridge.[1] William and Mary also followed the
example of the English universities. Later colleges were guided by
both English and American precedent.

The foundations of the classical curriculum were, of course, Greek,
Latin, and mathematics. These might well comprise the entire course
of study for the first two years, although the colleges' responsibility
for the training of clergymen led many to add training in writing and
public speaking under such titles as rhetoric, composition, debate,
forensics, and oratory. In the upper classes mathematics might extend to astronomy and natural philosophy (physics), and even
chemistry and geology. But only rarely could a student explore the
developing field of biological sciences within the regular college curriculum. Philosophy and religion were appropriate subjects for upper class-

* From H. Martineau, *Household Education* (Philadelphia, 1849), p. 155.

72

men, and the senior year was quite regularly crowned with courses in moral and mental philosophy given by the president. The content of these varied with the interests of the teacher, but they were often the student's only introduction to the social sciences. English literature, modern languages, and history, other than ancient and Biblical history, were all marginal subjects. Political economy and government, except as they crept into the course on moral philosophy, had no place in the curriculum, although in time pressure from the legal profession resulted in isolated courses in law and government.

It is clear that such a curriculum bore little relation to the education being offered to young ladies of that era. Latin and mathematics were taken seriously only in the seminaries concerned primarily with teacher training, and even here the offerings were small. At Mount Holyoke Seminary, for instance, Latin was an "extra" in the early years, given by special request, and mathematics ended with algebra and geometry. Rarely if ever did a girls' school offer Greek. The girls were trained in the modern languages rather than the classics, and in biological more than in physical sciences. Art, music, and English literature were essential to a lady's education, but not to the education of a gentleman. The girls' religious education, while not neglected, was not of the same caliber as that given to the future clergymen. Modern history and the social sciences were not regarded as important for either sex.

Even for men, however, the classical tradition was being challenged by the time that higher education of women was seriously considered. Union College in Schenectady had been noted for its liberalism from the first. Founded at the end of the eighteenth century, its motto was in French instead of the usual Greek or Latin.[2] Science received far more emphasis here than at other institutions of the time, and a scientific course was offered very early as an alternative to the traditional classical course. Students dissatisfied with their training elsewhere transferred to Union in sufficient numbers to make the enrollment in the upper classes greater than in the lower. President Nott, whose regime lasted from 1804 to 1866, was largely responsible for this.

This development came a little earlier than the founding of the University of Virginia, where Thomas Jefferson introduced the free elective system which he had observed in Europe. He had tried earlier to reform William and Mary, but without success.[3] The free elective system not only permitted students to choose different courses of study, but it broke the lock step of the classical system. A student could graduate when he had completed the required number of courses with acceptable grades. Under the classical system, as in our grade schools today, students were promoted one year at a time. If a man's work was not satisfactory in all courses, he might be forced to repeat an entire year of studies. By the same token there was no possibility of accelerating his progress. The University of Virginia also had a different objective from that of the church-founded colleges. It was designed, as a state institution, primarily to prepare men for government service.

This offered a real challenge to the established curriculum. It spread rapidly in the South, but only slowly in the realm of Harvard, Yale, and Princeton. Professor Ticknor of Harvard, as a result of his acquaintance with German universities, became interested in the free elective system. He was unable to persuade his colleagues of its worth, but he received some encouragement from President Quincy and was allowed to adopt it within his own department.[4] President Wayland of Brown, who had been one of Nott's students at Union, made a point of visiting the University of Virginia to study the system, and later was successful in introducing it for a time at Brown. In 1850, faced with declining enrollments, the trustees and faculty reluctantly let him experiment with the elective system. He even experimented with adult education, providing chemistry courses in the evening for the local jewelry manufacturers.[5] Enrollments nearly doubled in four years with the free elective system.[6] But after Wayland's retirement in 1855, his successor was persuaded to give up the "cheap" degrees that could be earned without Greek or Latin and in less than four years.[7] Only when Eliot succeeded in putting it into effect at Harvard, by slow degrees in the seventies and eighties, did the elective system become respectable.

The shift from the fixed curriculum to the elective system came gradually. The first relaxation of the program was to offer a scientific course in addition to the classical course. The former usually differed from the latter in reducing the Greek and Latin requirements, substituting modern languages, and increasing the scientific content. Sometimes a literary course, emphasizing English and modern languages, was also offered. And the classical course itself began to include new subjects as the growth of scientific knowledge brought new pressures. Each curriculum was comparatively rigid, but at least the student had the option of two or three curriculums. As the field of knowledge widened, the new subjects forced the introduction of some electives in all courses, gradually reducing the number of required subjects, particularly in the upper years. Thus it was not such a long step to an elective system which still contained a core of required subjects.

The free elective system at its peak took various forms. It usually required a major, which was controlled by the department concerned and which provided some degree of continuity and specialization. But in its extreme form students were allowed to elect the majority of their courses without control. In my own experience as an undergraduate at Stanford University, when the elective system was in full sway, a minimum of my elections was dictated by my major department. Even here there were generous alternatives. Beyond this the whole range of course offerings was mine to try. Formal prerequisites to courses were sometimes absent even when they were in fact essential. I clearly recall my difficulties when I found myself in a course requiring more mathematics and physics than I had at my command. This was my problem; if I did not know better than to take a course for which I was inadequately prepared, I could suffer the consequences. I survived; and in its way the experience itself was educational.

It was in this period of change that many of the new women's colleges were founded. The classical tradition still prevailed, but it had been challenged and new vistas were opening up. Besides it could be argued that, whatever was good for men, a woman's education should be different. The women's colleges were not training for the ministry—or for the law or government service. They were training future housewives and teachers. Finally, they had no tradition of their own to hold them back.

The lack of precedent had disadvantages, too. There was no evidence to prove that any particular system was better or worse than another. And among those who believed that women's education should be different, there was no agreement as to the nature of the difference. Moreover, the critics of higher education for women had to be silenced, and the only way to prove that women were as able as men was to put them through the same course. Z. C. Graves, the first president of Mary Sharp College, made it clear that the only innovation at his college was providing for women the same education as men. According to the first catalogue, in 1853, this was to be "a school for young ladies of a higher grade than any previously known to exist . . . a college where ladies may have the privilege of a classical education."[8]

Elmira, on the contrary, introduced a modified system in 1857. Latin and Greek were required, but only a year and a half of Latin (based on a prerequisite of two years in the preparatory course) and one year of Greek. The modern language requirement, in French and German, was a minimum of three and one-half years. Mathematics was required for the first two years, followed by astronomy. The science requirements began in the freshman year and continued throughout the course of study, covering practically every known science, although there was little opportunity to get beyond the introductory stage. There was still time for history, political science, political economy, logic, and more English literature than I have found in the curriculum of any men's college of the time. And music, drawing, and painting were also offered as a concession to the "elegancies" expected of women. Finally, there was, of course, religious study, including a systematic reading of the Bible once a year; and that special presidential course given in almost every college of the time, moral philosophy. Mental philosophy was added a few years later.[9]

Choices were apparently limited to languages. A student taking the regular course, after taking both introductory French and German, could in her senior year choose between these two languages. And a student electing the scientific course instead of the classical could omit both Latin and Greek, taking modern languages instead. This, however, was not encouraged. Occasional changes were made in individual offerings in the ensuing years, but the program remained basically the same for some years. It was a simple curriculum that could be printed complete with texts on one side of a page. Today the Elmira curriculum, serving not so many more students, covers sixty pages. Like all the rest, Elmira has adopted the elective system.

Milo Jewett, the man who persuaded Matthew Vassar to give his fortune to the founding of a women's college instead of to a hospital, and who served as the first president of Vassar College, wanted a modified elective system instead of the classical curriculum. He had had opportunity to observe both in the South where he was head of Judson Female Institute for many years, and in Europe where he spent some months studying the European educational system.

Jewett argued that to put everyone through the same course lowers standards, because students who are able in some studies may lack aptitude for others. Provision should be made, he thought, for diversity in ability and interests.[10] Moreover, he believed it an error to assume that "certain peculiar subjects" alone can train mental faculties. In his judgment a wide range of subjects were suitable for this purpose.[11]

These arguments, generally accepted today, were heresy at the time. Eliot was not yet president of Harvard. Brown University had just abandoned its brief experiment with such "shoddy and second-rate" education. The president of Princeton had recently pledged that "we shall not aim at innovation. No chimerical experiments in education have ever had the least countenance here"; and as late as 1872 one of Princeton's most distinguished professors was boasting that "not a single new idea had come out of Princeton" in the fifty years that he had been there.[12] Still later, another president of Princeton, McCosh, engaged in public debate with Eliot of Harvard on the subject. This was in 1885.[13] Yale was to hold out until President Hadley's regime, which began at the turn of the century.

Why Jewett modified his program is not clear. It was approved by a committee of the board of trustees in 1863 and was favored by Matthew Vassar.[14] Probably Jewett was influenced by practical considerations. An elective system inevitably requires a considerable range of choice in courses and a correspondingly larger faculty, and rising building costs during the Civil War were making heavy inroads on Vassar's large endowment. In any event Jewett's final specific proposals left very little choice. They did, however, offer more variety than the strict classical curriculum. To quote him directly, "We would, therefore, abridge the College Course in Mathematics, Ancient Languages, and Metaphysical and Political Philosophy, and thus secure more time to our own and other modern languages, to Natural History, Domestic Economy, Music, Drawing and Painting."[15] With one exception this is what the first curriculum provided. The exception was domestic economy.

Jewett also stressed the importance of health measures. He pointed out that since women did not have to spend their time getting professional training they could afford to get a more thorough grounding in physiology than was being offered in the men's colleges. He wanted "hygiene in its largest sense, physical and mental." He also emphasized, outside of "intellectual instruction," physical education. Of the whole field of health, inside and outside of the formal course of study, he says: "Of such transcendent moment do I hold this element of feminine study that I would be glad to see it take first place in our institutions."[16]

Matthew Vassar, at the first meeting of his Board of Trustees, had the following to say with regard to the curriculum:

I wish that the Course of Study should embrace, at least, the following particulars. The English Language and its Literature; other Modern Languages; the Ancient Classics, so far as may be demanded by the spirit of the times; the Mathematics, to such an extent as may be deemed advisable; all the branches of Natural Science, with full apparatus, cabinets, collections, and conservatories for visible instruction; Anatomy, Physiology, and Hygiene, with practical reference to the laws of health of the sex; Intellectual Philosophy, the elements of Political Economy; some knowledge of the Federal and State Constitutions and Laws; Moral Science, particularly as bearing on the filial, conjugal, and parental relations; Aesthetics, as treating of the beautiful in Nature and Art; Domestic Economy, practically taught, so far as possible, in order to prepare the graduates readily to become skillful housekeepers; last, and most important of all, the daily, systematic Reading and Study of the Holy Scriptures, as the only and all-sufficient Rule of Christian faith and practice.[17]

The subjects listed may have been dictated by Jewett, but it is clear from the modifying clauses where Matthew Vassar's interest lay. He was prepared to bow to tradition "so far as may be demanded" and "to such an extent as may be deemed advisable." But the arts and sciences, with their accompanying tangible equipment, were what caught his fancy. And the importance of health, homemaking skills, and religion was to him very real.

Milo Jewett met with the displeasure of some of the trustees, and in the end, of Matthew Vassar himself, and he resigned before the college opened. The course of study, as it appeared in 1865, was the product of his successor, John Raymond. However, it resembles Jewett's final version very closely. Latin, mathematics, and French (in place of Greek) were required of all freshmen. And then, according to the catalogue, freshmen were allowed a choice between ancient history and English grammar. No further reference to the history course has been found and it seems doubtful that it was actually offered. Later statements are to the effect that all freshman courses were required. If ancient history was not given, it was not for lack of good intentions. Perhaps there were not enough students to justify it. Or, more likely, since there were problems of staffing that first year, no suitable instructor was found. Greek was not offered at any point in the regular four-year course, but there was a teacher of Greek for those who wished to take it as a special course.

Sciences were plentiful. There is no science offered at Vassar today that was not offered in the original curriculum. Four of the eight original professors were in the field of science. These included the distinguished astronomer, Maria Mitchell; Dr. Alida Avery, who doubled as college physician; Professor Tenney, an Amherst graduate who had studied under Agassiz at Harvard; and Professor Farrar. These last two taught an entire group of sciences, for many of these were represented by a single semester course or just a series of lectures. Great specialization was not thought to be necessary. Farrar was trained as a lawyer, but he was teaching science so successfully at Elmira that President Raymond felt justified in offering him more than twice his Elmira salary to lure him to Vassar.[18] The lack of formal training in science was not unusual among the early scientists. The classical curriculum left no room for that kind of specialized training. Benjamin Silliman, one of the most distinguished scientists of this period, had, like Farrar, been trained in the law, and had no intensive scientific education at the time he was invited to teach in this field at Yale. Vassar's Maria Mitchell was educated by her father and her own self-directed study.

Vassar's equipment for teaching science was of the best. One of the three original buildings was the observatory equipped with the "third best" telescope in the United States. And the Main Building contained laboratories for natural philosophy, chemistry, and natural history, as well as "scientific cabinets" with collections for geology and the biological sciences. Few colleges could compare with this. A description of Brown's scientific equipment as of 1870 states: "Brown has one ghastly skeleton and two or three small charts, and a few promiscuous bones! Natural Philosophy is also destitute of means for making the subject interesting, if it is possible to make it so. Juniors are edified with a clothes-line and a broken fiddle.[19] In 1871 the professor of science at Elmira wrote: "Our apparatus in Optics inventories at only 5½ dollars at present. A Microscope would be a vast help in Physiology, Botany, Natural Philosophy, etc. Vassar College owns three. Cost of a good one, about 150 dollars."[20]

While Vassar was oriented toward science, as were the other women's colleges of the time, other subjects were not neglected. The course of study included English Literature, logic, rhetoric, political economy, government, natural theology, and evidences of Christianity. History, as a regular part of the course, had to await the appointment of Lucy Salmon, the college's first trained historian, in 1887.

In the junior and senior years the students were given a considerable range of choice of subjects, although mental and moral philosophy were required as in the standard classical course. But domestic economy was not offered. The prospectus of 1865 explained that practical work was not feasible for so large a group, but that "theoretical instruction through text books and lectures by a competent instructress would be given." It never was given, and it received no further mention.

President Raymond was practical in his approach. He leaned toward the classical curriculum, but he was willing to experiment within reason, and make any modifications that experience might prove desirable. His own education had been at Columbia College. It is true that he obtained his degree at Union, under President Nott, but he had transferred there, not because he was dissatisfied with his course at Columbia, but because he had been expelled for some student prank and only Union would take him in that late in his course.[21] His stay at Union was brief and he appears to have been little influenced by it at the time. However, as President of Vassar he made extensive study of other outstanding colleges and was well acquainted with the changes in the course of study that were being so widely debated.

After two years of the original curriculum, with only minor modifications, Raymond introduced a classical and a scientific course in 1867. The scientific course was usually the first break from the classical curriculum, but this step at Vassar meant, rather, a move in the direction of the classical course. In the latter, Greek was introduced for the first time as a part of the regular curriculum. In another two years the scientific course, as such, was dropped, although the privilege of substituting French for Greek, which was the most important difference between the two programs, was retained.

This does not mean that Raymond was rigidly committed to the older system. On the contrary, he writes:

My own faith on this subject is briefly this: that, while the education for men has outgrown the old college system, and is demanding room for expansion and free development in various directions, that for women has but just grown up to it, and needs for a season the bracing and support of its somewhat narrow forms. And I think we shall commit a serious, if not fatal, mistake in our policy for the College if we overlook this important distinction.[22]

I assume that this meant (although other interpretations are possible) that he felt that women must first prove to themselves and to others that they were capable of mastering the course that was still regarded by the majority of educators as the only rigid discipline in thinking. He did not himself doubt their capability. Thus the Vassar program of studies came closer to the traditional curriculum of the men's colleges year by year. And we find Maria Mitchell complaining: "We do things that other colleges have done before. We wait and ask for precedent. If the earth had waited for a precedent, it never would have turned on its axis."[23]

There were, however, some important differences between the women's college programs, including Vassar's, and the men's. This can be seen by analyzing the programs of study of men's and women's colleges in New York state, as reported to the state Board of Regents and published in their *Annual Report* of 1868. There were four women's colleges at this time authorized to grant the A.B. degree— Elmira, Vassar, Ingham University, and Rutgers Female College. A comparison of the courses of study of these four institutions with those of nine liberal arts colleges for men shows two important differences. The women's colleges offered more modern languages and less Greek than the men's. And they offered more sciences, particularly more biological sciences. These same differences appear when Vassar's course of study is compared with those of Yale and Harvard at approximately this same period. The emphasis of the women's colleges on the biological sciences was in part, but not entirely, due to their preoccupation with matters of health. It should be noted, also, that while art and music rarely appeared in the regular course of the women's colleges they were always available as special studies.

None of the women's colleges was offering domestic economy at this time. Rutgers Female College, in its report to the Board of Regents in 1868, elaborated in some detail on a Department of Domestic Economy, including such subjects as physiology, anatomy, hygiene, and the culinary arts. But then it was explained that they had not been able to establish this department as yet. In later reports of this college no further mention is made of this project. Smith introduced a one-point course in household chemistry in the late eighties as its concession to this field, but did not continue it. As late as 1891-92 we find Wellesley introducing a department of home economics, which apparently flourished for two years. The importance of this innovation and its great success were emphasized in the president's reports for these years. But the instructor resigned and no suitably trained person was found to replace her. On this subject the women's colleges have always been somewhat ambivalent. They have recognized their obligation to prepare their students for the profession of homemaker. But how to do this on the high intellectual plane on which they must operate has never been clear.

By the time Smith and Wellesley opened in 1875, Harvard, under Eliot's leadership, was multiplying courses and moving toward the free elective system. Smith and Wellesley were near neighbors of Harvard, and they could not fail to be influenced by these developments. Smith, however, had chosen to require Greek for entrance— the highest standard (or the most rigid, depending on one's point of view) that any women's college had set up to that time. President Taylor of Vassar said that Vassar's entrance requirements in that year were as rigid as those of the men's colleges, *except* for Greek.[24]

Nor did Smith provide any preparatory department to which students without the required entrance subjects could be diverted. And with only fourteen qualified students in the first year there was no possibility of free electives. The size of the student body precluded choice. The students studied Greek, Latin, English, and Biblical Literature in the first term. Mathematics, French, and German were added in the second, as additional teachers were secured. Chemistry and physics followed in the second year. And before the first class graduted they were instructed in mental and moral philosophy. Not only had they been given the traditional education for men; they had been instructed in part by Amherst professors who testified that the average performance of the Smith students exceeded that of the Amherst students.[25] Their health was not impaired. And the college enrollments were increasing fast. This was the final proof, if proof was still needed, that women were capable of the same intellectual performance as the men.

President Seelye addressed the first graduating class in Latin, but the commencement speaker, who was substituted for the usual senior essays and orations, was President Eliot of Harvard. He told his audience, after congratulating the college on its high admission standards, that he found generally recognized "but one mental acquisition as an essential part of the education of a lady or a gentleman—namely, an accurate and refined use of the mother tongue."[26] He went on to say that experience might well prove that the higher education of women should be different from that for men. The shift to a more varied curriculum and increased electives came gradually at Smith as enrollments increased. The most extensive revision of the curriculum, which may be used to date the complete acceptance of the free elective system, went into effect in 1899.[27]

Wellesley, with a larger student body than Smith, started with more faculty and a greater array of courses. Students in their freshman year were required to take Latin, German, French, and history, but they were given the most unusual privilege of one elective in the freshman year. And while required courses continued in later years, a considerable number of free electives were permitted. Wellesley's course of study as a whole was much like those of her sister colleges. Henry Durant had taken some pains to acquaint himself with those of Vassar and Mount Holyoke. The only unique feature, still found at Wellesley, was a required course in Biblical history. Starting with this degree of freedom, the shift to the elective system was less radical for Wellesley than for the other early colleges.

Bryn Mawr, opening in 1885, is the earliest of the colleges whose courses of study I have had opportunity to examine that offered a free elective system in its opening year. No one can say that Bryn Mawr did not maintain high academic standards from the beginning, yet Greek was not required for admission. Latin was required for admission, and a reading knowledge of Latin, French, and German, and "some acquaintance" with Greek for graduation, but students might acquire this knowledge in various ways. After three years, even the limited Greek requirement was waived for science students.

The only courses required of all students were two years of English, which covered the history of English literature from its Anglo-Saxon beginnings to the present; and one year of philosophy, which included logic, philosophy, ethics, Biblical study, hygiene, and human physiology! Beyond this there were some limited choices of the kind referred to today as distribution requirements; a choice of various sequences of courses known as major courses; and, finally, a certain number of completely free electives. Thus Bryn Mawr led her sister colleges who were already weighted down with an established order that was hard to dislodge.

The elective system was introduced at Vassar under President Taylor. It began gradually in the eighties with the introduction of an increasing number of courses and a correspondingly greater choice of electives. This in turn resulted in pressures to free the students from required courses. Beginning in 1890 there were fifteen departments of instruction, compared to the eight listed in the first catalogue. Some of these resulted from subdivisions of old departments; some of them represented new subjects; but all reflected multiplication of course offerings. The final step to an elective system comparable to that adopted by Bryn Mawr in 1885 was taken in 1903 after four years of debate by the faculty. President Taylor, reporting the results to the trustees, commented: "The process of making it [the new curriculum] has been a long and weary one and has not contributed, in my opinion, to the best relations of members of the faculty." It was not long before this brought new worries. In 1908 Taylor reported to the trustees what he believed to be an "undue multiplication of electives" under the pressure of departmental competition. It was a tendency, he felt, that would need watching.

Mount Holyoke, which did not achieve full college status until 1888, offered a classical, a scientific, and a literary course, with differentiated degrees. There were limited choices within these courses, but it does not appear to have offered the freedom of Bryn Mawr's course of studies. It was still a compromise between the two systems.

The course offerings of the coordinate colleges were dictated by different considerations. These, being attached to large universities and drawing on their faculties, had the advantages and limitations of a large potential curriculum over which they had little control. Radcliffe, the first of these coordinate colleges, was limited for its instruction to such Harvard faculty as were willing to repeat their courses for the women students. This offered some difficulties in organizing a consistent curriculum. However, the Harvard professors were generous in their response, although the additional remuneration was modest. In the first year twenty-nine classes were formed for the benefit of twenty-five students.[28] In the second year, twice as many courses were offered as were finally elected by the students. No complaint has been found that the students were denied important courses. The courses were the same, however, as those offered to the men. There was no question of adapting the work to any special needs of women. The requirements for the Radcliffe degree were Harvard's requirements.

Barnard, starting in 1889, was in a somewhat different position. The Barnard students were offered a Columbia degree from the beginning, on the condition that the students passed the Columbia examinations. No provision was made by the university for their instruction, but they obtained Columbia faculty. The number of courses was more limited than those available at Radcliffe. The Columbia faculty seem to have been less generous than the Harvard faculty, or perhaps the funds available were more restricted. In the end, however, Barnard won the right to appoint her own faculty and to make her own specifications for admission and degrees. This was subject to the approval of the Columbia authorities, but it did not mean identical requirements with those of Columbia College. In the early years, however, Barnard did not have a free hand in shaping the curriculum. Both these colleges had the advantage of drawing on distinguished faculties. And no one could question the quality of the women's work, since they were being judged by the same faculty and on the same courses as the men. But the opportunities for experimentation under this system were limited indeed.

Such was the early history of the development of courses of study in some of the older and larger women's colleges. A careful study of the curriculums of the major women's colleges in 1918 concludes that they were not marked by any particular originality; they were, rather, a "safe imitation" of those of the men's colleges.[29] This is true for the most part. The pressures that the women's colleges were under to prove themselves did not provide a favorable climate for exploration. And by the time that they were accepted they had become, like the older men's colleges, set in their ways. There were, however, some important differences in emphasis, as has already been noted.

One cannot but wonder if it might have been different. If, say, Milo Jewett had not been forced to resign, or to revise his original plan to fit Vassar's shrinking finances, might not the women's colleges have been at least a little in the lead in adopting the free elective system? If they had had a free elective system earlier, might they not have been freer to experiment with new subjects that appeared to be of special interest to their students? And of interest to men students, too, once they had broken with tradition? This assumes, of course, that Vassar's lead would have been followed by the later women's colleges, but this is not improbable. Vassar was one of the earliest and largest of the women's colleges. And the newer colleges always looked to their predecessors for ideas. They wanted to experiment, but they also felt the need of precedent. Just educating women was radical enough! However, the first need may have been to establish self-confidence among the women themselves. This was doubtless best accomplished by demonstrating to friends and enemies alike that they could do exactly what the men could do.

When all the women enrolled in schools of higher learning during the second half of the nineteenth century are considered, the importance of what one or another of the private women's colleges was doing shrinks considerably. At no time during this half century did the private women's colleges enroll as many as half of the women taking work beyond the secondary school level. At the end of the century, only 24,000 of the 85,000 women in schools of higher education were in women's institutions, and one-third of the 24,000 were in women's normal schools and Catholic colleges. Less than one woman in five was in a private women's liberal arts college where church influence was relatively small.

More than half of all the women continuing their formal education beyond the secondary school level were in normal schools and teachers colleges. The courses of study in these varied widely from those in the liberal arts colleges. They had a specific aim—preparing teachers; the subjects these teachers would be teaching were more likely to be arithmetic than calculus, and English grammar rather than Greek grammar. Also, the normal schools for the most part had less rigid requirements for admission than those set up by the liberal arts colleges; the majority did not yet offer a four-year course leading to a degree. They, too, were in the experimental stage. The desirability of formal preparation for teachers was not yet completely accepted, and the usefulness of some of the courses in techniques of teaching, as contrasted with courses in the subjects to be taught, could be challenged. In fact, the whole program advocated by the "educators" was scorned by many women's colleges. They might offer a course or two in education under the sponsorship of a department of philosophy or psychology, but that was as far as they were willing to go in preparing their students specifically for the profession that most of the students were destined to pursue, for a few years, at least.

The split between the women's colleges and the normal schools was so complete that the graduates of some of the well-known women's colleges could not get a teacher's certificate without an additional year of study. The effect of this in later occupational activities is marked. Vassar College appears to have made the fewest concessions in this respect. It never had a department of education. And Robinson reports that among the alumnae of five eastern women's colleges, class of 1912, Vassar had fewer teachers than any of the other colleges—31 per cent as compared with from 57 to 74 per cent for the graduates of the other colleges.[30]

The big universities, on the contrary, had departments of education, or even complete teachers colleges. And many of the women enrolled in these institutions—some 5,000 around 1900—were preparing for teaching. These were in addition to the 45,000 women in normal schools. The gulf between the women's colleges and the teacher training institutions has narrowed in recent years. The normal school is rapidly being replaced by the teachers college with a four-year course that has incorporated increasing amounts of the liberal arts program over the years. And the women's colleges and the state departments of education have worked out programs, each side making some concessions, that enable the graduates of these colleges to get teachers' certificates with a minimum of additional training.

Woman's other important occupation is homemaking. This was generally regarded one hundred years ago as something to be learned at home and not at school—certainly not at college. When home economics began to be taught in the lower schools, the state universities and teachers colleges introduced departments of home economics, not so much for the prospective homemaker as for the prospective teacher of homemaking.

The early attempts to introduce home economics in the leading women's colleges met with failure, as has been noted, although many women's colleges did introduce it later, particularly the public and the private southern colleges. Home economics more surely than teaching was woman's sphere, but by the same token it was judged to be less demanding intellectually than the subjects studied by men. Training in this field, like training in education, has changed with the years. Sociology and child psychology, as well as physiology and chemistry, are important fields which the two courses of study have in common; but home economics as such is not found in most of the larger eastern women's colleges.

It is easy to argue that the women's colleges were right in avoiding these subjects in a period when the colleges were on trial, and when the subjects themselves were more concerned with skills than basic principles. It is also possible to argue that they shirked a responsibility or missed an opportunity for pioneering in these fields. Those steering the course of the older women's colleges were aware of these questions, and they were in disagreement as to what should be done about them. But in the end they left it to other institutions, mostly public, to find the answers to them.

With the development of the state agricultural colleges there was demand for training in home economics. If farmers could profit by scientific training, the farm families reasoned, so also could the farmers' wives. Iowa State College at Ames was the pioneer, offering "Domestic Economy" in the Ladies' Course in 1871.[31] The State Agricultural College of Kansas followed, offering, in the middle seventies, courses in "Household Management and Economy," "The Management of Children and Their Private Instruction," and "A Knowledge of the Laws of Health and Nursing the Sick."[32] By the turn of the century, instruction in this area was offered in many of the agricultural colleges and a few liberal arts colleges.

It is often assumed that the women in the coeducational institutions —and they constituted 70 per cent of all women in schools of higher education in 1900—were receiving just the same education as the men. It is true that they were offered the same opportunities, or most of them. But they had choices. And insofar as the men selected engineering and agriculture, and the women education and home economics, they were likely to be studying in segregated groups even while occupying the same campus. Of the 61,000 women enrolled in coeducational schools in 1900, 43,000 were in teacher training courses and 2,000 were majoring in home economics; approximately three-fourths of the education students and all but a handful of the home economics students were women. Thus while the women's colleges were offering women the same education as that provided by the men's colleges, many of the coeducational institutions, and particularly the state universities and colleges, were providing women with something different.

The free elective system offered increasing possibilities for experimentation. A new subject could be introduced without revising the whole course of study. This gave those who were interested in trying out new ideas a chance to try them without much resistance from the defenders of traditional courses. Perhaps even more important was the greater opportunity it gave to students of shaping the curriculum through their relatively free choice of courses.

The combined course offerings of Mount Holyoke, Smith, Vassar, and Wellesley doubled in the twenty years between the eighties and the first decade of the twentieth century.[33] In the next thirty years they more than doubled again. That about ended the period of expansion. The "undue multiplication of electives" that Taylor had feared is now recognized and some of these colleges have been pruning their courses in recent years. But the total offerings are still between four and five times what they were seventy years ago. Smith offers about twenty times as many courses as a student would normally elect in a four-year course. Or, to put it another way, it would take her nearly eighty years of study to exhaust the course offerings. There seems to be room for a more drastic reduction of courses than any that has been made to date. To quote Sidney Hook: "This process of historical accretion has many causes but few good reasons."[34] And

Robinson: "An overloaded curriculum is not the guarantee of a useful one."[35]

The kind of education that women have had is perhaps better reflected by actual student elections than course offerings. The shifts in student elections at Vassar College, where they can be traced over a period of ninety years, are very marked. This is shown in Table 4. Four-year periods have been used for these comparisons to avoid the temporary fluctuations that often occur in a single year.

Table 4.

PERCENTAGE DISTRIBUTION OF STUDENT ELECTIONS, VASSAR COLLEGE 1865–1869 TO 1953–1957

Groups of Studies[a]	1865-1869	1901-1905	1927-1931	1953-1957
Sciences	39.3	25.4	19.7	16.5
Classics	21.2	16.3	4.1	1.7
Modern languages	20.6	15.3	18.3	14.9
Arts	11.6	23.3	29.0	29.4
Social Sciences	7.2	19.7	28.9	37.4
Total	100.0	100.0	100.0	100.0

[a] The classification of subjects is that used in the Vassar course of study. Psychology, which is included in both sciences and social sciences, has been divided equally between the two divisions. Student credit hours are the measure used.

A more detailed breakdown for the later period, based on student majors, is given in Table 5. The major as a fairly concentrated field of study has been in existence at Vassar only since the early 1930's.

The arts and social sciences combined accounted for less than one-fifth of the total student elections at Vassar in the earliest years of the college. Today they account for two-thirds of the total. Modern languages show the smallest relative change, but the decline in the classics is sharp. The great decrease came with the removal of required courses in this field in the 1920's. Sciences have dropped sub-

Table 5.

TRENDS IN MAJOR STUDENTS, VASSAR COLLEGE
1931–1957

Department	Average Annual Number of Senior Majors[a]		
	1931-1934	1943-1945	1954-1957
Chemistry and physics	15	21	10
Mathematics	12	17	10
Geology	3	3	2
Biological sciences	9	23	14
Psychology	6	7	9
Total science	45	71	45
Classics	11	4	2
French	26	8	12
Other foreign languages and literatures	10	11	9
Total foreign languages	47	23	23
Art	11	14	21
English and drama	54	53	60
Music	11	9	9
Total arts	76	76	90
Child study	12	26	30
Economics, sociology, and anthropology	22	34	32
History and American Culture	32	29	28
Political science and international relations	11	7	25
Philosophy and religion	7	4	11
Total social science	84	100	126
Total	252	270	284

[a] Each group comprises the senior majors for four classes. The acceleration of the war period resulted in four classes in the three years 1943-1945.

stantially, but even so account for one-sixth of total elections.

The extent to which these trends represent changes in student interests between the 1860's and the 1950's, and the extent to which it is merely adjustment to existing student interests with the removal of rigid requirements cannot be measured, although it can be demonstrated that the removal of a specific requirement brings substantial changes in course elections in a short space of time.

With the removal of requirements it is possible to compare the interests of men and women students at a given period. Table 6 compares the percentage distribution of earned degrees in 1956 in different groups of subjects for men's and women's colleges, and for men and women in state universities. The eight colleges selected for this comparison are liberal arts colleges in the same geographic area—New England and New York state. The six state universities are among the largest in the country, and none is located in the east.

The variations among individual colleges for men and women are greater than the differences between the men's colleges as a group and the women's colleges as a group. The differences between the two groups represent a difference in men's and women's interests rather than any chance emphasis of a particular college. The women are found in the arts, mathematics, modern languages, and religion in much larger numbers than the men, and the men greatly outnumber the women in the physical sciences, economics, and philosophy. Differences in other subjects are not as marked. In general, it is apparent that where the students are not specifically preparing for such professions as engineering, business, home economics, or nursing, but are for the most part specializing in fields that interest them without regard to their professional possibilities, the differences in masculine and feminine interests are not very great. This conclusion is supported not only by the data given in Table 6, but by detailed study of individual colleges. To illustrate, in spite of the preponderance of men in physical sciences, there were more chemistry majors at Mount Holyoke than Amherst, and more English majors at Amherst than Mount Holyoke in this year. Other instances of this can also be found in the detailed data.

When professional schools are compared, the differences between men's and women's interests or choices are striking. Women are not yet flocking to engineering or men to home economics or nursing.

Table 6.

FIELDS OF CONCENTRATION FOR CLASS OF 1956 IN SELECTED MEN'S AND WOMEN'S LIBERAL ARTS COLLEGES AND STATE UNIVERSITIES[a]

Field of Concentration	Percentage Liberal arts colleges		Distribution State universities	
	Men	Women	Men	Women
English and drama	15.3	21.6	5.7	17.3
Art and music	4.0	10.9	1.8	5.1
Total arts	19.3	32.5	7.4	22.4
Mathematics	1.2	2.6	1.4	1.1
Physical sciences	11.4	5.7	5.4	.9
Biological sciences	7.0	6.2	7.5	4.7
Psychology	3.7	4.6	2.2	3.1
Total science	23.3	19.1	16.5	9.8
History	13.2	11.6	2.7	3.3
Political science	8.3	10.0	3.1	2.2
Economics	14.6	3.1	4.0	.8
Sociology	1.8	3.5	1.6	3.4
Philosophy	5.4	1.9	.6	.3
Religion	.6	2.2	.1	b
All other	4.2	2.6	3.5	7.6
Total social science	48.1	36.9	15.6	17.6
Classics	.3	.3	.1	.1
Modern languages	2.6	5.6	.7	3.3
Total foreign language	2.9	5.9	.8	3.5
Professional training	6.5	5.6	59.7[c]	46.7[c]
	100.0	100.0	100.0	100.0
Students with majors listed	1,367	1,401	13,018	5,829
Major not classified	92	48	513	341

[a] Colleges: Amherst, Colgate, Dartmouth, Williams; Mount Holyoke, Smith, Vassar, Wellesley. Universities: California, Illinois, Michigan, Minnesota, Texas, Wisconsin. Data from United States Office of Education, "Earned Degrees Conferred by Higher Educational Institutions, 1955-1956," Circular No. 499, 1957.

[b] Less than 1/10 of 1 per cent.

[c] This includes education degrees, which account for 28.5 per cent of the women and 6.4 per cent of the men.

The large numbers of men and women in the state universities who are taking professional or pre-professional courses at the undergraduate level reduces the proportions in most of the nonprofessional fields, as compared with the liberal arts colleges. But the relative differences between men and women are much the same in the universities and colleges compared.

It is frequently stated that in the coeducational institutions a great preponderance of men or women in a particular subject will deter members of the minority sex from electing subjects that really interest them. It is argued that Amherst students, for example, are more likely to elect English courses than men students in a coeducational institution. And the students in a women's college are more likely to elect physics than women in a university where the physics students are predominantly men. The minority sex will either be intimidated by the majority or will feel that such studies are inappropriate to their sex. It was on this ground that President Van Hise of the University of Wisconsin proposed separate sections for men and women in those subjects with enough students to require division into sections.[36] The experiment was never seriously tried. However, the data in Table 6 give some support to this belief. The proportion of men majoring in English is 33 per cent of the proportion of women in the universities as compared with 77 per cent in the colleges. And in the physical sciences it is found that the proportion of men is six times the proportion of women in the universities and only double the proportion of women in the colleges. In view of all the variables this cannot be accepted as conclusive evidence that coeducation may intimidate the minority sex in any given field. The variations among individual universities, as among individual colleges, are very large. And the students attracted to the different institutions in the first place may well have different kinds of interests.

The above discussion has assumed that the student elections have been guided by student interests rather than college requirements. This is in general true, but the college requirements are still an appreciable factor in determining student choices, particularly in private

Table 7.

REQUIRED COURSES IN WOMEN'S COLLEGES
1931–1932 AND 1956–1957[a]

Subject	Percentage of Colleges Requiring Subject		
	1931–1932	1956–1957	
		Including Catholic Colleges	Excluding Catholic Colleges
English	97	83	82
Religion	47	45	37
History	70	40	34
Health and hygiene	26	32	37
Philosophy	34	25	11
Psychology	38	11	3
Mathematics	33	6	3
Classics	25	6	—
Number of colleges	76	47	38

[a] Catholic colleges have been included in the 1931–32 figures approximately in proportion to their numbers at that time. These figures cover the majority of women's colleges for 1931–32. The 1956–57 figures include about two-thirds of the non-Catholic colleges and a smaller proportion of the Catholic colleges, in order to hold the proportion of the two groups of colleges approximately the same in the two periods. The differences in the requirements of the two groups is very marked. The data for 1931–32 are from S. H. Walker, *The Women's Colleges* (Mimeographed report), September 1932, pp. 5-6. The data for 1956-57 have been compiled from catalogues of that year.

colleges. The extent to which specific course requirements have prevailed in the more recent period in the women's colleges is shown in Table 7. Even when the specific course requirements are small, however, there is usually a large array of distribution requirements. The student need not take any particular science or language, but sciences and languages she must have. The choice of the major is free, but the choice of courses within the major field is sometimes quite limited.

Even the colleges that tailor their programs to individual needs and interests may give individual advisors dictatorial powers. The extent to which these requirements have affected student elections would be difficult to measure.

It is apparent from the data in Table 7 that while specific requirements have declined substantially in this twenty-five year period, the requirements in health and hygiene have increased. The great decline in history is partly due to the substitution of courses in American civilization which are only in part historical. Mathematics and psychology show marked declines. The classics, for the non-Catholic colleges, have disappeared completely. Physical education has not been included in the comparison because it is often a requirement for which no credit is given. It was required by all but one of the forty-seven colleges in the 1956-1957 sample.

Among the women's colleges I have found three that have no single course required of all students—Bennington, Sarah Lawrence, and Vassar. Bennington does not even have a physical education requirement. Sarah Lawrence and Vassar have such a requirement, but without credit. Bennington and Sarah Lawrence depend largely on individual advice to steer the individual student. Vassar, in addition to an extensive advising system, has elaborate distribution requirements and a good many restrictions on the major. Neither too much nor too little specialization is permitted. The actual degree of freedom that students have depends on the individual department and the flexibility of individual advisors. At the other extreme, Scripps has a substantial core curriculum required of all students. These are not the requirements of the classical curriculum, and free electives are available even in the freshman year, but the course does represent a marked withdrawal from the free elective system.

There are other ways, also, of controlling student elections. Specific prerequisites to specific courses have grown. These are in addition to major and distribution requirements. Such trends are not peculiar to the women's colleges, however.

One of the arguments for women's colleges has always been that they can adapt their educational program to women's special needs more readily than the coeducational institutions. But the discussion thus far suggests that they have done this to a very limited extent. Home economics, as it was earlier defined, is found in a large number of women's colleges today, but it had its earliest and greatest development in the state universities and agricultural colleges; the eastern women's colleges had no part in its early expansion. Nor did they participate in their early years in developing courses of study for nurses, teachers, or other women's professions. They have, however, shown some interest in social work, although more as a field for volunteer service than as a professional opportunity. The first course offered in this field at a women's college appears to have been a course in "Charities and Corrections" given at Bryn Mawr by Franklin Giddings in 1888. Vassar introduced it in 1894. But the earliest course in this field seems to have been offered at Cornell in 1885.[87] In other words, the women's colleges did not invent it, but were quick to see its virtues for their students.

A second field that is presumably of particular interest to women has been marriage and the family. Herbert C. Mills introduced a course in the family at Vassar in 1916, the first that I can find for a women's college. But such courses did not originate at Vassar. Edward A. Ross was teaching a course in this field at Wisconsin in the first decade of this century; and Mary Roberts Smith gave a seminar in "Family" at Stanford as early as 1894. This, so far as I can learn, was the first such course in our colleges. Today these courses are found in practically every women's college, and also, of course, in the coeducational institutions.

In recent years the question has been raised as to whether this field is of peculiar interest to women. Men, too, are concerned with family life. When Radcliffe and Harvard became completely coeducational in 1947, Radcliffe reserved the right to offer courses of special interest to women. In the following year, taking advantage of this provision, they offered a course in "Sex and Marriage" and were surprised to find that some twenty-five Harvard undergraduates had elected it.[38] Whatever the motives of the men students they were allowed to remain. Today a course in "Sociology of the Family" (perhaps a less enticing title) is open to all. Moreover, a number of men's colleges, among them Amherst, Bowdoin, Dartmouth, Haverford, and Union, offer courses in marriage and the family. It is well known that young men are taking an increasing interest in and responsibility for family problems, as their wives are taking increasing responsibility for support. The old division of labor between the sexes is in some measure breaking down.

Child psychology and child study are other fields that have received special encouragement in the women's colleges. These courses have usually been attached to psychology and education departments, respectively. Most of them were introduced in the 1920's and later, although some of the early education courses included some of the material of child study. Child psychology was introduced at Vassar as a separate course in 1918. These subjects are now quite generally found in both coeducational and women's colleges—complete with nursery schools. They have not yet been established in the courses of study of the men's colleges, as far as I can learn.

Student interest in these fields is genuine. The Department of Child Study at Vassar, for example, has been among the three largest, in the number of majors enrolled, in recent years. How much of this is due to interest in teaching, and how much to preparation for their future roles as homemakers, it would be hard to say. The fact that it prepares for either eventuality is, no doubt, a consideration. But there is also a tendency for the "intellectuals" to sneer, or to question whether the new field has the content and disciplinary value of the sciences and humanities—or if it has, whether this is a useful rearrangement of the content of the established disciplines. Every new field must meet this type of criticism. It takes time for a new subject to acquire the content and techniques that earn respect, and this field is still in its infancy. Not all such experiments succeed, but without them the educational process is likely to stagnate.

The most complete flowering of work in this field, as far as I can learn, is to be found at Antioch, a coeducational college with a "family studies" department. This covers the usual range of courses in family and the child, as well as consumer economics, nutrition, fashion and technology, and food. Correlated studies are found in physical education, psychology, the arts, and other fields. Vassar College, with her tradition of euthenics courses, has an entire department of child study, courses in nutrition in the Physiology Department, and the family and consumer economics in the Department of Economics, Sociology, and Anthropology. In one place or another in the Vassar curriculum most of the courses listed in the related fields of the Antioch family studies are to be found. But these courses are not formally grouped, as at Antioch, and the courses in food and clothing are missing.

Vassar's Euthenics contemplated such an interdepartmental venture as Antioch's family studies; but two of the three departments originally selected for this refused to cooperate, and what remained of the project shortly split into Euthenics and Child Study. Child Study survived and prospered, partly because it fills the gap left by the absence of a department of education. Euthenics is no longer a part of the regular curriculum, although a summer institute flourished for many years. The summer Euthenics Institute, it should be noted, was primarily adult education, and coeducational.

The field of study in which the women's colleges clearly pioneered was health. Courses in hygiene and physiology were standard offerings in nearly every women's college from the beginning. They were usually required at a time when they were rarely found in the men's colleges. Many of these required courses were sacrificed to the free elective system, but it is worth noting that health and hygiene is the one field for which the number of required courses has increased in recent years, a period when the general trend has been away from required courses. Outside of the academic curriculum, such courses were reenforced by required physical education and required physical examinations. Women in the coeducational institutions, also, were sometimes provided with medical services before these were provided for men. In the University of Wisconsin, for instance, the students in Ladies Hall had medical care for some years before this was extended to the men.[39]

Required physical education and required physical examinations have spread to the men's and the coeducational colleges over the years, but the women's colleges led the way. Physiology has become a regular academic department in many institutions, although required courses in this field have practically disappeared and the subject is often combined with other biological sciences in departments of biology.

Many of the women's colleges are pursuing some of the newer trends—the individual honors programs, required courses in the great tradition, field work programs, and others. Bennington, Sarah Lawrence, Scripps, and Keuka can be named as being in the vanguard in one or another of these experiments. But one can also name Swarthmore, Antioch, Reed, St. Johns, Goddard, and Chicago. Experimental programs are not, of course, necessarily an improvement on the more conventional ones, but they are likely to open the way to progress. Unfortunately, the new colleges tend to be more experimental than the old, and except for the Catholic colleges there are no longer new women's colleges.

NOTES

[1] S. E. Morison, *The Founding of Harvard College* (Cambridge, 1935), Ch. 3.
[2] D. R. Fox, *Union College, An Unfinished History* (Schenectady, 1945), p. 13.
[3] R. F. Butts, *The College Charts its Course* (New York, 1939), pp. 88-91.
[4] H. B. Adams, *Thomas Jefferson and the University of Virginia* (United States Bureau of Education Circular of Information No. 2, 1888), pp. 122-125.
[5] F. and H. L. Wayland, *Memoir of the Life and Labors of Francis Wayland* (New York, 1868), vol. 2, p. 101.
[6] *Ibid.*, pp. 95-96.
[7] G. P. Schmidt, *Liberal Arts College* (New Brunswick, 1957), p. 66.
[8] T. Woody, *A History of Women's Education in the United States* (New York, 1929), vol. 2, p. 142.
[9] G. Meltzer, *The Beginnings of Elmira* (Elmira, 1941), Ch. 6.
[10] M. Jewett, "Origin of Vassar College." Manuscript.

[11] M. Jewett, manuscript, probably Milo Jewett's original paper to Matthew Vassar.

[12] Schmidt, *op. cit.*, p. 67.

[13] Butts, *op. cit.*, p. 210.

[14] H. R. Lloyd, ed., *Life and Letters of John Howard Raymond* (New York, 1881), p. 566.

[15] M. Jewett, "Origins of Vassar College." Manuscript.

[16] *Ibid.*

[17] *Proceedings of Trustees of Vassar Female College.* Meeting, February 26, 1861. p. 16.

[18] W. C. Barber, *Elmira College* (New York, 1955), p. 93.

[19] W. C. Bronson, *History of Brown University, 1764-1914* (Providence, 1914), p. 370.

[20] Meltzer, *op. cit.*, p. 88.

[21] Lloyd, *op. cit.*, p. 56.

[22] *Ibid.*, p. 584.

[23] P. M. Kendall, *Life, Letters, and Journals of Maria Mitchell* (Boston, 1896), p. 174.

[24] J. M. Taylor and E. H. Haight, *Vassar* (New York, 1915), p. 66.

[25] L. C. Seelye, *The Early History of Smith College, 1871-1910* (Boston, 1923), p. 51.

[26] *Ibid.*, p. 48.

[27] *Ibid*, p. 98.

[28] Society for the Collegiate Instruction of Women, Commonly Called "The Harvard Annex," *Story of its Beginning and Growth* (Cambridge, 1891), p. 11.

[29] M. L. Robinson, "Curriculum of the Woman's College," (*United States Bureau of Education, 1918*), *no. 6*, p. 108.

[30] *Ibid.*, p. 120.

[31] B. Morgan, *A History of the Extension Services of Iowa State College* (Ames, 1934), p. 9.

[32] *Biennial Reports of the State Agricultural College.* Manhattan, Kansas.

[33] For Mount Holyoke, the first year of its existence as a college was used for this comparison.

[34] S. Hook, *Education for Modern Man* (New York, 1946), p. xi.

[35] Robinson, *op. cit.*, p. 107.

[36] M. Curti and V. Cardensen, *The University of Wisconsin, A History, 1848-1925* (Madison, 1949), vol. II, p. 81.

[37] W. T. Hewitt, *Cornell University, A History* (New York, 1905), vol. 2, p. 131.

[38] *New York Times*, April 15, 1948, p. 21.

[39] M. Curti and V. Cardensen, *op. cit.*, vol. I, p. 686.

A COLLEGE IS NOT ONLY A BODY OF STUDIES BUT A MODE OF
ASSOCIATION; . . . A FREE COMMUNITY BUT A VERY REAL ONE,
IN WHICH DEMOCRACY MAY WORK ITS REASONABLE TRIUMPHS
OF ACCOMMODATION, ITS VITAL PROCESSES OF UNION.

WOODROW WILSON*

6. Study Is Not Everything

THE ACADEMIC work week is not as definite as that of the ordinary job, and it probably falls a little short of the forty-five hour expectation of the typical undergraduate course. It certainly does not occupy half of the average student's waking hours. What the students do with this free time has always been a matter of concern to the college authorities; and the residence college, particularly, has regularly used it to improve the manners and morals of the young people, if not their minds. The students, too, have filled odd moments with their own group activities.

Parents often send their sons and daughters away to college when there is an equally good institution within reach of home because they want them to participate in the social life of the college. The students themselves frequently explain that "study is not everything." For many, the nonacademic activities are as important as the course of studies. The women graduates, in particular, stress the value of the

* From Woodrow Wilson, "The Spirit of Learning," Phi Beta Kappa address, Harvard University, July 1, 1909.

friendships made in college, and the development of social skills (presumably outside the classroom) during their undergraduate years. Even the college authorities have emphasized, in the picture books, and in the handbooks and catalogues, the social and educational value of extracurricular activities. The current Vassar catalogue, for instance, in its introductory statement, gives about equal space to the "Academic College" and the "Residential College." In discussing the latter it says:

Residential life contributes significantly to the college's educational program. It provides a miniature and, in many ways, ideal society in which young women learn about the nature, aims, and problems of social groups and of society at large. . . . We believe that life in the residence halls should be, in quality, equal to the life of the classroom, that intellectual and spiritual values and attitudes subscribed to in the one should be mirrored in the other, that in a college community manners, as the reflection of morals, are the proper responsibility of both faculty and students.[1]

The residential college was a necessary development in a period when population was scattered and an institution of any size had to attract students from great distances. But today it is regarded by all concerned as having special educational values of its own. The college sets social as well as academic standards for its students; and it provides opportunities for training outside of the strictly academic program. It controls their environment and most of their activities. It used to decide how long the students should sleep. In Mount Holyoke's early seminary days, for example, students were not allowed to get up before five or after six, and had to be in bed by ten.[2] In view of these around-the-clock programs it is not surprising to find that it is the small residential college, rather than the university, that has emphasized the development of the whole person.

In the earlier period the students' entire week was neatly scheduled. Each day began with morning prayers, sometimes as early as five o'clock. Meals, recitations, study hours, recreation hours, religious services, and more prayers followed in regular rotation, every student doing the same thing at the same time, with lights out at nine or ten.

Vassar's first weekday schedule provided two "recreation periods" of forty minutes each, and two unscheduled hours that presumably took care of concerts, special lectures, exercise, and perhaps some additional recreation of the students' own choosing.[3] But even on Sundays the student had little unscheduled time. The Wellesley student of 1876 arose at seven on Sunday mornings and retired at 9:30 in the evenings. During these hours she participated in three prayer meetings, a Bible class, church, and two "silent hours" (actually only fifteen minutes each). There were also three formal meals that could not be disposed of in the fifteen or twenty minutes that today's students allot to such ceremonies.[4] Yet 1876 was in a comparatively late and sophisticated period.

Many of the college regulations are in lieu of parental controls, and are primarily for the protection of the student. Others are essential to group living. The rules for the early women's colleges were numerous, although the men's colleges, too, had many regulations. It was thought best to err on the side of safety. Mary Lyon explained that "at first the law of love was enough" but as the students increased, and were less mature, she found that she had to be more explicit.[5] By 1839 the regulations, later known as the "book of duties," had expanded to 106 items. Among the forbidden activities were riding "with a gentleman alone," studying during recreation hours, and staying in a room "over a fourth of a minute after the bell sounds." Under "things that should seasonably be said" were such items as the desirability of daily baths, "proper conduct in back buildings," and "gentle footsteps over stairs."[6] The students appear to have accepted these rules with amusement, but without rebellion.

Protective measures have become fewer year by year, in keeping with the increasing freedom which parents themselves allow their children today. But they may still include a limited number of weekends away from college, and where (if at all) a student may consume alcoholic beverages. Such controls are usually relaxed as the student progresses from the freshman to the senior year. This is part of the growing-up process. Other regulations, such as quiet hours, are as essential to group living today as they were earlier. When a protesting Bryn Mawr student asked, with regard to some new, student-initiated rules concerning quiet hours, "Will the President define what is meant by noise?" she was told by the presiding student officer: "Noise is what disturbs other people."[7] Such regulations are important for all concerned but they are not primarily educational.

The educational features of the extracurricular program are many. Those most frequently mentioned are (1) religious training; (2) a manual-work program; (3) a college lecture and concert program; (4) training in "behavior befitting a gentleman or a lady;" (5) student government; (6) student-initiated activities; and (7) the opportunity to associate informally with other intelligent and educated people, whether students or faculty. All these have been consciously fostered by one or another residential college as factors contributing to the end product—a well-rounded personality.

Religious education outside of the college curriculum has always been stressed. In those colleges established by the different religious denominations this has often taken precedence over the academic program, as well as being in some measure incorporated in it. In many of the early colleges the president was not only an administrator; he was professor, college chaplain, and probably minister of some local church as well. Today, on the contrary, the religious program in most colleges is voluntary. There is usually a full-time chaplain, but no prayer meetings and no compulsory chapel. It remains an important part of some students' programs, and is ignored by others. The visiting ministers must compete for student time and interest with other college-sponsored events; and the religious clubs must compete in the same way with other student organizations.

In recent years interest in religious activity has increased, as it has in the world outside of the college. I recently overheard a student saying to her companion as they left the college chapel, "I don't know how I am going to explain this to my parents. They don't go to church." Those who have worried about the antireligious influence of higher education can be reassured. Those who would promote the spirit of inquiry no matter where it may lead are now the ones who worry.

Required manual-work programs have been a relatively infrequent part of the educational plan. A few of the early college founders made a fetish of required labor, and some educators today insist that manual work should be a part of every student's experience to insure that well-roundedness which the college has set as its goal. Others, however, have felt that there is ample opportunity to obtain this kind of training elsewhere, and that to incorporate it in the total college program is to take time and energy that might better be devoted to intellectual pursuits. The latter group has usually prevailed. And in practice few colleges have adopted such a program for educational purposes.

When Mount Holyoke opened as a seminary each student was required to work an hour a day at some domestic task. This was not a part of the educational program, however, as Mary Lyon repeatedly explained. It was necessary because domestic help was scarce and because it was important to keep costs at a minimum. As soon as circumstances permitted, it was to be abandoned.

One or the other of these considerations—financial need or scarcity of labor—accounts for most of the college work programs. Ordinarily, the colleges today provide such self-help opportunities as waiting on table, shelving books in the library, and sorting mail, for those students who must earn a part of their expenses. Some of the early men's colleges employed "charity students" on the college farms during vacations. But these activities have limited educational value, particularly for the poorer students who have worked before, and are regarded by all concerned as a solution for financial problems rather than as an educational device. As far as the college is concerned such work is optional.

When, however, a war or other emergency creates a shortage of workers, colleges have frequently followed Mount Holyoke's early example in introducing a required work program. Under these conditions they have sometimes insisted that this is not only unavoidable, but that it has educational value as well. Even Mary Lyon sometimes argued that her domestic system afforded healthy physical exercise and preserved student interest in home duties.[8] And Henry Durant regarded the hour each day which Wellesley required when it opened as an important measure for promoting democratic feeling among students from families of different income levels.[9] It was retained at Wellesley for twenty years.

The colleges introduced volunteer work programs, rather than required labor, as a result of the labor shortages of World War I. The Vassar students, after some preliminary skirmishing with dandelions in the college lawns, formed a group of farmerettes to work on the college farm and neighboring farms during the summer. Similar programs were to be found at other women's colleges—all volunteer.

With World War II, however, a required hour each day was instituted at Vassar for waiting on table, cleaning rooms, messenger service, and other essential jobs. This was explained in the *Vassar Student Handbook* of 1946 simply as being necessitated by the labor shortage. The 1948 handbook, however, describing a somewhat more limited program, explains: "The Committee believes that the co-operative system has contributed substantially to the education of Vassar students. . . . The Committee wishes to emphasize that the educational values do not lie in learning how to do any specific piece of household work. . . . It offers invaluable experience in learning how to handle people, in learning to know and work with others of different ability and background."[10] This was a faculty committee but it was not an exclusively faculty point of view. I recall one student who expressed real enthusiasm for the system, explaining that she didn't mind the work at all and it was worth an hour a day "just to see Margie have to get her hands dirty." Today, with a cafeteria service, the work load has been reduced to one hour a week, and is explained in the current handbook as being required "chiefly for practical reasons, but it also teaches each student to share with others the responsibilities of community living."[11]

Another type of work program, which is an integral part of the educational offering, is the required work period away from college.

Such programs are found for instance, at Antioch, Bennington, and Keuka. These, however, are a definite part of the academic program, and are usually performed outside of the college community. Consequently, they have no place in the discussion here.

The arguments for including manual or clerical work in every student's program, except as it keeps the cost of education down or is required because of labor shortages, are less cogent today than they were when Henry Durant introduced his domestic labor at Wellesley. Household service today is rare, and most students have been called upon to help with the housework at home. Also, a paid job in summer is almost routine for today's undergraduate. Five out of six students of the 1958 graduating class at Vassar had worked in paid jobs at least one summer during their college course. One-fourth of them had worked all three summers, and many had held paid jobs before they entered college.

While the earlier records are incomplete, there is enough evidence to indicate that not over one student in ten worked in a paid position in summer in the early 1920's. A job after college was respectable enough at that time, for that was the day of the career girl. But working at odd jobs during one's college course was not usually regarded as desirable training for a career. Today, however, such educational value as the simple manual and clerical jobs afford is obtained by the great majority of students outside of the college program. In consequence, whatever requirements the college may make in this respect will be due primarily to the difficulties of obtaining hired help.

The large coeducational institutions with most of the student body living off of the campus have not been in a position to require a work program for all students. Also, with a somewhat less sheltered student body the educational values that Durant and others have seen in such a program are less apparent. A larger proportion of the women in the universities have worked to contribute to their own support than in the more expensive private colleges. The universities have made some effort to provide self-help opportunities; but that is all. The contrast between the girl from a wealthy family who lives in a sorority house and her classmate who works her way through college, at least in part, and who economizes by living in a small room and cooking on a hot plate, or eating her food cold, is more apparent than any to be found in the small residential colleges with no sororities and a limited work program for all. Which experience is better training for life is a matter of opinion.

Turning to things of the mind, most colleges have regularly provided an extensive series of lectures, concerts, art exhibits, and other events to stimulate and extend the students' intellectual interests and horizons. Attendance is usually voluntary, except as individual instructors may decide that some particular event will contribute directly to the work of a specific course. Formerly, a list of such events at Vassar was included in the president's annual report to the trustees. Today such a list would fill a small book. The calendar for a single week covers two or three printed pages. The offering for a two-week period, selected at random, includes six film programs, three different plays produced by the students, two concerts, two art exhibits, two outside lectures, and four miscellaneous events. There is also a regular chapel service six days a week. All these are open to the entire college community. The big state universities are in a position to provide even more opportunities of this nature, and regularly do so. Such events are within easy reach of all the students of a residential college. Students who live away from the campus find it more difficult to avail themselves of these educational advantages.

It seems to be generally agreed that there are too many of these activities, although a certain number are an important part of the students' education, and others serve as a pleasant form of recreation. But I have found no serious evaluation of this part of the college program. The women's colleges have occasionally stressed the importance of bringing distinguished women to the college as a way of encouraging and stimulating the able and ambitious student, but such programs have been sporadic and their effect seems not to have been measured. The one test that is occasionally applied to these programs is attendance, and perhaps this is as satisfactory a test as can be made.

In any event they have continued and multiplied.

Closely associated with the extracurricular lectures, concerts, and other general college programs is the training in the social graces which the early women's colleges, at least, accepted as their function. Women must be good conversationalists, although not orators; hopefully they should have some proficiency in musical performance and painting. Among the accomplishments listed in the 1865 *Prospectus* for Vassar College are conversation, reading, the "beautiful arts," and "letter writing and other forms of elegant composition." And of course the students must always behave like ladies. Even today a student may be reminded that when she is away from college she is still representing the college in the minds of those she meets and should behave accordingly.

When Vassar opened, the lady principal was second in importance only to the president. Her salary was double that of the women professors. The president directed the religious and academic instruction of the students, while the lady principal took care of their manners and morals. Hannah Lyman, the first of the lady principals, was impeccable in her own dress and set rigid standards for the students. Everyone must change her dress for supper. "You may," she said, "take off one calico frock and put on a fresh one of the same kind, if you can do no better, but some sort of change is essential."[12] Gloves had to be worn on formal occasions, including such events as the reading of one's own essays to college classmates. Miss Lyman personally inspected hemlines for platform appearances, particularly for commencement. A sagging skirt was not tolerated. And while it was the function of the teachers, who lived on every corridor and headed the tables in the dining room, to correct the students' manners and faults of speech, Miss Lyman herself was known to point out, on occasion, faulty posture and errors in speech. Her requisites for a good teacher (the faculties of that day were divided into professors and teachers, and all of the latter were women) were: "First she must be a lady; second, she must be a Christian; third she must have the faculty of imparting knowledge, and lastly, knowledge."[13]

Concern with these matters today is not as apparent as it was ninety years ago. But as late as the 1930's a number of changes were made at Vassar to promote "gracious living." One of these was to reduce the number of students at a table from ten to six to promote good conversation and (hopefully) table manners. Its success was uncertain. I once asked a student whether, in the interest of economy, tables for ten could be restored, and was told it was out of the question because "we couldn't reach; we'd starve to death."

Today little is said about this aspect of college life and the rules are simple. Vassar students must wear skirts off campus, at dinner, and on a few other occasions, and maintain "decent and respectable appearance" when sun bathing. No further reference is made to dress in the ninety-page handbook. Good conduct is expected, but it is not spelled out in detail. It is left to the students' judgment.

There is another phase of the training of "ladies" that has perhaps differentiated the women's colleges from the others. Partly because women are assumed to appreciate the refinements of life more than men, partly because they are more protected, the women's colleges have made more effort than others to house their students on campus, and to provide attractive, even luxurious, surroundings. Achievement of the latter has been somewhat spotty because the women's colleges, unlike some of the men's colleges, could not afford to provide them. Some of the men's dormitories at the Ivy League colleges are more luxurious than those of any women's college. I recall one young man whose family had difficulty persuading him to come home for vacations because at home he did not have a private bath. That is more luxury than any women's dormitory that I have seen provides.

Nevertheless, the women's colleges as a whole have provided better dormitory facilities, and more elaborate gardens and grounds, than other colleges. The economizing is done elsewhere. The parlors of the women's dormitories, at least, are apt to be redecorated at frequent intervals by professional decorators, even though the classrooms, which account for more student hours per week than any parlor, remain dingy and unattractive. If faculty reside in the student dormitories their quarters are more elegant than anything their colleagues achieve on their own salaries; and faculty offices tend to be as bare as monks' cells. There seems to be a real difference in emphasis, in this respect, between the women's colleges and the others. Whether or not this arises from the fact that higher education of women is still not quite as serious a matter as the higher education of men, or whether the women themselves have rated these things higher, is not clear.

It has always been regarded as more important to protect women students than men, and in consequence the coeducational institutions have made more effort to provide dormitories for their women students than their men students. In fact, in the early years some universities insisted on providing dormitories for women before they would admit them at all although no such concern had been shown for housing men. Also, deans of women were usually appointed before deans of men. The president presumably performed the duties of the latter office along with his multitudinous other activities, but it seems improbable that he could give the time to these duties that even a part-time dean of women could give. But dormitory accommodations in the larger institutions, particularly the big state universities, have never kept pace with the growing enrollments, even for women, and the problem of living quarters has been left, for the most part, to the student's own initiative. Private rooms and boarding houses are always available and the students can adjust their living expenses to their financial resources more readily than when living in college dormitories with a relatively limited range of charges.

With the recent mushroom growth of many of these institutions the inadequacies of private living quarters have become increasingly apparent even in urban areas. Not only is there often an acute shortage of living quarters of any kind; the economies of off-campus living have sometimes been at the expense of health, and the scattered and unsupervised residences create social problems. In consequence, the university authorities have extended their supervision over living arrangements, and have provided more housing for women than men. They have also recognized the changing needs and mores of the students. New dormitories often house both men and women students—usually in separate wings, but with common social rooms and dining facilities. Also, apartments for married students are provided with increasing frequency. Stanford University, for example, is providing apartments for students with up to three children. Those with four have to fend for themselves.

The growth of student enrollments, however, has usually outdistanced the public and private resources available for housing. This is particularly true in the state universities, which have less control over the number of students admitted than the private institutions. The University of Wisconsin, for example, originally assigned a dormitory to women students which was ample to house all who came. In 1952, on the contrary, only 23 per cent of its women students were in university houses. The number living at home was 13 per cent, the number in sorority houses was 11 per cent. And more than half—53 per cent—were living in private rooms, boarding houses, and apartments. San Jose State College, in California, is not at present housing any of its several thousand women students, and sororities and the homes of parents and relatives take care of only about half of the total enrollment. The college has plans for some dormitories, but not enough from the administration's point of view.

The students themselves do not always welcome college housing, even when it is clearly superior to the alternatives available. They sometimes resist even the minimal rules essential for community living. And they can sometimes save money and perhaps get meals more to their liking with a hot plate.

The number of women who are making great personal sacrifices, and even risking their health, for a college education is probably fewer than in earlier years because the office job has become a satisfactory and less demanding alternative to teaching for those who must make their way. And marriage is an even better and more probable alternative for support, without the effort of obtaining a bachelor's degree. Also, for those who persist there is help to be had from the multitudinous deans who supervise living arrangements when the university fails to provide its own housing, and from well-staffed personnel services and the scholarship programs.

Turning to the student-initiated activities, the first in importance is usually conceded to be student government. This more than any other extracurricular activity is assumed to be effective training in citizenship in a democracy. It has often been stressed as a unique virtue of women's colleges, since only in the absence of men are women likely to hold the more important and responsible positions.

Student government can be traced to the medieval universities of Europe. In fact, students have never had comparable powers since. These universities started as groups of students and faculty, without endowment. The students organized them and administered them. The rectors of the universities of Bologna and Padua, for example, were students.[14] As the universities achieved permanence, however, controls passed to the faculty. The student population was transient and the faculty remained. But as long as the custom of paying fees directly to individual faculty members continued, the students retained powerful controls. This system was still in effect at the University of Glasgow in the middle of the eighteenth century. The story is told that when Adam Smith resigned his professorship early in the academic year he insisted on returning the fees to his students in spite of their protests that they had already received full value for their money.[15] At this time, however, the fees were in addition to a salary from the university; and in the English universities fees went directly to the university or college treasury. The English colleges were well endowed and tuition fees did not constitute the major part of their income.

Harvard started with an endowment, following the Cambridge precedent, and its government was divided between the Board of Overseers, and the president and faculty. The students had no part in it. The university was training clergymen, not statesmen. Student self-government was a comparatively late development in most American colleges, and it is still limited in scope. Although nine out of ten institutions have some form of student participation in government, the authority delegated to them is likely to be small.[16]

The beginning of formal student government was apparently at William and Mary immediately after the Revolution. The students at that time took over some of the problems of discipline and later adopted an honor system. But it was at the University of Virginia. early in the nineteenth century, that the first comprehensive system of student government was instituted. Jefferson was concerned with the training of statesmen for a democracy, and he believed that one of the most effective devices for this end was to give the students responsibility for self-government while in college.[17] They were given control of most student activities, including the honor system for examinations and the handling of most disciplinary problems. This became a model for student government that gradually spread to other institutions in the United States, but there is no standard pattern and the extent of student control varies widely from one college to another. With few exceptions the powers granted to students during the nineteenth century came as a result of student demand rather than any conviction on the part of college authorities that this was a valuable educational device. The real growth of student participation came in the early twentieth century. Woodrow Wilson was one of its most eloquent supporters during his presidency of Princeton.

Self-government has, on the whole, been more extensive for women than for men. Frances E. Willard introduced the honor system at Evanston College for Young Ladies before it was adopted at Northwestern, with which the women's college was affiliated. Wisconsin gave its women students responsibility for social regulations in 1898, whereas it was another ten years before men students assumed these responsibilities. And coeducational institutions have frequently given their women students more control over social regulations and problems of discipline than they have conceded to men students. This was true at Stanford University in the early years of student government. Furthermore, the group of colleges which pioneered in this field in the years between 1890 and 1910 contained more women's colleges than was to be expected from their number in the total college population.

The earlier colleges did not, for the most part, start with any program of student government. As has already been noted, most of the systems now in effect have come at the instigation of the students, although the extent of student control is likely to depend on the degree of cooperation that the administration has been willing to give. There has been a tendency to grant the students responsibility without control; that is, they have been charged with enforcing rules made by others. Such a system works only if the rules of the authorities meet the approval of those administering them; and the students have, in fact, had a real voice in social regulations in many instances in which they have been granted no specific control simply because enforcement of unacceptable rules broke down.

Bryn Mawr pioneered in granting students rule-making as well as rule-enforcing powers. The announcement by the administration that a written code of regulations was to be prepared as a result of widespread violations of unwritten, but presumably well-understood rules of behavior, led the students to request a voice in making the rules. Carey Thomas, then dean, cooperated with the students in setting up a formal student government, in 1892, which gave the students legislative powers in the field of social regulations.[18] This became a model for other women's colleges. When Wellesley, which had made earlier unsuccessful attempts to establish effective student government, decided in 1901 to institute a system with wide powers, the president of Bryn Mawr's student association was invited to consult with the Wellesley students.[19] Barnard students obtained some legislative powers in 1894.[20] The Vassar student association received a charter in 1901 granting limited legislative authority in social matters. They had previously had considerable executive responsibility, but no legislative authority. In another ten years most of the women's colleges had legislative powers; and the importance of self-government as training for citizenship was being emphasized. President MacCracken of Vassar expressed this point of view in a speech on "The Students Share in College Government" as follows:

The new America is likely to be governed in far greater measure than formerly, . . . from the ranks of college graduates. If we want the worst kind of petty tyranny and personal self-seeking . . . we shall continue the present system of college administration which denies the student government all authority except over the most trivial aspects of student life. . . . If we want a truly liberal state . . . we shall begin their training in college by granting to self-government all the power it can enforce and maintain.[21]

While the area of student control has usually been quite limited, the student councils have often provided the students with the opportunity to express and even enforce their wishes. It was the pressure of the student governments that first brought permission for women students to smoke on college premises (with many safeguards, of course, in the interest of fire hazards and public opinion). Bryn Mawr led in this, too, with Vassar close behind. And with adequate precedent established, the New England colleges followed.

While students usually win in the end, in the interim between their demand for changes and the administration's acquiescence students inevitably feel that their powers do not match their responsibilities. They cannot enforce rules that the majority of students oppose and that the student officers themselves may not regard as reasonable. An occasional complete breakdown of student government can usually be traced to such a situation. To illustrate, before the prohibition of smoking was abandoned at Mount Holyoke, two-thirds of the students admitted that they smoked—many in their college rooms.[22] Some had smoked with their mothers at home, and might even be embarrassed by a mother or sister appearing on the campus, lighted cigarette in hand.

It is frequently proposed that student powers be extended beyond the social regulations, with which they have been primarily concerned, to the academic program. Some colleges have student curriculum committees which have been active in gathering student opinion in this area and communicating it to the authorities. And at least one college, Antioch, invites students as well as faculty to meet candidates being considered for teaching posts, although they have no votes.[23] In practice, the introduction of the free elective system has given students almost as much control over course offerings and faculty as the medieval system. If an elective course is not acceptable to students, it will not be given. This indirect control has sometimes been overlooked in discussions of student government, but it probably accounts in part for the unconcern which students often exhibit toward having a voice in this field. An unpopular required course arouses protests quickly enough.

Some of the newer developments in self-government are legislative bodies for certain activities with representation from faculty, administration, and students. These usually widen the area of participation by the students. But the educational value of any system will be commensurate with the real powers and responsibilities granted to the student body, and the joint faculty-student participation runs the risk of being dominated by the faculty. It is also important for the college administration to recognize that it can sometimes profit by student judgment. Serious consideration of student recommendations, before decisions are reached, will sometimes prevent the students from feeling that they have no real powers, and so prevent the complete breakdown of student government.

The extent to which women students were entrusted with their own government in the early period was not matched by their participation in outside government. They were given more control than most of the men students enjoyed before they had won the vote in national, state, or local affairs. Whether this was due to greater interest or greater dependability is not clear. It does not appear to have been greater need of training for citizenship. There are problems still, but one of the newer problems seems to be the danger that, as with the faculty, the proliferation of committees will lead to "busy work" that is less useful than time spent in the library, the laboratories, and on field-work projects.

Another important aspect of campus life is the multitude of specialized activities carried on by student initiative—athletics, drama, debate, innumerable clubs, and a variety of newspapers and literary magazines. These activities have developed quite spontaneously as one or another group of students has felt a lack in the total campus offering. In Vassar's first year President Raymond was astonished by the request of some students to be permitted to hold a meeting with no faculty or officers present.[24] They merely wanted to discuss a matter of current interest by themselves. In this same year the Philalethean Society, now engaged in play production, was organized for the writing and reading of original compositions. Three years later there was a musical organization, and clubs for religious inquiry and for gardening. These were followed by organizations for French conversation, natural history study, the fine arts, Shakespeare reading, madrigal singing, and a glee club. In ten years time the catalogue lists only the largest organizations, adding significantly, "etc., etc." Student publications also started almost at once and multiplied.

The virtue of these activities has frequently been emphasized. The students participating learn to organize and direct their own projects, to develop special skills, and to take responsibility for seeing things through. Over the long run the principal student activities, in all kinds of institutions, have been issuing newspapers and literary magazines, religious organizations, drama, athletics, debate, music, and clubs in fields of special interest, often connected with their studies.

The women's colleges have had all these, but athletics have never dominated student interests as they have in the larger men's and coeducational colleges. President Nielson of Smith used to remark that one of the great assets of the women's colleges was that they had "never lost a football game."[25] There has been very little intercollegiate rivalry, and the women spend very little time sitting on the side lines merely cheering. One intercollegiate debate a year in the first quarter of this century was a high point of student activities in some of the eastern women's colleges; but this has long since disappeared. Except for an occasional intercollegiate conference, which is not a competitive affair, or the merging of men's and women's choirs for a concert, activities are intramural. The women's colleges have been at a disadvantage in play production. In the early days women taking men's parts had to wear skirts. Even when they were permitted to wear trousers the illusion was never complete. Today real men are usually imported for the occasion. The special virtue of the women's colleges in such student affairs, as in student government, has been that women are in complete control. They have been presidents and editors-in-chief as well as secretaries and assistants. In recent years, however, women can be found in coeducational institutions as editors of the college papers and in other high positions. Whether this is due to decreasing discrimination or the declining importance attached to these activities is not clear.

Some 96 different student activities are listed in the current *Vassar Student Handbook*. These include eleven musical organizations, seven religious organizations, and nine activities that take the student into the larger community in which the college is located. These latter include political clubs and work in community centers. This type of activity was impossible in the days when going to Poughkeepsie, even to shop, involved finding a chaperon. How active all these organizations are is problematical. Tradition dies slowly. Such extracurricular activities used to be pursued mostly on weekends, but today the college week, even in the residence college, is more nearly five days than seven. With improved transportation and unlimited weekend leaves (for upper classmen at least), students are likely to seek their entertainment elsewhere. The majority of those on campus over the weekend are probably writing papers, catching up on their assignments in the library and laboratory, or perhaps entertaining a weekend guest.

Some of these activities still serve a useful function. Others only clutter too crowded schedules. They were a more important ingredient of the average student's education fifty years ago than now. Today students are socially more mature. They are less sheltered by parents before they come to college than was formerly true. Also, many have run school papers, helped to produce plays, and engaged in political discussion in high school. And many have learned to see a job through by holding paid positions in summer. Moreover, college courses themselves have encroached on the students' preserve. Courses in dramatic production can be more satisfying, as well as more educational, than the purely amateur effort. And field work in the social sciences has a touch of reality that the discussions of the social problems clubs often lacked.

On the whole, the activities that have shown the greatest vitality are those with the greatest cultural and educational possibilities. The more childish extracurricular activities die first. Alumnae who regret the disappearance of one or another student activity probably have not fully taken into account the changing scene. My own observation is that the students can be trusted to keep what is useful to them, and add new activities as new interests arise. I am less sure that they can be trusted to discard the old when it becomes outdated. The young are conservative, and they hesitate to abandon a well-established tradition.

These are the organized activities of the residence college, but judging from comments of both students and alumnae none of them is as important to the majority of students as the opportunity of finding congenial companions among their classmates. In no other place is a young woman so likely to come into contact with as many others of the same age group. And the fact that the group has been selected for intelligence, and presumably some interest in intellectual pursuits, increases the probability of finding friends with common interests. The faculty sometimes worry about there being too little variety in the social classes from which the students come, but this is rarely a worry of the students themselves.

Women college graduates, when asked, repeatedly mention friendships made in college as one of the most important things they got from their experience. And the time studies to which students are frequently subjected regularly show more hours per week devoted to "just talking" than to all the organized extracurricular activities combined. The organized student activities may be used primarily as a way of extending one's circle of friends, or as a pleasant way of spending time with them, but it is the friendships that count.

The women's colleges more often than the others have managed without sororities or other societies with limited memberships. They have tended to pride themselves on this democratic feature of campus life. The reasons for this rather special feature of the women's colleges appear to be, first, their very adequate dormitory facilities. In colleges where many students live in boarding houses the sorority house has a greater appeal and often fills a real need. When Stanford University first provided adequate housing for its women students it was able to ban the sororities. Second, many of the women's colleges have established reputations for giving social prestige to their students. Why, is not completely clear; but as long as being a student of a specific women's college lends social prestige the need for sorority status is not greatly felt. For the same reason there is easy acceptance by the students of these colleges of any college classmate without much concern about family background.

One of the great virtues of the residence college is supposed to be the continuous contact with the faculty, as well as fellow students. To encourage this, Vassar has faculty fellows and their families living in all residence halls. Students frequently insist that they want even more contacts with the faculty; but when these are provided few students take advantage of them. In crowded schedules, faculty contacts beyond those essential for the pursuit of the academic program do not have high priority.

This fact is supported by the findings of the Mellon Foundation research at Vassar College. Mervin Freedman reports that the student culture "is the prime educational force at work in the College."[26] While most students are "interested, even enthusiastic, about at least some of their courses and academic achievements," the "central core of values" and habits of life of the student body, which the students accept, "is relatively independent of the more formal academic influences."[27] This student culture assumes friendly relations with the faculty, but it "discourages genuine relationships of a kind that might challenge the basic values of students. . . . It even offers instruction in how to keep the faculty at a distance."[28] Apparently the house fellows, who were also instituted by the Mellon Foundation, have not achieved their purpose.

The average student, like everyone else, wants to be accepted by the group in which she finds herself, and "all that is required for acceptance by fellow students is that one act pretty much like the rest."[29] This has certain virtues. It minimizes differences as long as the students from different classes and different family backgrounds can conform to the expected behavior. But it does not encourage the independent thinking and intellectual integrity that is an important aim of the liberal arts education.

This raises important questions for the residence college. Are self-reliant students, reaching independent and considered judgments, less apt to develop in a community where students are in continuous and close contact with each other than in an institution where students have more outside contacts and the student body itself affords greater diversity—in age groups, at least? Or is it possible to influence the student culture itself so that the ends which higher education has in view are incorporated in the culture? Or do the students, however important the values of the student culture may seem to them at the moment, shed them readily when they grow older, and retain, in spite of all, some of the basic values that their college education is assumed to offer? These are unanswered questions.

The one thing that is sure is that whatever the virtues or the short-comings of the residence college, they are of decreasing importance in the whole development of higher education. A continually diminishing proportion of students attend residence colleges of the kind assumed in the above discussion. The proportion today is about one student in ten. Moreover, the college week in these residence colleges is a five-day rather than a seven-day week. It is true that the majority of students can still be found on campus on any weekend. But it is also true that they are away enough to restrict greatly their nonacademic activities. And guests are frequent enough that contacts and interests with other groups than college classmates are maintained. Also, their extra-curricular activities are increasingly related to the larger community. Local churches, community centers, and political groups welcome the students, and the students welcome participation from outsiders in some of their affairs. This is most obvious in play production, where a cast of young women does not afford the necessary variety, but it is found also in weekend conferences, musical performances, and other areas. In other words, the residence college is not the self-contained community it used to be.

One of the difficulties of any transition period is that the new is often added to the old instead of substituted for it. The total college calendar offers undue stresses and strains. It has been proposed at Vassar recently that all student organizations and all faculty committees be abolished, with the understanding that if any of them are missed, they can be restored with the appropriate formalities. This does not mean that most of them have outlived their usefulness, but it would insure that those that meet no important current need would not linger indefinitely. It is hardly necessary to add that this proposal has not been given any serious consideration.

The important additions to the academic program that the extracurricular activities provide appear to be a college government in which students play a significant role, and the opportunity to find congenial friends. A few student-initiated activities are doubtless useful, but this usefulness is limited by the increased opportunities for such activities in both the secondary schools and the larger community, and the invasion of this field by academic courses. It seems quite possible, however, that these new developments will encourage the desired faculty-student contacts quite naturally. Faculty and students can work together on problems of college government, in play production, concerts, conferences on international affairs, and on through the list. And they can share in the activities in the wider community, whether in the churches, the community centers, or the political clubs.

The contributions of extracurricular activities to the students' development are not peculiar to women's education, as contrasted with men's. But they appear to have been somewhat more prominent in the women's colleges than elsewhere, partly because the women in the early days had fewer opportunities for outside contacts than the men. Whether this intensive training is responsible for the outstanding achievements of the women's college graduates in later life in community affairs is not clear.

NOTES

[1] 1959-1960, p. 9.
[2] A. C. Cole, *A Hundred Years of Mount Holyoke College* (New Haven, 1940), p. 78.
[3] F. A. Wood, *Earliest Years at Vassar* (Poughkeepsie, 1909), p. 21.
[4] F. Converse, *Wellesley College, A Chronicle* (Wellesley, 1939), p. 29.
[5] S. Stow, *History of Mount Holyoke Seminary* (South Hadley, 1887), p. 119.
[6] Cole, *op. cit.*, pp. 74-75.
[7] C. Meigs, *What Makes a College?* (New York, 1956), p. 56.
[8] Stow, *op. cit.*, p. 91.
[9] F. Converse, *Story of Wellesley* (Boston, 1915), p. 93.
[10] Pp. 43-44.
[11] *Vassar Student Handbook*, 1956-57, p. 32.
[12] Wood *op. cit.*, p. 22.
[13] *Ibid.*, p. 39.
[14] F. E. Falvey, *Student Participation in College Administration* (New York, 1952), p. 35.
[15] J. Rae, *Life of Adam Smith* (London, 1895), pp. 169-170.
[16] H. H. Lunn, Jr., "The Students' Role in College Policy-Making," *A Report . . . of the American Council on Education* (Washington, 1956), p. 3.
[17] Falvey, *op. cit.*, p. 39.
[18] Meigs, *op. cit.*, pp. 54-56.
[19] Converse, *Wellesley College, A Chronicle* (Wellesley, 1939), p. 130.
[20] L. S. B. Saunders, "Government of Women Students in Colleges and Universities," *Educational Review*, December 1900, pp. 475 ff.
[21] *Vital Speeches*, January 14, 1935, p. 252.
[22] Cole, *op. cit.*, p. 287.
[23] Lunn, *op. cit.*, p. 36.
[24] J. M. Taylor and E. H. Haight, *Vassar* (New York, 1915), pp. 92-93.
[25] M. F. Thorp, *Nielson of Smith* (New York, 1956), p. 240.
[26] M. B. Freedman, "The Passage Through College." *Journal of Social Issues*, vol. 12, no. 4, 1956, p. 14.
[27] *Ibid.*, p. 15.
[28] *Ibid.*, p. 17.
[29] *Ibid.*, p. 15.

A TRULY DEMOCRATIC IDEALISM WOULD SEEM TO INVOLVE, NOT LOWERING THE STANDARD SO THAT EVERYONE COULD FIND SOME INTERESTING MEANS OF SECURING A DIPLOMA, BUT RATHER GIVING EVERYONE A CHANCE TO MEASURE UP TO AN EXACTING STANDARD.

NORMAN FOERSTER*

IT SEEMS TO ME THAT THE VITAL SOCIAL QUESTION IN AMERICAN EDUCATION TODAY IS NOT, HOW WELL CAN WE DO WITH SPECIALLY QUALIFIED GROUPS OF STUDENTS? BUT RATHER, CAN OUR YOUNG PEOPLE AS A WHOLE BE LIBERALLY EDUCATED?

ALEXANDER MEIKLEJOHN**

7. The Students

THE SUCCESS of higher education will depend on the quality of students going to college far more than on the quality of the educational offering. The faculty can greatly assist in the learning process, but learning is something one must do for oneself, and able students sometimes obtain a good education under the most adverse circumstances. I met a young German woman after World War II who was doing outstanding research in economics. Yet her entire university course had been pursued during the Nazi regime when instruction in the social sciences was at low ebb. I asked her how, under these conditions, she had been able to learn, and she answered simply: "I read books."

A recent estimate states that only one-fourth of the women capable of profiting by a college education are in fact going to college; and only one in three hundred of those capable of earning a doctor's degree pursues her education that far.[1] This is a much smaller pro-

* From N. Foerster, *The American State University* (Chapel Hill, 1937).
** From A. Meiklejohn, "Wisconsin's Experimental College," *The Survey*, June 1, 1927.

portion of the potential college group than is found among the men. Moreover, there is evidence that those who do go to college are not necessarily the top fourth of the group capable of going. It is important, therefore, to consider both the factors that determine whether certain women apply for admission to college or not, and the admissions requirements of the colleges.

The students' reasons for going to college have already been considered. It is sufficient here to note that professional training appears to have been, from the beginning, one of the dominating reasons for continuing formal education to this point. It continues to be important, as demonstrated both by the reasons the students themselves give for going to college and by the courses they elect. A second factor is that college is a pleasant way of passing the time between school and marriage. Last, but not least is the urge of intellectual curiosity. This particular reason for going to college is likely to be developed by the educational process itself when conditions are favorable; partly because of this and partly because of the process of selection, it will be stronger among graduate than among undergraduate students.[2]

Reasons for not going to college are many. Relatively low mental ability is an obvious reason why some girls end their formal education at the high school level. For these, the effort of learning is too great, or perhaps they are not admitted if they apply. Money is the deciding factor in many cases. When the family income is small the sons, rather than the daughters, will be sent to college. This is because the daughters are less likely than the sons to use their education, in the early years of marriage at least, to contribute to the family income. Also, the girl who has graduated from high school can usually get a good office position, and the satisfaction of immediate income of her own is likely to outweigh the more remote possibilities that a college degree offers. The teaching position, to which the college degree often points, may not provide much greater income or much greater prestige than the office job.

The family backgrounds of the students give some idea of the groups that send their daughters to college. In the early period, when college education for women was still on trial, the families that sent their daughters to college were likely to be those in which the father had been to college. This meant that they were, for the most part, from the professional and wealthy business classes.

Mary Lyon made every effort to keep the cost of education low at her seminary, but such records as I have found of the earliest students refer to a "preacher's daughter," the daughter of a bookshop and bindery proprietor, and specific students from well-known families, such as Emily Dickinson, and Louise Torrey, the mother of William Howard Taft. Special mention is more likely to be made of the daughters of prominent families than the others, of course, and there must have been some daughters of poor farmers, like Mary Lyon herself, among the teachers who came for further education. But even Mary Lyon spoke scornfully of students who, like mill girls, spent their time reading novels.[3]

Matthew Vassar, in contrast to Mary Lyon, saw no necessity for keeping the cost of college low. He believed that students should pay what their education cost, although he modified his position enough to provide for a scholarship program. Of this program, he wrote in a letter to the Reverend Thomas T. Devan, September 26, 1860:

A liberal and gratuitous education to the indigent is *one* of its chief elements, but in the selection of such we shall not be confined to creeds or classes but aim to bestow our benevolence as far as practicable upon those who give the greatest evidence of capacity to receive moral and mental culture. . . .

He later set aside a scholarship fund. But the recipients of scholarships were few and Vassar was regarded from the beginning as a rich girls' college. The cost of attending Vassar then, as now, was relatively high and the scholarship program has always been used to help the daughters of professional families of modest income rather than the daughters of manual workers. This has not, of course, been explicit college policy. But the daughters of relatively low-income professional families are more likely to apply than the daughters of manual workers of the same income level. All the more expensive women's colleges draw on the same social and economic groups.

The record of the occupations of fathers of the early Vassar students is incomplete, but among 139 (of the 185 college students) reporting their fathers' occupations in 1870, all but six were the daughters of professional and independent business men.[4] This indicates that there has been little if any change in the social groups from which Vassar students have come in the entire period of the college's existence.

A comparison of the occupations of fathers of Vassar students in 1910—the earliest year for which complete data are available—and 1956 shows that in both years 88 per cent of the fathers were either professional or business men, and only 12 per cent were minor officials in business establishments, clerical workers, or manual workers. Only 1.5 per cent in each year were the daughters of manual laborers. Neither increasing scholarships nor better job opportunities have changed the circles from which the college draws. Yet at least two-thirds of the girls of college age are the daughters of the group represented by 12 per cent of the Vassar college population.

Data from Mount Holyoke show that in spite of Mary Lyon's early emphasis on reaching women of modest incomes, the college today is reaching much the same group as Vassar. The Mount Holyoke classification of occupations of fathers does not permit detailed comparison with the Vassar data, but the present Mount Holyoke student body comes in somewhat larger numbers from the professional classes—44 per cent compared with Vassar's 37 per cent—and probably in correspondingly smaller numbers from the business group. Mount Holyoke reports that 2.5 per cent of the fathers of their students (or mothers, since the occupation of the family breadwinner is the one recorded) are in clerical occupations, as compared with 1 per cent for the fathers (or mothers) of Vassar students.

The small proportion of "blue collar" families represented in these colleges is partly due to the fact that a college education for daughters, and even for sons, is not likely to seem as important to parents who have not themselves gone to college as it seems to parents who have had some higher education. The *Fortune* Survey cited earlier reports that whereas among college educated parents 80 per cent want their sons to go to college and 73 per cent want their daughters to go to college, among noncollege parents these percentages drop, to 58 and 46 per cent respectively.[5] These proportions make it clear that the college educated parents regard it almost as important for daughters to go to college as sons, whereas the noncollege parents lay much less stress on higher education for daughters than for sons. The deciding factor is not solely the level of family income. It has been stated repeatedly that "college professors earn less than plumbers." Yet even to the extent that this is true the college professors' daughters will be sent to college—hopefully on scholarship—whereas the plumbers' daughters will more probably seek office positions when they graduate from high school.

It cannot be assumed, of course, that the daughters of blue-collar families rarely go to college just because they are not found in large numbers at Mount Holyoke or Vassar. Comparison of the Vassar data with data from a private women's college that offers professional training as well as a liberal arts course shows that 26 per cent, as compared with Vassar's 12 per cent, come from families where the breadwinner is a clerical employee, manual worker, or minor official in a business establishment; the daughters of manual workers alone constitute 8 per cent of the total compared with 1.5 per cent for Vassar. Data for a state teachers college, where costs are lower and the emphasis on professional training even greater than the private college just cited, show a much greater difference. More than half of the women students of this college come from "employee" families, including 30 per cent from the manual worker group. This is shown in Table 8. Even this college, however, has a disproportionate number of the daughters of the professional and business classes as compared with the total population.

Education is, of course, closely related to the occupational distribution. Samples from recent and current college classes show that 83 per cent of the fathers of Vassar students are college educated, as compared with 56 per cent of the fathers of students in the other private

Table 8.

OCCUPATIONS OF FATHERS OF COLLEGE STUDENTS[a]

Occupation	Percentage Distribution		
	Vassar College Classes of 1957–1960[b]	Other Private Women's College Class of 1961[c]	State Teachers College Classes of 1958–1961[d]
Professions and semi-professions	40.8	29.9	21.0
Business men	45.4	41.7	22.2
Farmers	1.2	2.0	2.3
White collar workers	10.9	18.5	24.1
Manual workers	1.5	7.7	30.3
Total	100.0	100.0	100.0
Number of student records	1,682	247	261

[a] In a few instances where the mother was the breadwinner for the family her occupation has been recorded.
[b] Data are for entire student body of that period.
[c] Data are for entire class.
[d] Data are for a sample of the four classes; women students only.

college cited above, and 27 per cent of the fathers of the women students of the teachers college. Two-thirds of the mothers of Vassar students are also college women. Comparable data for the other colleges were not obtained.

Another factor interfering with college education for women is the increasingly early age of marriage. Today half of the young women of this country are married by the age of twenty, that is, before they can graduate from college. Women students marrying near the end of their college courses often remain to graduate. But those who marry before their senior year are not likely to continue their college courses unless they are attending the same college as their husbands. Those students who drop out of college because they marry are not a complete measure of the inroads that the earlier age of marriage is making on the higher education of women. The probability of early marriage makes college education seem less important as preparation for a job, and it also reduces interest in intellectual pursuits. This affects the daughters of the well-to-do and the well-educated as much as the others.

As stated at the beginning of this chapter, the quality of its students is the most important single factor in determining the success of any college. The institution will be judged by its graduates, and if it fails to attract able and highly motivated students in the first place, the best education it can offer will not result in distinguished alumni.

The importance of this has been widely recognized by the colleges and they have endeavored not only to weed out the unfit through appropriate admission requirements, but also to attract able students through scholarship programs and advertising. The Carnegie Report of 1911 states that "in no other civilized country do the institutions of higher learning compete for students. Nowhere else are the allurements and advantages of the college training so advertised. . . . College education in America is a commodity that is sold somewhat after the manner of life insurance and patent medicines."[6] In the early nineteenth century this was partly due to the rivalry among the different religious denominations which founded the colleges. They were seeking not merely able students, but any students at all in order to convert them to their faith; and since their efforts to compete resulted in an oversupply of colleges, they also wanted numbers to keep the institutions afloat. This did not lead to high standards at first. But it probably did contribute toward making young people "college conscious." And this in turn swelled enrollments to the point where the better colleges could set high standards.

The earliest women's colleges had the advantage of offering a commodity in short supply, since the number of coeducational institutions was negligible. This, together with the fact that women's colleges still had to prove themselves, led them to set standards of admission equivalent to those of the better men's colleges although not identical with them. They were handicapped by the inadequacies of the secondary schools for girls and by the lack of dependable tests. And these factors, plus the feeling that women's education should, perhaps, be different from men's, led to more flexibility in admission requirements than was to be found in the well-established men's colleges. But that kind of flexibility would hardly be regarded as a sign of weakness today. And lack of adequate preparation was compensated for, in part, by the fact that mediocre women students were not often tempted to set out on so questionable a venture. Vassar accepted students at first that did not measure up to the standards that the college had set, but with a little experience it proved possible not only to maintain the official standards but to raise them.

The nineteenth century colleges had to administer their own examinations for entrance, often after the student had arrived for the opening of college. In time these were supplemented in other ways. Vassar, for instance, gave its own examinations from 1865 through 1916. By 1877, however, it was felt that the college had sufficient experience to trust the schools whose recommendations had been tested by the success of their former students. Thus certifications by schools without examination were accepted also, from 1877 through 1918. In 1879 the New York Regents' examinations became available for New York students and these examinations, too, were accepted. And from 1882 to 1895 the Harvard examinations for women were also used. The College Entrance Board examinations were available beginning in 1902. In addition, of course, the college continued to specify required entrance subjects.

These developments in admission requirements were not peculiar to Vassar or to the women's colleges. The women's colleges were only following the trends in other institutions. And with similar admission standards—identical, of course, in the coeducational schools—the only factor that could have resulted in either lower or higher average ability of women students, as compared with men, were the inferior preparation of the girls on the one side, and the doubts as to women's capacity for intellectual growth, which must have operated as a selective factor, on the other. Both these differences disappeared with time.

For many years all students who could meet the standards set were admitted gladly by the colleges. College education, except for the women in the very early period, was in oversupply. There was room for all the students that wanted to come and could meet the relatively modest requirements. The sooner the college departments could be expanded, the sooner the preparatory departments could be abandoned.

By the end of the nineteenth century most of the preparatory departments had been closed, and early in the twentieth century the applications for admission to the college course began to outrun the number of students that could be accepted in the better colleges. By the second decade of this century the leading women's colleges were closing their admissions lists two years or more in advance of admission, and were in the unhappy position of turning down clearly exceptional students because they had applied too late. To meet this problem they shifted gradually to a completely competitive system. Bryn Mawr, Mount Holyoke, Smith, Vassar, and Wellesley all made this change during the 1920's. Before the change had been completed the lists, except for the gradually increasing number of places reserved for the competitive group, were closed between four and five years in advance of entrance. Anxious parents sometimes registered their daughters at birth.

With applications of these proportions to select from, the shift to the competitive system made it possible to raise standards materially. By this time there were many good preparatory schools for girls as well as boys, and the great majority of public high schools were open to boys and girls alike. In fact, it seems probable that with the competitive system in full effect the women's colleges were able to demand higher standards of work than some of the better known men's colleges which continued to give priority to the sons of alumni provided they could meet the minimum requirements.

Meanwhile the subject matter requirements were changing. With the free elective system the relevance of the earlier fixed requirements was no longer clear. The range of acceptable subjects inevitably broadened. One study notes that over one hundred different subjects were acceptable for admission to *some* college by 1922.[7] "Hours of exposure" became less important than results of examinations. And "gaps" in preparation, and even occasional lapses in performance in examination, might be forgiven if the scholastic aptitude tests and other evidence of worth appeared to justify making an exception. In short, increased emphasis was placed on the students' potential ability, as far as this could be ascertained, and decreased emphasis on past performance. This broadened the base from which the college could select its students.

There is little doubt that the quality of the students admitted improved as a result of all these factors. But the more expensive colleges, particularly, continued to draw their students from limited circles. A study made in the 1920's indicated that about half of the students applying for admission to any college were good risks, and that a quarter of those not applying were also good risks. If these proportions can be applied to women there were at that time about five times as many good risks among the women who never tried to go to college as among the small minority who did.

Although it was recognized that many potentially brilliant students were not applying, and college scholarship programs were being expanded to meet the cost of college for some who could not otherwise afford to come, the upsurge in college enrollments in the 1920's led the colleges to emphasize methods of selection from among those students who were applying, rather than to stimulate further applications. When Vassar first went completely over to the competitive system, three times as many students applied as there were places for, and as far as the admission office skills permitted, only those in the top third were admitted. The multiple registrations that plague admissions offices today were almost unknown. Ninety-nine per cent of the students that Vassar accepted in the first year of its completely competitive system actually came to college in September. Most of the better colleges that restricted their numbers were in an equally favorable position.

This happy state of affairs was short-lived. First, the depression made it necessary for many students to withdraw after they had been accepted by the college, and later the trend toward coeducation cut deeply into the number of applications received by the women's colleges. Moreover, the number of women going to college did not keep pace with the number of men. The number of women students has doubled since 1930, but the number of men students has tripled. Enrollments in women's colleges as a whole have declined. The problem for the women's colleges has become, in consequence, less a problem of selection from among the applicants, and more a problem of broadening the group from which the applicants come.

Data for nineteen of the larger women's colleges for the class entering in the fall of 1957 show that no college of this group was in the position that Vassar was in in 1929 of accepting as few as one-third of its applicants.[8] Fourteen of these nineteen were accepting more than half. The men's colleges could be more selective. Data for twenty-one of these, also for the class entering in 1957, show that only one-third accepted more than half of their applicants, and better than one-third accepted less than one in three. It cannot be concluded from this that the men's colleges are getting better students than the women's, since the proportion of men attending college is approximately double the proportion of women. In other words, while they had more applicants to select from, it seems probable that the greater pressure on men to go to college results in a greater number of mediocre applicants among the men than among the women. Nevertheless, the quality of students going to the women's colleges cannot be maintained unless present trends are reversed.

The state universities have never been able to be as selective as the stronger private colleges in their admissions policies. To refuse students whose parents, as taxpayers, are supporting the institution is more difficult than to refuse students whose parents pay only if the student is admitted. In consequence, there is a tendency to do such sifting as is done on the basis of the student's record after entering college. Under these conditions it is to be expected that women students will have as good a chance of admission to these institutions as men, and no evidence of preferential treatment for the men has been found. But the greater pressure for a man to go to college than for a woman to go probably results in fewer mediocre women than men applying in the first place. In any event records of the women attending often show a higher average than the records of the men. In Michigan, for example, in 1956–1957 the average grades were 2.7 for the women and 2.5 for the men.

The relatively small increase in the number of women attending college, coupled with the trend toward coeducation, is responsible for the decline in applications to the non-Catholic women's colleges.[9] Data for five of the high-ranking coeducational colleges that draw on much the same group of young people as these women's colleges show that four out of five accepted less than one-third of their women applicants in 1957. None of the nineteen women's colleges rejected such a large proportion of its applicants. Also, these coeducational colleges were rejecting a larger proportion of women than men applicants in every case. In some instances the number of men applying was larger than the number of women and in some instances smaller, but in no instance was the number of men admitted smaller than the number of women.

The fact that large numbers of the students accepted do not come is due to multiple applications, which have increased as the mounting college attendance makes admittance less certain. This is not peculiar to the women's colleges. It applies to the "national" colleges, rather. Those drawing on an essentially local clientele have a high percentage of the students they accept actually enrolling. For the nineteen women's colleges noted above, only nine had more than half of the group that they accepted actually enrolling. The best record was made by a college that attracts a large number of local students, but even this one did not have two-thirds finally enrolling. Compare this with the 99 per cent that enrolled at Vassar in 1929. The men's colleges had a somewhat better record, a median of 56 per cent, but the difference is not marked. Twenty-two coeducational colleges show a median of 59 per cent for men and women students combined.

The question as to whether the students coming to the women's colleges are of as high quality as those of some thirty years ago, when a smaller proportion of the applicants was admitted, can be debated endlessly. Some of my colleagues believe that they can detect some deterioration over the long period; but some people always paint the past in rosier colors. My own impression has been that the students are much the same. However, the unmistakable trend toward coeducational institutions, if it continues, will create a problem for the stronger women's colleges, as it already has for the weaker ones.

There are two other trends that may well concern the future of the eastern women's colleges. One is a preference for a college near enough home to make it possible to maintain some social contacts with one's friends. A Pacific coast girl who goes east to college will lose touch even though she can get home by plane for vacations, and perhaps for an occasional weekend. If she returns to the west at the end of her college course, she then loses contact with many of her college friends. Considering the mobility of population in these days —particularly among the professional and business executive groups —the wider circle of friends may be to her advantage in the end. But it is hard to convince her of this at the age of seventeen. And with the multiplication of colleges there is always a good college reasonably near home.

The second trend is away, not only from the national college, but from the residence college. The residence college is a phenomenon of a rural society. With sparse population and very few young people going to college, a wide area was required to support a college, and few students could hope to find one near home. Today, with colleges in every large population center, and improved means of transportation, most people live within commuting distance of some college. The cost of a college education is much less if the student can live at home.

And this is an important factor for middle and low income families.

Insofar as these factors are increasing in importance the circle from which the "national" colleges located on the eastern seaboard can draw is narrowing. A comparison of Vassar students in 1870 (excluding the preparatory group) and 1956 shows the same proportion of the group, 27 per cent, from the west and south in both years. In 1890 the proportion from the west and south was substantially larger— 34 per cent. Yet the proportion of the population of the United States living in the west and south has increased in the meantime.[10] Moreover, the greater ease of travel today should favor drawing students from greater distances. Instead of parting from family and friends for at least the full college year, as was formerly the case, the students from the far west and south usually get home for all vacations. They are even given travel time—that is, an extended vacation—for the purpose.

Among the eastern women's colleges that have made an effort to draw on a wide geographical area for their students, Wellesley at present has the largest proportion of students from the west and south —38 per cent in 1956—with at least one student from every state, although in several instances only one. This is in spite of the fact that it is located farthest north and east of any of this group of colleges. Of the other women's colleges of this area for which the data have been found and tabulated, two have increased the proportion of their students from a distance since 1910. Three others, however, are drawing more heavily on nearby areas than they did earlier in this century. Increasing efforts to attract students from a distance, including expanded scholarship programs, have failed to offset the pressures that encourage students to attend colleges near home. There is every evidence that drawing students from a distance is increasingly difficult.

The reasons for encouraging a "national" student body appear to be two. The first is to reach a larger circle of young people, thus making it possible to select abler students. The second is the assumption that bringing together students from different areas is in itself of educational value. Another reason used to be given: the obligation to spread culture to the less favored regions; but no one would be so presumptuous as to offer this reason today. The current objectives are valid enough. But if an eastern college selects a girl from California in place of one from New York for the sake of varied backgrounds, and gives her $500 more in scholarship because of her travel expenses, has it really been worth the extra cost? Particularly if it turns out, as often happens, that the California girl's family lived in the east until recently and still has many eastern ties. Or if a college accepts the only good candidate that applies from Mississippi, Montana, or Nevada, just to round out the number of states represented in the student body, when someone from Massachusetts could have been accepted who was a shade better, will the quality of education be improved? Might not the effort and money be better spent selecting the best of the local clientele?

For all these problems there is no definitive answer. The fact that the population of the United States today is increasingly mobile, particularly among the professional and business executive groups whose daughters make up the largest part of the student body in the private residential colleges, makes it seem doubtful that there are any very significant regional differences in customs or points of view.[11] Foreign students are another matter. No one would question that the colleges can make a real contribution in cultural interchange by encouraging a considerable number of foreign students to come. Also, the opportunities to study in other countries are so limited that the chance of getting really superior students is excellent. But as far as native Americans are concerned, it seems probable that the doctor's daughter from New York and the doctor's daughter from California will be more alike, both in ideas and social usages, than, say, the daughter of a doctor and the daughter of a manual laborer from the same community. The intellectual ability and the differences in viewpoints that is sought through the wide geographic distribution of the student body might perhaps be found near at hand if more effort were made to find it there.

The better known private colleges have, perhaps, overemphasized their special contributions to students in providing a community of young people with varied backgrounds. Not only is geographic distribution inadequate insurance for varied backgrounds; the larger state universities have also attracted students from wide geographic areas. A perusal of recent catalogues shows that while the majority of students are residents of the state in which the university is located, a very substantial minority comes from out of the state. This is in spite of the fact that the higher tuition for out-of-state residents militates against the "foreigner." Not only is every state in the union likely to be represented in these universities, but also more foreign countries than I have found in the student body of any private college. It may be easier to insulate oneself against foreign contacts in a sorority house on a large state university campus than in a women's college dormitory where one has no control over one's neighbors; but for the student actively seeking variety the state university would appear to be the better hunting ground.

In stressing the efforts of the women's colleges to obtain wide geographic distribution for their student body, it should not be overlooked that they have also tried to get wide distribution for economic groups as well. The scholarship programs, which have expanded greatly, have been used to make it possible for students to come from low income families. Scholarships have, on the whole, more than kept pace with costs. A recent report from Wellesley on its financial aid program states that scholarships have grown from four in 1878 to around 300 in 1957—enough for more than one student in six.[12] At the same time the amount of aid per student has been increased, averaging about $1,000 per student in this year. Furthermore, the possibilities of remunerative summer employment have increased, so that students from low income families can earn part of the cost. In fact, it has become an established custom for women students, as well as men, to take summer jobs. There are not only new opportunities opening up; the social pressures that used to prevent young women from working for pay if their parents could afford to support them no longer interfere. And a final factor is that the daughters of skilled workers are no longer handicapped by poverty. The family income is often comparable to that of professional families.

The data given earlier, however, make it clear that the women's residential colleges are not attracting the daughters of manual workers or white collar workers in large numbers; and the Vassar data for 1910 and 1956 respectively indicate that neither scholarships nor job opportunities have changed the circles from which the college draws. The reasons for this are fairly clear. The daughters of noncollege fathers (and most of this group are the daughters of high school graduates) are less likely to want to go on to college or to be urged to go than the daughters of college graduates. There is no college tradition. And there are plenty of opportunities for employment for the high school graduate between school and marriage. School teaching is no longer the only respectable opening. It is often one of the less remunerative ones. Also there are lingering doubts as to whether education beyond high school may make a girl less marriageable.

Many, of course, do go to college. But they are more likely to go to a public than a private institution. Even when a family can afford the latter the parents are still apt to regard it as an extravagance. Students from these families are also likely to live at home during their college course rather than going to a residence college. And if a residence college is within reach of their homes, the college itself, in its emphasis on its residential features, has tended to discourage them. And finally, many of the women's colleges, in particular, are thought of as rich girls' colleges where others might feel out of place. This attitude has been fostered by the relatively high cost of the women's residential colleges, and by the large proportion of students from the private preparatory schools that make it their business to meet specific college requirements.

The picture books regularly published by the public relations departments of the colleges do little to combat the stereotype of the rich girls' college. They try valiantly to depict the academic process, beginning with libraries which are usually reasonably photogenic. But the fact is that things of the mind do not lend themselves readily to pictorial description. Besides, the residence college wishes to emphasize the special virtues of group living. And in the end, intended or not, as one leafs through these books one is left with a strong impression of a country club. The college plays are there. And so are all the sports—tennis, golf, horseback riding, swimming, skiing, and the others, complete with appropriate and expensive costumes and equipment. Even the California colleges feel that they must feature skiing along with all the other sports. There is always a prom, as well as informal gatherings that include plenty of well-set-up young men. Foreign students are occasionally featured for variety; but I have found no identifiable Negro students in these books, not even in the classroom or the choir, although Negroes do appear as white-capped maids in the dining rooms, or subjects in the nursery school, or being interviewed by sociology students on a field trip. Is it any wonder that potentially able but unsophisticated students from families of moderate means feel that they would be out of place and are not persuaded to apply, even by generous scholarship programs?

Moreover, the undue emphasis on endowment has sometimes led the colleges to favor the daughters of the wealthy in the hope of increasing alumnae contributions in the future. This policy, if carried to extremes, results in subsidizing the rich girls of today in the hope that they in turn will subsidize the rich girls of tomorrow. It was the danger that President Raymond recognized when he said: "It would be sad if the prediction should even in part be realized that Vassar is destined to become a place where rich men's daughters may get a first-class education at a low rate, while those very young women . . . on whom the country must depend to supply its demand for thoroughly educated female teachers, are shut out through poverty."[13]

It is clear that the private residential colleges, and particularly the women's colleges, are reaching a relatively limited group of young people geographically, and even more limited in terms of occupational groups. I do not want to stress unduly the trend away from national, residential, and segregated men's and women's colleges. I know students who are still crossing the continent because they are sure that a particular college has the science program they want; or because they have learned that the arts faculty is exceptional; or because they are convinced of the value of a particular honors program. The women's colleges as a whole have stressed the quality of teaching with good effect, although the older ones have sometimes been slow to experiment with new programs and have sometimes lagged in consequence. I also know students who prefer a women's college. The varying interests and needs of the students leave room for a wide variety of institutions. Neither the residence college nor the women's college has outlived its usefulness. But some of these colleges have failed to reassess the changing needs which they should be prepared to meet.

It is entirely appropriate for American colleges to advertise their advantages. This has long been accepted practice. But while the colleges are publicity conscious I believe that they have not always stressed the right things. The women's colleges, particularly, have from their origin been on the defensive. They have had to explain that college education does not impair the students' health or their feminine charm. And by the time these facts had been established the students began to indicate a preference for coeducation. This has tended to make college publicity negative rather than positive. In recent years the picture books are likely to suggest that the women's colleges are just as good as coeducational, in their social life at least. Young men appear in the pictures on nearly every page. And this in turn has led to emphasis on the social side of the college.

Also, in their enthusiasm for educating the whole person—a very legitimate concern—the college authorities have sometimes seemed to imply that participation in extracurricular activities is more important than academic performance. In fact, they have sometimes acted on this assumption, choosing the well-rounded candidate in preference to one with unusual intellectual leanings. It is one thing to take some responsibility for using the educational process as a means of developing the whole person. It is quite another to insist that she be well-rounded before she is admitted. I once heard a professor from a sister college remark, "Thank goodness, a few queer ducks still slip through."

I am inclined to think that a more positive and less apologetic approach is needed. More emphasis might be placed on the positive values of higher education, together with the specific contributions of the institution in question; and less emphasis on the fact that it will do the student no harm, and she will be just as healthy and happy as if she had stayed at home. I also think that we sometimes worry too much when a student with strong intellectual leanings takes little interest in extracurricular activities, concerning herself primarily with intellectual problems. We cultivate conformity even while we deplore it. What if a few escape the trend and devote their lives to some profession, and perhaps do not even marry? Women are a hardier lot than men, we have discovered at long last, and there aren't enough men to go around anyhow.

And one thing more. If the trend away from segregated colleges should continue, the segregated colleges might find—as many already have—that coeducation is quite possible. It makes it easier for those who marry young to finish their education. And it opens the way to young people of the sex that happens to be excluded by a particular college, because this is the only college within reach of home where, for one reason or another, they must remain. The important function of a college is to give the best education it can to the ablest students it can find. If insistence on segregation of the sexes, residence, national representation, or some other factor should prove a handicap rather than a help toward this goal, it ceases to be a contribution to the educational process.

It is sometimes assumed that the quality of the college students will decline as the proportion of young people going to college increases. This is true only if the applicants up to now have included all the more brilliant students, which is not the case. The University of Wisconsin recently reported that the entering class of 1957 included a larger proportion of students who had been in the upper quartile of their high school class than entering classes some years ago when the numbers were much smaller.[14] College does attract the better students in the families that assume that a college education is desirable and worth the time and cost; but there are still large sectors of the population that, partly although not entirely for financial reasons, do not consider the possibility of a college education at all.

In conclusion it should be emphasized that the potentially able college students who do not go to college are far more numerous among the girls graduating from high school today than among the boys. How many of these could be persuaded to go to college before they marry is uncertain. But the college recruiting methods could certainly be improved. And perhaps more attention should be given to reaching local women in their thirties, whose children are in school, and who probably will also be needed in school to teach the large numbers of children whose education is already suffering from the teacher shortage.

NOTES

[1] National Manpower Council, *Womanpower* (New York, 1957), p. 33.

[2] Reasons why parents want their daughters to go to college, as reported by the *Fortune* Survey "The Public Looks at Higher Education" (June 1949, p. 259), are: professional training 48 per cent; better fitted to lead a full life, 20 per cent; social advancement, 18 per cent; knowledge, 16 per cent; preparation for marriage, 9 per cent. For sons the reasons are: professional training, 66 per cent; better fitted to lead a full life, 19 per cent; knowledge, 15 per cent; social advancement, 10 per cent. (Reasons exceed 100 per cent because more than one reason is sometimes given.)

[3] A. C. Cole, *A Hundred Years of Mount Holyoke College* (New Haven, 1940), p. 94.

[4] J. Orton, "Four Years in Vassar College," *National Education Association, Proceedings,* 1871, vol. 14, p. 112.

[5] Pp. 163, 171.

[6] Carnegie Foundation for the Advancement of Teaching, *Sixth Annual Report,* 1911, p. 73.

[7] H. C. McKown, *The Trend of College Entrance Requirements* (Washington, 1925), p. 95.

[8] Data obtained from letters from individual colleges.

[9] Many individual colleges are getting more applications than earlier because of the growing custom of applying at several institutions in order to be sure of

getting into one. Among the private non-Catholic women's colleges, however, the majority apparently have fewer applicants who will come, if accepted, than they had a few years back.

[10] West and south are defined to cover all states outside the New England states, New York, New Jersey, Pennsylvania, Delaware, Maryland, and the District of Columbia.

[11] A sample of 111 Vassar students shows that six out of ten no longer live in the city or town in which they were born, and eight out of ten have at some time lived in another city.

[12] *Wellesley Alumnae Magazine*, January 1958, p. 82.

[13] H. R. Lloyd, ed., *Life and Letters of John Howard Raymond* (New York, 1881), p. 630.

[14] *New York Times*, February 2, 1958. A letter from the Registrar of the University of Wisconsin states that the proportion of entering Wisconsin freshmen graduated in the top quarter of their high school class increased by 7 per cent between 1948 and 1957, and the increase between 1955 and 1957 was 4 per cent.

TO GIVE WISELY IS HARD. . . . THE CHEMIST SHOULD HAVE
HAD A LABORATORY, AND THE OBSERVATORY SHOULD HAVE
HAD AN ASTRONOMER; BUT WE ARE TOO APT TO BESTOW
MONEY WHERE THERE IS NO MAN, AND TO FIND A MAN
WHERE THERE IS NO MONEY.

MARIA MITCHELL*

8. Financing Women's Education

STRINGFELLOW BARR, in his novel *Purely Academic,* remarks
that education has been "the only business in the country in which
the customer regularly got what he ordered at less than cost."[1]
Higher education was never a business, of course. It has always been
a philanthropy. But it is true that the beneficiaries—the students and
their parents—have been able to dictate the terms in a degree not
ordinarily found in philanthropic enterprises. This is a result of the
early competition among the different religious denominations for
ministers and church members. It is also a result of the American
enthusiasm for education which increased the opportunities faster
than the number of students justified. And when state universities
began to offer higher education at little or no cost to the students,
only a heavily endowed private institution could hope to compete
successfully. But compete they must, or close their doors. The mor-
tality has been high, and many of the survivors have led a pre-

* From P. M. Kendall, *Life, Letters and Journals of Maria Mitchell* (Boston,
1896), pp. 183-184.

carious existence. Only the elite among the colleges have been able to set up rigid standards of admission, and even these have hesitated to charge what it costs. The state universities, with more adequate funds for both faculty and equipment, and often only nominal tuition charges, have proved formidable competitors to the private institutions.

Today demand has overtaken supply, but one consequence of the long period of cut-throat competition is that the customers are not prepared to pay what higher education actually costs. Neither are the taxpayers or the philanthropists. Another factor that adds to the reluctance to meet the full cost is the intangible nature of the product. It is difficult to distinguish between good education and bad, particularly when so much depends on the ability and enterprise of individual students. It is neither possible nor desirable to turn out a standardized product. Moreover, success in our free enterprise system is measured largely in terms of money; and the value of an education is measured, in consequence, in terms of how much it will contribute to one's earning power. A recent estimate of earnings for men of different educational levels places the lifetime earnings of the college graduate more than $100,000 above the earnings of the high school graduate.[2] But while the general public is convinced that the degree has monetary value, the returns are so remote and problematical at best that parents are not prepared to make anything like an investment of $100,000 even when they could afford to do so. Consequently, the problem of financing higher education appears to be as acute as ever.

Financing women's education presents much the same problems as financing the men's, but the women suffer from greater handicaps. In the first place, the attitude that earning power is the important test of the value of an A.B. degree militates against charging the full cost to the students for women even more than for men. Women have, on the average, received substantially lower salaries than men when they have had comparable positions. And while it might seem worthwhile to educate a daughter so that she could get a teaching position, if the cost is not too high, it hardly seems worth while to educate her for the unpaid job of wife and mother. The possibility that some college education may lead to a (financially) better marriage is sometimes recognized, but this is uncertain, at best.

It is primarily for this reason that parents often are not willing to spend as much on their daughters' education as their sons'. Many will send a son to the best engineering school that they can find and economize by sending his sister to a second-rate college near home. Or they will settle for two years for the daughter—enough to give her the college "label." Or, more probably, they will be satisfied to have her work in an office and live at home from the time that she graduates from high school until she marries. This is not through any lack of concern for the daughter's welfare. It is rather a conviction, often shared by the daughter, that higher education has little value for her. It is difficult to persuade parents to pay what a good education costs for their sons. It is even more difficult when it is the daughter's education that is under consideration.

A second handicap in meeting the cost of women's education is that women are not in as favorable a position as men to contribute to the costs themselves. The average earnings of men students, as reported by an Office of Education study for 1952-1953, were $389 for summer and $486 for the school year. For the women these figures were $296 and $265, respectively. Moreover, a larger number of men than women contributed to their educational costs from current earnings—approximately two-thirds of the men and half of the women —during the school year.[3] The men also depended more on loans than the women. It is one thing to borrow when the college education will result in a higher paid job, and quite another to borrow when early marriage means that the obligation will fall on one's husband's earnings rather than one's own.

Thus, in spite of the fact that the actual expenditures of women students averaged $1273 per year as compared with $1462 for the men, the cost falling on the parents averaged $817 for the women and only $727 for the men.[4]

Women from low income families have compensated in part for their lower earnings by going to less expensive colleges. For families with incomes under $8,000, women pay less than men for tuition, and for room and board. For families with incomes over $8,000, on the contrary, women pay more than men for all college charges. The expenditures for recreation are regularly higher for men at every income level, and those for clothing are regularly higher for women.[5]

This puts the women's colleges at a financial disadvantage. Since it is considered to be less important for a girl to have a good education than a boy, and since the girl is not usually in a position to contribute as much to the cost of her own education as the boy, there is less willingness to meet the cost of a good education for women than for men.

This is not a problem for the coeducational colleges, since they are quite content to educate more men than women. In fact, one of the early arguments against admitting women was that there was not enough money to educate both sexes, and many of them opened their doors to women in the first place only because those interested in promoting the higher education of women offered them special subsidies for the purpose. In other words, the women *bought* their way in. Women were admitted to the University of Michigan and to the Medical School of Johns Hopkins University when women succeeded in raising $100,000 for each of these institutions, and made the gifts conditional on the admission of women. The University of Rochester first admitted women when $50,000 was raised for the purpose, largely through the efforts of Susan B. Anthony. The gifts that opened the doors of Cornell University to women came from Henry W. Sage. Once women were admitted, however, there could be no differentiation between the financing of women's and men's education in these institutions.

The financial problems of the early women's colleges were discussed briefly in the account of their development. Most of them opened without enough money for the essential buildings, and income-producing endowment was almost unknown. Matthew Vassar had originally planned for such endowment, but the Civil War inflation and his own enthusiasm for the best in material equipment consumed practically all of the original gift. This was not peculiar to women's colleges. Vassar and Wellesley, at least, were handsomely endowed according to the standards of the day. Very few of the colleges had any substantial income from productive funds. That was a later development.

A comparison of costs of education in men's and women's colleges in recent years, however, shows some real differences in both expenditures and income. The principal differences in costs can be traced to three factors: the higher standards set for living conditions in the women's colleges; the smaller number of students per faculty member in these; and the larger proportion of women on the faculty. On the income side of the accounts, the women's colleges have had less income per student from productive funds. These factors will be considered in turn.

The women's colleges have usually undertaken to house all their students. The men's colleges have rarely provided enough dormitories for the whole student body, leaving fraternity houses and local rooming houses to fill the gap. In the women's colleges, in consequence, expenditures for the maintenance of residence halls and dining rooms play a more important part in college budgets than in the men's colleges. This does not in itself increase the cost of the students' education. Fees paid to the college for living costs need be no higher than room and board elsewhere. On the contrary, since the buildings are likely to be gifts, and the college does not operate its dormitories and dining rooms at a profit, the costs to students might be lower than off-campus accommodations. The Hollis study shows, however, that while the highest expenditures were incurred by students living in fraternity, sorority, and other club houses, and the lowest expenditures were incurred by students living at home, as is to be expected, the remainder of the students spend more if they live in college dormitories than if they live in private homes (other than their own) and rooming houses.[6] This higher cost is primarily a phenomenon of the private, liberal arts college. In public universities, students living in dormitories spend less than those living in private houses.

The women's colleges have, in practice, usually charged a flat rate to all students, and have sometimes provided a more expensive standard of living than the poorer students can afford. Where living quarters are off of the campus the students can adapt the cost to his or her means in considerable measure.

Charges for board and room in the 33 largest private, liberal arts colleges for women are uniform for all students in 27 of the 33 institutions, whereas only eight of 24 such colleges for men list a single rate, and in some of these eight colleges alternative living arrangements are indicated. Sixteen give either a range of living costs or an average. A comparison of the median charges of these colleges is given in Table 9. In both years listed the median charge for the women's

Table 9.

MEDIAN CHARGES FOR TUITION AND ROOM AND BOARD IN SELECTED MEN'S AND WOMEN'S COLLEGES 1955–1956 AND 1958–1959[a]

| | 1955–1956 | | 1958–1959 | |
	Women's Colleges	Men's Colleges	Women's Colleges	Men's Colleges
Number of colleges	33	24	33	24
Overall fee	$1,730	$1,555	$1,900	$1,740
Tuition	800	840	950	1,000
Room and Board	900	680	920	712

[a] Data for 1955–56 are from American Council on Education, *American Universities and Colleges* (1956 edition, Washington, 1956). Data for 1958–59 are from catalogues, letters, and newspaper notices. For those colleges that quote an overall fee without breakdown, tuition is taken to be the amount charged nonresident students. Required incidental fees have been included with tuition unless they are directly related to living costs. For those institutions that do not have a uniform charge for board and room, the average quoted in the catalogue, or the average of the range quoted, has been used.

colleges was about $200 higher than that for the men's.

Where the college provides both education and living for all of its nonresident students, the separate figures for tuition and living do not necessarily reflect the costs of these different functions. In general, it is assumed that the operating costs of the dormitories are not subsidized from endowment income, although the gifts for building the residence halls may represent a considerable subsidy. There is no uniform practice in college accounting, however. The distribution of overhead costs is a matter of individual judgment, and other considerations than costs may influence the breakdown of the total fee. Some colleges, for instance, have kept tuition charges low with the deliberate intent of attracting students living in the community. Some have even educated local residents free. This is because the college has felt that it owes something to the community in which it is located, or perhaps agreed to do this in return for a local subsidy early in its history; and also because the local students are taken on as "extras." Unless there are large numbers of them it may not even be necessary to employ additional faculty for their instruction. Classes will be a little larger, and that is all.

Other colleges, faced with the necessity of increasing fees, have considered what will seem more reasonable to parents rather than actual costs. In one instance the increase was added to tuition because it was feared that if it was added to living costs the parents would complain of the quality of the food. In another instance it was added to board because everyone would understand that the price of food had increased. In neither case was the additional income applied specifically to the budget designated. Nevertheless, it seems probable that the difference in the median charges for board and room in the men's and women's colleges represent a real difference in college expenditures for these purposes.

This assumption is supported by the fact that operating costs for residence halls are usually the determining factor in setting charges for board and room, and also by the higher standard of living that is typically set for women. There are living quarters in some of the wealthier men's institutions that are more luxurious than any I am acquainted with in the women's colleges, but on the whole, the women are better housed than the men, and are provided with more service. Until recently cafeteria service was unthinkable in the women's colleges. The students were served by white-capped maids. The common rooms of the dormitories are usually furnished tastefully, and often expensively. The grounds, too, are sometimes as well kept as those of a millionaire's estate. These niceties would be wasted on men. They are part of the education of a lady. The women, too, are usually provided with more protective services than the men— from house mothers to night watchmen.

In recent years the rising costs and the difficulty of obtaining dependable service have led to the abandonment of many of the former attributes of gracious living. And as the students are given more freedom, and seek their recreation off campus in larger measure, the differences between the men's and the women's living arrangements will probably diminish. There is already some indication of this. In both 1955-1956 and 1958-1959 the charges of the women's colleges for board and room were higher on the average than those of the men's colleges. But in 1955-1956, living costs exceeded tuition in all but seven of the 33 women's colleges used for the comparison in Table 9, whereas in 1958-1959, tuition fees equalled or exceeded room and board in 17 of these colleges. Thus the division of costs is coming a little closer to that in the men's colleges, which regularly charge more for tuition than for room and board—or at least as much. The relatively small increase in charges for room and board in this three-year period is due in part to reduced services, such as cafeteria service, central dining rooms, and the reduction of maid service in the care of student rooms.

No tendency is found among the women's colleges to follow the pattern of the men's in providing, or permitting the students to seek, different accommodations at varying costs. The accommodations provided by the women's colleges are by no means uniform, but it is good luck rather than dollars that brings a student one of the better rooms. The custom of uniform charges in the women's colleges seems to have arisen from the fact that in the original dormitories rooms were much alike. Differences have arisen only as new dormitories are provided. The differentials found in the men's colleges resulted from the fact that the college did not provide living quarters for all of the men.

The practice of uniform charges is defended today by the colleges that maintain it on the ground of democracy, although the colleges that have varying charges make the same claim to democracy on their campuses as the others. Some of the critics of the uniform charges believe that the effect is to exclude students from low income families rather than to contribute to democratic living. Those favoring uniform charges insist that scholarships take the place of low cost quarters. My own impression is that the differential charges in the few women's colleges that have them have not led to any serious social discrimination against the students who occupy the lower cost rooms. Scholarships adjusted to need are not completely democratic either. But although I, as an undergraduate, attended a university which had differential charges, and have taught in a college that does not, and have also talked with others who have had experience with both types of charges, my information is not sufficient to be sure of my impression. It should, however, be both possible and worth while to get fairly adequate evidence on this point. And if it should prove that the students in low-cost rooms suffer no obvious social discrimination, the advantage would appear to be in favor of the differential charges. For a relatively poor student to draw an inferior room by chance may well leave her with the feeling of being cheated, even though she may have a scholarship. And some of the students from middle-income families, and no scholarships, might be glad to have this kind of saving. This is also a device for charging the wealthier students more nearly what their college education costs.

Before leaving this point it is important to note that most of the women's colleges with uniform charges for the great majority of their students do in fact have some kind of self-help houses where a small number of students, by doing the house work themselves, including the cooking, can reduce living costs. These are generally approved, but they provide for very few students and are rarely open to freshmen; in some instances the possibility of reducing the cost of a college education in this way is not even pointed out in the catalogues and other literature sent to prospective students.

The important contribution of the women's colleges in the matter of residence is the fact that they have for the most part undertaken to house all nonresident students. This has insured healthy living conditions, and it has given all students equal opportunity to participate in social and other campus activities. These factors, in turn, have made the sorority superfluous. It has been comparatively easy, in consequence, to ban all special invitation societies and clubs, which often create unfortunate social distinctions. This most of the women's colleges have done. If, in achieving this, they have erred on the side of uniform charges and some needless luxuries, they can be forgiven. I have found no one who would prefer to turn the students loose to fend for themselves, whether in private rooming houses or in sororities.

The second factor that makes the women's colleges somewhat more costly than the men's is the small number of students in proportion to faculty members. There are, of course, some men's colleges, and some coeducational colleges, with a smaller number of students per faculty member than some women's colleges. But this is in general a characteristic of women's colleges, and one that adds materially to the cost. Historically, there appear to have been two reasons for this. The first was that the women's colleges have been smaller, on the average, than men's and coeducational institutions. And the small college typically has a low ratio of students to faculty. It is difficult to offer a sufficient variety of courses without giving a large number of (by normal standards) under-elected courses. Being small, the colleges have made a virtue of necessity and featured individual instruction. The claim of the women's colleges that they have put good teaching above all else is based largely on this factor.

The comparatively large number of faculty has not been the extravagance it would have been at the men's colleges because the employment of women on the faculty of the women's colleges made lower salary scales possible. But as the women's colleges compete increasingly with other institutions for men faculty, this promises to be a luxury that they can no longer afford. Most of the savings of the lower salary scales of the women's colleges have been eaten up by the larger number of faculty in proportion to enrollment. In 1940, for example, when the differences in salary scales were larger than at present, instruction expenses per faculty member in the women's colleges were only 78 per cent of those in the men's colleges. But instruction expenses per student were 91 per cent of those in the men's colleges. The number of students per faculty member at this time was 8 for the women's colleges and 10 for the men's. In view of the greater competition for faculty today, the lower salary scales cannot continue without seriously impairing the quality of teaching. Small classes with dull teachers are not conducive to good education.

Another factor responsible for the relatively larger teaching staff of the women's colleges is that in their early history the women teachers lived in the dormitories with the students and were charged with a good many social and disciplinary duties in addition to teaching. They were actually only part-time teachers. In more recent times the nature of these duties has changed, but a rather elaborate advising system is prevalent in these colleges, and there are still faculty residents in the residence halls, although their obligations are different, and also less onerous, than in the early years. Some of the men's colleges have introduced similar systems, and they are generally approved. The more frequent and less formal contacts between faculty and students that this provides, as compared with the classroom, are supposed to stimulate intellectual interests in the students—and probably do in some measure. But it requires a larger faculty in proportion to enrollment, and if the students demanding admission to our universities and colleges outrun the new recruits to the faculty, as is predicted, it may not prove feasible to use trained scholars in this way. In fact, it seems probable that the women's colleges have gone farther than the men's in assigning non-classroom duties to their faculty because the women faculty have been cheaper than the men, and the necessity for economizing in their use has not been so apparent.

It is of some interest to note that this has never been a characteristic of the public women's colleges. On the contrary, when there were still a substantial number of these, in 1940, the number of students in proportion to the faculty was larger, in almost every state, than the number for the corresponding men's college in that state.

The statement that women faculty members have been cheaper than men needs further elaboration in view of the fact that the salary scales are uniform for both, at least nominally. This uniformity is, however, a comparatively recent development—an accompaniment of published salary scales.

When women first entered the teaching profession the preference for men, even in the lower schools, was so strong that the differential between men's and women's salaries was very marked. And by the time that women took over this field for their own, at least in the grammar schools, the lack of alternative employment for educated women gave them little bargaining power. Lucy Stone once taught in her brother's school during his illness, and the trustees cut the salary from $30 a month to $16. That was enough for a woman, they explained.[7] But this differential was small for that period. Susan B. Anthony taught for fifteen years, rising to headmistress of a girl's academy, without receiving any increase in her $2.50 per week salary. She had to pay board from this sum. At the same time her father, whose experience had been mostly in the field of business, was able to command $10 per week as a teacher. Such a differential between men's and women's salaries was standard for the period.[8] The daughter was regarded as a very successful teacher, but more than once she replaced men receiving four times her salary.

This was in the 1840's. In the latter half of the nineteenth century, state school boards regularly reported average salaries for men and women separately, and in the New England and Middle Atlantic states the men's salaries were about double the women's. In Connecticut, for example, in 1866, the average for women was $23 per month and for men $49; and in 1905 these averages were $46 and $107, respectively. Even as late as the 1920's some states continued to report average salaries for men that were double those for women. It is true that this was partly because men were found mostly in the higher positions; but it does not follow that the women were not equally qualified for the higher positions.

Among the early women pioneers in higher education, Sarah Josepha Hale argued that if education was to be universal it must be cheap, and that women could manage with lower salaries than men.[9] Lydia Sigourney urged that young women should teach for nothing if they could afford to do so.[10] And Mary Lyon accepted low pay as inevitable. She was a missionary at heart, and she expected her teachers, and the students that she was training to be teachers, to live lives of sacrifice. She set them a good example by accepting the meager salary of $200 a year plus living expenses, after having given her services for nothing for three years while promoting the seminary, and spending $1,000 of her savings from earlier teaching, in addition.[11] Catherine Beecher, on the contrary, insisted that if teachers are underpaid "the profession will be as it has been, the resort of the dull, stupid and shiftless."[12] She wanted to charge the students enough to cover adequate salaries and provide scholarships for the needy.

President Raymond of Vassar agreed with Beecher. He deplored the attitude that regarded "those in educational professions as the servants or beneficiaries rather than the benefactors of the public, giving from their stores of heart and brain and nerve treasures of supreme worth, and receiving the most meager return."[13] He himself declined the presidency when Matthew Vassar first offered it at a salary of $3,000. He said that he could not come for less than $5,000, a sum that he felt the college could not afford. In the end he settled for $4,000, plus living quarters for himself and family at the nominal rental of $100.[14] He also established a salary of $2,000 for men professors in the first year. This was good for that period. Brown University paid no more than this, and Amherst, Dartmouth and Bowdoin paid much less. Professors at Amherst were paid $1200,[15] and Dartmouth increased professors' salaries in the year that Vassar opened from $1100 to $1300.[16] Bowdoin increased its salaries from $1100 to $1500 in 1867.[17] By that time Vassar was paying $2500.

Raymond's high standards did not extend to women, however. Eight professors were appointed in the first year, two of them women: Maria Mitchell and Dr. Alida Avery. Maria Mitchell was recognized at the time as a person of distinction. She was approached some months before the college opened by one of the trustees, and a salary of $1500 was suggested. President Raymond later expressed his hope that she might be persuaded to come if the college could "afford such a costly luxury."[18] But the salary finally offered was $800 plus living for herself and her father. Dr. Avery received $700 plus living. It is true that the $2,000 salaries of the men professors did not include living, but examination of the early ledgers of the college shows that rent, groceries, and coal combined amounted to about $650 per family. (The college served as landlord and merchant as well as employer.) Thus the net salary comparable to Mitchell's $800 must have been at least $1300.[19] Moreover, in the second year the men's salaries were raised to $2500, and one man received in addition a reduction in rent from $400 to $100. The two women continued to receive their original salaries.[20] Teachers—all women—were paid $400 to $500, also with living. It was several years later that some adjustments were made after Mitchell and Avery offered their resignations, not only because of the lower salaries, but also because Raymond had neglected to ask them, as he asked the men, to report their scientific publications, and had also failed to appoint them to committees.[21]

It was not surprising that the women's viewpoint was overlooked in the earliest women's colleges, since both the boards of trustees and the presidents were men. Boards of trustees had to be solid citizens —bankers, lawyers, and successful business men, leavened by a sprinkling of clergymen. The assumption that college presidents should be ministers, together with the obvious advantage of having college-educated individuals in this post, barred the possibility of women administrators at this time. No woman had received a Ph.D. from an American university when Elmira, Vassar, Smith, and Wellesley opened, and only ten such degrees for women are recorded by the time that Bryn Mawr opened in 1885. There were a few women ministers, but these had not achieved general approval.

Wellesley's first president was a woman, a graduate of Mount Holyoke Seminary. She was succeeded by Alice Freeman Palmer, who graduated from the University of Michigan and had done some graduate work there, but had no graduate degrees. M. Carey Thomas, who had a doctor's degree from Zurich, seems to have been the first woman college president with a Ph.D. She was inaugurated in 1894. The eastern women's colleges that employed the largest proportion of women on their faculty in 1890 were the two with women presidents —Mount Holyoke and Wellesley. Whether this was because they had women presidents or whether the women presidents as well as the faculty were economy measures is not recorded.

Maria Mitchell and Alida Avery were probably not the first women members of a college faculty to protest against discrimination, and certainly were not the last. These protests have borne fruit. Today in the women's colleges there is no obvious differentiation in rank and salary scales. The men may be placed a little higher than women of equal qualifications when they are first employed, and they may push ahead a little faster, but this would be hard to prove. Several of the Radcliffe Ph.D.'s whose comments on discrimination are recorded in the study *Graduate Education for Women,* specifically state that there is less discrimination in the women's colleges than in the coeducational institutions. One or two report that they have found none at all in the women's colleges.[22] And there is no doubt in the minds of those with whom I have discussed this matter, who have had experience in both coeducational and women's colleges, that there is a sense of discrimination among the women in the former that is entirely lacking in the women's colleges.

This is an achievement for the women's colleges to be proud of, particularly in view of the extent of the earlier discrimination. But it raises new financial problems. With equal—or almost equal—pay for men and women, and a decreasing number of women applying as a result of early and all but universal marriage, the financial advantage that the early women's colleges enjoyed from employing women is disappearing. In 1940, 72 per cent of the faculties of the 22 largest private women's colleges were women, as compared with 3 per cent of the faculties of the 21 men's colleges of the same size group (over 450 students and under 3,000). Expenditures for instruction per faculty member were $3,385 in the men's colleges and $2,658 in the women's; thus the average salary paid by the men's colleges was 27 per cent higher than that paid by the women's colleges.[23]

By 1955 the proportion of women on the faculties of these women's colleges had dropped below 60 per cent, and the proportion of women on the faculties of the men's colleges had dropped below 2 per cent. Fragmentary data on current salary scales indicate that there is still a considerable differential between the salaries of the two groups of colleges. This differential cannot continue without a material decline in the quality of faculty in the women's institutions. There is no longer a large number of women with graduate degrees and the freedom to go where they can find the best openings. For those who are trained and free to go where they please there are opportunities opening in research positions with the government and private industry that were not formerly available. It seems probable, also, that opportunities for women will increase in the universities with the growing shortage of trained personnel.

On the income side of the balance sheet, the women's colleges complain that it is easier to get endowment for men's colleges than women's. The facts support this contention. In 1955 the amount of productive funds per student was $17,724 for 42 private liberal arts colleges for men, and $7,311 for 53 comparable colleges for women.[24] But while the women's colleges had less than half of the endowment per student that the men's colleges had in this year, they had more than twice the endowment per student that the 304 coeducational colleges had. The funds for these came to $3,189 per student. In the fifteen years from 1940 to 1955 the endowment per student increased more for the women's colleges than for either the men's or the coeducational institutions. This was primarily because of the relatively small increase in the number of students in these women's colleges. But even in 1940 the endowment per student was larger for the women's colleges than for the coeducational colleges—$3,016 as compared with $2,424. The number of colleges with more than $10,000 per student in 1955 is shown in Table 10.

Table 10.

PRODUCTIVE ENDOWMENT PER STUDENT ENROLLED, 1955[a]

Amount per enrolled student	Number of Colleges			Per cent of Colleges		
	Men's	Women's	Coeducational	Men's	Women's	Coeducational
$20,000 and over	9	4	4	21.4	7.5	1.3
$10,000–19,999	6	3	15	14.3	5.7	4.9
Under $10,000	27	46	285	64.3	86.8	93.8
Total	42	53	304	100.0	100.0	100.0

[a] Private colleges not directly governed by a church. *American Universities and Colleges,* 1956 edition.

A large part of the gifts received by the women's colleges has gone into buildings and equipment. Largely because of their efforts to house the entire student body, the women's colleges have had a somewhat higher investment per student in buildings than either the men's colleges or the coeducational colleges. This, too, has probably accounted for their small productive funds, as compared with the men's colleges. Endowment per student increased substantially in the period from 1940 to 1954, but the cost of education increased even faster. The percentage of current income of privately controlled institutions coming from endowment dropped in this period from 18 to

9 per cent. Moreover, endowment income is often earmarked for uses that are not closely related to the basic educational program; and sometimes the programs which these funds were designed to encourage draw other unearmarked revenues away from the main college function.

Very little relation is found between the endowment income and tuition fees. It might be expected that the less well endowed colleges would have to charge higher tuition. The fact appears to be, however, that the richer colleges provide a more expensive, and presumably a better education. Table 9 shows that the men's colleges have higher tuition charges than women's. The women's colleges, in turn, have higher tuition charges than the coeducational colleges on the average. These latter are not shown in Table 9 because with the large numbers of colleges in this group and the rapid changes in fees it is difficult to obtain a dependable average figure for the group as a whole. But the data for earlier years, and a small sample for recent years makes it clear that the average is still somewhat lower for the coeducational than for the men's or women's colleges.

In summary, the total charges for the women's colleges have been higher, on the average, than those for the men's colleges—partly because the women's colleges have had a somewhat smaller endowment income, partly because residence costs have been higher. Instruction costs have been approximately the same for these two groups of institutions, the women's colleges having taken advantage of lower salary scales to employ a larger faculty in proportion to student enrollment. Both groups of colleges have higher fees, as well as larger endowments, than the average private coeducational college. They are providing a more expensive education.

The women's colleges have enjoyed a greater increase in endowment per student in recent years than other institutions, as noted above, largely because of the much smaller increase in their student enrollments. Even so, endowment income has not kept pace with rising costs. And with the more direct competition with other colleges for faculty—owing to the decreasing number of women applicants for such positions—the advantage of lower salary scales, which they enjoyed in their early history, is no longer available to them. Moreover, the growing preference of women students for coeducational institutions makes it difficult for the women's colleges to attract the abler students at the same time that they are charging higher fees. The increasing difficulty of getting into coeducational colleges may insure the women's colleges of a numerically adequate student body, but it seems doubtful that they can continue to attract the same quality of students that they have so successfully attracted in the past unless the differential charges can be reduced. Consequently, if they are going to compete successfully with other institutions in the future, it seems probable that they will have to economize in the two areas where they have been, on the whole, more lavish than other colleges. These are the residence expenditures and the relative size of their faculties.

The financial position of the women's colleges is more vulnerable than that of other institutions, but this is not due, as frequently assumed, to the inadequacy of their endowments. The relative decline in endowment income is characteristic of all private institutions; and while the women's colleges cannot compare with Harvard and Yale in endowment, only about one in twenty of the private independent colleges today can compare with Wellesley, Scripps, Bryn Mawr, and Vassar in endowment per student. The real financial problem of the women's colleges is the greater reluctance of their clientele to pay what it costs for women's education than for men's; and the gradual disappearance of their special financial advantage: the low salary scales made possible by their willingness to employ women on their faculties. I stated earlier that the success of an educational institution will depend on the quality of its students more than any other single factor. But if it is to attract outstanding students, it will have to provide them with outstanding teachers.

NOTES

[1] S. Barr, *Purely Academic* (New York, 1958), p. 5.

[2] Paul C. Glick and Herman P. Miller, "Educational Level and Potential Income," *American Sociological Review*, June 1956, p. 310.

[3] E. V. Hollis and Associates, "Costs of Attending College," *United States Office of Education Bulletin, 1957, No. 9,* 1958, pp. 48, 51.

[4] *Ibid.*, pp. 31, 48.

[5] *Ibid.*, p. 12.

[6] *Ibid.*, p. 37.

[7] F. J. Hosford, *Father Shipherd's Magna Charta, A Century of Coeducation in Oberlin College* (Boston, 1937), p. 85.

[8] K. Anthony, *Susan B. Anthony* (New York, 1954), p. 7.

[9] *Ladies Magazine*, March 1829, p. 133.

[10] L. H. Sigourney, *Letters to Young Ladies* (New York, 1835), Letter XI.

[11] A. C. Cole, *A Hundred Years of Mount Holyoke College* (New Haven, 1940), p. 70.

[12] *Ibid.*, p. 26.

[13] H. R. Lloyd, editor, *Life and Letters of J. H. Raymond* (New York, 1881), p. 506.

[14] Lloyd, *op. cit.*, p. 509; and *Vassar College Ledger, 1865-1866.*

[15] C. M. Fuess, *Amherst: the Story of a New England College* (Boston, 1935), p. 183.

[16] L. B. Richardson, *History of Dartmouth College* (Hanover, 1932), vol. 2, p. 526.

[17] L. C. Hatch, *History of Bowdoin College* (Portland, 1927), p. 214.

[18] Lloyd, *op. cit.*, p. 528.

[19] Subtracting $700 for the living costs which the men had to meet from their salaries.

[20] *Vassar College Ledgers, 1865-1867.*

[21] H. M. Wright, *Maria Mitchell: Sweeper in the Sky* (New York, 1949), pp. 181-182. The Vassar ledgers of the early 1870's show that Maria Mitchell and the other women professors received the same salaries as the men.

[22] Report by a Faculty-Trustee Committee, Cambridge, 1956, Ch. 3.

[23] Compiled from data in United States Office of Education, *Biennial Survey of Education, 1938-40,* "Statistics of Universities and Colleges."

[24] Compiled from data in American Council on Education, *American Universities and Colleges,* 1956 edition (Washington, 1956).

CHOICES NEVER DREAMED OF A HUNDRED YEARS AGO HAVE
OPENED TO A WOMAN IN BUSINESS AND THE PROFESSIONS.
THE GOING IS STILL ROUGH, HOWEVER, AND SHE MUST BE
BETTER PREPARED THAN A MAN IF SHE IS TO MEET HIS
COMPETITION.

NANCY LEWIS*

9. The College Woman and the Job

THE DISCUSSION thus far has been concerned primarily with the
institutions that have provided higher education for women; their
aims; the kind of training they provide; the kind of students they
attract; and their apparent successes and failures. This chapter and
those immediately following are concerned with what the women who
have gone to college have done with their lives, in the hope of showing
the influence of their education on their later activities.

All education is supposed to help to prepare young people for
"life." In the days when college women either married or pursued
a career the problem was to guess which direction each student would
go in time to prepare her for her particular life. Today, when it is
fairly clear that she will marry and rear a sizable flock of children,
as well as work outside the home for a considerable period of time,
and that she will also participate in community affairs, the problem
is not which to prepare her for but whether she can be prepared for

* From N. Lewis, "College Women and Their Proper Spheres," *American Association of University Women Journal*, May 1954, p. 208.

everything in the short space of time that is available before an early marriage. There is one comforting thought, however; whatever the preparation may be, if it is useful for the purpose intended, it will not be wasted.

This chapter will be devoted to exploring the success of higher education in meeting the aim of professional or vocational training. The extent to which other aims have been realized will be explored in later chapters.

To get some perspective on the part that higher education has played in preparing women for jobs it is important to sketch the main trends of women's occupations during the period that higher education has been available to them. No large number of women worked for wages outside the home when the agitation for higher education for women began. The home itself was a workshop that could easily use the time and skills of all the women in the family. And if the home was on a farm, as it frequently was, there was more than enough work to occupy every able-bodied member of the family. Harriet Martineau, writing in 1837, claimed that there were only seven occupations open to women: teaching, needlework, keeping boarders, working in the cotton mills, bookbinding, typesetting, and domestic service.[1] Actually a good many agricultural laborers were women, and some shopkeepers. But it was true that most women working for wages were concentrated in a few occupations.

The first comprehensive Census of Occupations in the United States was that of 1870. At this time the proportion of women working outside the home was considerably less than half of the proportion working outside the home today. Most of those who had paid employment in 1870—four out of every five—were domestic servants, agricultural laborers, seamstresses, and laundresses. Nearly half were in domestic service alone. In short, they were doing much the same thing that they would have been doing at home. The other two important occupations for women, accounting for half of the remaining women workers, were teaching and work in the textile mills. Teaching was the most respectable occupation for a young woman from a middle class family, but the New England mill girls were also recruited from middle class families. In fact, many of them alternated mill work and teaching, the school year of the period often being only a few weeks in length.

The only important occupation that required even a grammar school education was teaching. This employed approximately 5 per cent of the working women in 1870. But even this did not require a college education. Normal schools were still new and by no means universal, and large numbers of their students did not continue beyond one year. Most teachers were high school graduates at best. Office girls and sales girls, for whom literacy, at least, is essential, were negligible in numbers. These were still men's occupations.

The women workers of 1870 were mostly unmarried and mostly young. Marriage brought them back to the home for the rest of their lives. Today women workers represent about three out of ten women over the age of 14. At the age of 18, and again at 50, nearly half of all women are working outside the home. Also, nearly half of the women workers are married "with spouse present," as the Census describes them. Whereas half of the adult women of this country never entered the labor force at the end of the nineteenth century, today those that never enter the labor market are only one in ten. Moreover, those who do have paid employment work for a larger part of their lives, on the average, than in earlier periods. And college women are more likely to have paid positions than those who do not pursue their education that far. Although only 5 per cent of women over twenty-five had had four years or more of college in 1950, college women constituted 9 per cent of the total women in the labor force. And at every age from 22 to 65 the proportion of college women who work outside the home is larger than the proportion of women who did not go beyond high school.[2]

The reasons for the increase of women working outside the home are first of all the usual economic ones. The unmarried woman is expected to be self-supporting, and under modern conditions of living she cannot pay her way by working at home. She is frequently expected, also, to support parents and other members of the family who cannot support themselves since she does not have a family of her own to provide for as her brother does. Even the married woman may become the sole support of her family if her husband dies or is disabled. It is no longer permissible for a ten or twelve year old boy to support his widowed mother.

More important, however, is the fact that it is now socially acceptable for a married woman to work. It no longer reflects on the husband's ability to support a family. This makes a vast difference; coupled with the fact that homemaking is rarely a fulltime job once the children are grown, and that the home itself is a lonely place in which to spend one's entire day, the job alternative which came earlier to unmarried women now appears both possible and desirable to their married sisters.

The fact that a working wife is quite respectable is one of the important factors which have encouraged early marriage. It is no longer necessary to wait five or ten years because the young man has not completed his education or been promoted to a position which would enable him to support a wife as her parents think she should be supported. Even when the husband earns a reasonable living the wife is likely to look for work when the children are no longer small, to make it possible to have all the costly labor-saving equipment in the home, to provide for the best education that can be had for the children, or even to buy luxuries.

One of the drawbacks to the employment of women that is frequently cited is their undependability because of family responsibilities and lack of ambition. It is true that marriage and the family come first. Few women today give up marriage because it might interfere with a professional career. And many fail to acquire the long training necessary for some of the professions, either because they marry before they finish their preparation or because they think that it is not worth while even to start. But it is also true that the older women, particularly those who have graduated from college, return to the labor market, and even make an effort at that time to get the necessary training for a professional position. And financial need, or the desire for the luxuries that the extra salary will provide, are not the only reasons. Even when salary is the deciding factor other motives are usually involved.

Professional women often place the satisfaction of the job itself first, and some stress the fact that it makes them better wives and mothers. One recent study shows that in spite of the fact that a considerable number of the college graduates interviewed had not been able to get the position they most wanted, only one in ten was working at a job that she disliked, and the majority definitely liked what they were doing.[3]

All this suggests that the new pattern will continue. It is difficult to imagine young people in the future waiting to marry until the man can provide for a family without his wife's assistance. Or to imagine the wife staying home alone with nothing to do. These are changes that those engaged in the higher education of women must take into account. For whatever their theories of education, all are agreed that education is training for life. And the woman's life is no longer, even ideally, to be completely absorbed by homemaking.

There have been important shifts, also, in the occupations that attract women workers. The women still tend to concentrate in a few occupations, in spite of the fact that at least one woman can be found in each of the several hundred categories listed in the 1950 Census. But there is less concentration than formerly, and the predominant occupations are different. Domestic service, which accounted for nearly half of the working women of 1870, accounted for only 8 per cent in 1950. Combined, all the four occupations which employed four-fifths of the 1870 women workers employed less than one-fourth of the women workers of 1950. The four leading categories combined, in 1950, account for considerably less than half of all workers. Also, two of these four occupations require a high school education, at least, whereas none of the four leading occupations of 1870 required any book learning.

Today women with only a grammar school education are found

as farm workers, factory operatives, sales clerks in stores, or in domestic and other service positions to a greater extent than women with more education; and they are found less frequently than their high school sisters in clerical work. They are less likely to be working outside the home than either the high school graduates or the college women. Women who had not reached high school constituted 46 per cent of the adult women of 1950, but they comprised only 37 per cent of the women in the labor force.

The old pattern has broken down. Marriage does not remove a woman from the labor market for life. Nor do unmarried daughters of well-to-do families stay home. As late as 1900 many families that sent their daughters to college objected to their working after graduation. They either had to prove that college education had not spoiled them for household tasks, or they had to prove that their fathers (or husbands) could support them. Today we are more likely to feel sorry for the girl who has to stay home than for the girl who works. Moreover, the jobs themselves require increasingly higher levels of education. The opportunities for girls without a high school education are distinctly limited.

A high school diploma usually opens the door to the office job. And office jobs provided work for about three out of ten women workers in 1950. Clerical work is the route by which 60 per cent of high school graduates, as compared with 25 per cent of the nongraduates, enter the job market.[4] This is one reason why girls finish high school in larger numbers than boys and then fail to go on to college in as large proportions as boys. The office position is respectable. It has short hours. It is clean. And one is likely to be associated with men of education and bright futures; hopefully, unmarried young men—there is always the chance of marrying a rising young businessman. College women themselves sometimes find the office job, in anticipation, more attractive than teaching even when the pay is no better. High school graduates are also to be found in large numbers in nursing, which is second to teaching among women's professions.

College women are found primarily in the professions. This is shown in Table 11. The leading profession is teaching. Today, the majority of states require an A.B. degree for teachers, even in elementary schools, and some require an A.M. degree for teachers in secondary schools. The proportion of teachers among working women is only a little larger than it was in 1870—6 per cent as compared with 5 per cent eighty years earlier. But the teachers today are college women. So are the members of most of the other professions where women are found in considerable numbers—as social workers, librarians, dietitians, and others.

Table 11.

OCCUPATIONS AND EDUCATION OF WORKING WOMEN, 1950*

	Percentage Distribution		
		Education	
Occupation	Four years or more of college	One to three years of college	No College
Professional	72	36	4
Clerical	16	36	23
Managerial	4	7	5
Sales	⎰	⎰ 7	9
Service and household	⎱	⎱	26
Factory operatives	⎰ 8	⎰ 14	25
All other	⎱	⎱	8
Total	100	100	100

* Women's Bureau, United States Department of Labor, Pamphlet 1, 1956. *Job Horizons for the College Woman*, p. 48. The data are for women workers twenty-five years of age and over.

Teaching has been the principal occupation of the college woman from the beginning. A study of the early graduates of Mount Holyoke Seminary, made in 1877, showed that approximately 70 per cent of the 2,341 former students for whom a record was obtained had taught; most of the remaining 30 per cent had never had a paid occupation.[5]

A study of self-supporting members of the American Association of University Women, made in 1909, showed that approximately three out of four were teaching.[6]

The proportion of college women who teach is, however, declining. The 1948 American Association of University Women survey showed that only 54 per cent of the more than 30,000 members who replied to the inquiry had ever taught; other studies indicate that the proportion teaching is smaller for the younger than for the older groups. Approaching this from another angle, the proportion of teachers who are women has declined from 12 out of 15 in 1920 to 10 out of 15 today. And there is every indication that it will continue to drop with the declining proportion of women among the college graduates and the early age of marriage. There appears to have been some revival of interest in teaching among the college women as a result of the emphasis being placed on this field today. A newspaper notice recently reported, as something new, that one-fourth of the Wellesley graduates of 1957 had gone into teaching or were taking graduate courses in preparation for teaching.[7]

The fact is that, in spite of large numbers of women who find teaching an absorbing and rewarding occupation, this has not been the ambition of the average college woman since alternative professions have become acceptable women's occupations. While teaching is high on the list of occupations when seniors are asked what they plan to do after graduation, it is low on the list when freshmen are asked the same question. The seniors are facing reality. An Educational Testing Service study of graduating high school students in 1955 shows that one-fifth of the girls who planned to go to college listed education as the probable field of study although only one-tenth indicated that this was their field of greatest interest.[8] When I recently asked a group of college seniors what they planned to do after their children were all in school (one never asks them any more what their immediate plans are since the immediate objective is almost always marriage), they were nearly unanimous in stating that they wanted to work in a business office; and they were obviously disconcerted by the question as to who they thought would teach their children if they did not.

Most college women are following well-trodden paths, not because of any special aptitude or inclination but because tradition and social attitudes make these the line of least resistance. The professional departments of the universities point that way; so do the school advisors who are often more concerned with directing their students toward the most probable job than the job that might interest them most. The B'nai B'rith survey in 1953 of 5,000 college women, cited above, showed that between 70 and 80 per cent of those who had expected to go into teaching, secretarial work, or nursing had attained their goal in the first job; whereas only 20 to 30 per cent of those who had aimed at personnel work, psychological work, music, or entertainment were able to get a job in their chosen field immediately.[9]

Nevertheless, teaching, secretarial work, and nursing are not the only practical job expectations. There is social work, a large variety of health services, and laboratory technicians. And among the traditionally masculine professions, 15 per cent of auditors and accountants are now women, and more than 10 per cent of chemists and natural scientists. Women have, however, made very little headway in the fields of medicine, law, and engineering, partly because of the weight of tradition which brings its special hurdles in getting both the training and suitable positions, and partly because of the long and expensive preparation which may seem of questionable value to women who are planning early marriage.

The great majority of college women now working outside the home are in professions requiring a college education. Sixty per cent are in teaching alone. Thus whether or not the college authorities intend to prepare them, the students themselves use their education for this purpose. The polls show that occupational training held first place in the minds of parents who were planning to send their daughters to college, and the fields of student concentration in college reflect the same concern. Among the women graduates of 1956, 45 per cent specialized in education. And adding to education all the fields directed specifically toward some occupation, including the healing arts and

medical sciences, home economics, business, social work, public administration, engineering, library science, and journalism, more than
three-fifths (63 per cent) of the women graduates are accounted for.
Nor does this include large numbers of students preparing for high
school teaching, since these usually major in English, mathematics,
history, sciences, languages and other subjects that they plan to teach.

The percentage of the members of some of the leading professions
who are women is given in Table 12. The universities offer special
degrees in all the professions listed in this table. It does not follow, of

Table 12.

PERCENTAGE OF WOMEN IN SELECTED PROFESSIONS[a]

Occupational Groups				Degree Recipients		
	1930	1950			1930	1956
Engineers	0.05	1.2	Enginering		0.02	0.3
Dentists	1.8	2.8	Dentistry		2.1	1.2
Foresters	0.2	3.2	Forestry		0.3	0.4
Lawyers	2.1	3.5	Law		4.8	3.7
Architects	1.7	3.8	Architecture		1.3	5.3
Clergy	2.2	4.1	Theology		5.6	1.5
Physicians and						
Surgeons	4.6	6.1	M. D.		4.6	5.2
Veterinaries	0.1	6.3	Veterinary medicine		0.0	1.8
Pharmacists	4.1[b]	8.2	Pharmacy		7.8	10.7
Social Workers	78.7	63.2	Social work		98.3	65.8
Teachers	81.0	74.5	Education		67.6	63.7
Librarians	91.4	88.5	Library science		93.3	77.4
Nurses	98.1	97.6	Nursing		100.0	99.1

[a] Data from *Decennial Census* and United States Office of Education, Circular
no. 499, *Earned Degrees, 1955-1956*. The professions discussed in the chapter
following on scholars and artists have been omitted here. Also, some for which
the classification has changed materially have been omitted. The professions listed
have been arranged in order of the proportion of women in each occupational
group in 1950.

[b] 1940; pharmacists are not separately classified in 1930.

course, that all the members of these professions have university degrees. In some, like nursing, university training is comparatively new, but it is increasingly expected in all. Those professions discussed in the chapter on scholars and artists, which follows, have been omitted here, although they show much the same trends as the professions included.

The most interesting trend shown by this table is the increase in the proportion of women employed in each of the nine "men's professions" listed, and the decrease in the proportion in "women's professions." Tradition and prejudice are, in some measure, breaking down, and neither sex has been able to maintain its monopoly, although the number of women in engineering, for example, is still quite small. The data on degree recipients show the same trends for most professions. In 1930 there was one profession, veterinary medicine, in which no women obtained degrees, and one profession, nursing, in which all recipients were women. In 1956 there were some men and some women in each of the categories listed. Among the degree recipients, however, there are three categories among the "men's professions" in which the proportion of women shows a decline. These are dentistry, law, and theology. This is partly a reflection of the decline in the proportion of women getting higher degrees, as compared with 1930. In fact, the gains in six of the professions, small though some of them are, are fairly impressive when it is recalled that they are running counter to the trend for degrees as a whole. Women are no longer as large a proportion of the degree recipients as they used to be.

The widening of women's opportunities and interests is less impressive when comparisons are made with women in higher education in Russia. In 1959 the percentage of women enrolled in universities and colleges was 35 in the United States and 51 in Russia. The percentage of women students in medicine was 5.5 in the United States and 69 in Russia. These percentages for engineering were 0.6 and 39 respectively.[10]

Any examination of the occupational activities of college women today should reassure those who worry lest women will never use their college education because they "just get married." They do get married but that does not remove them from the job market for all time. It is true that their working lives are shorter than those of the men, but today's women workers are expected to average from twenty to twenty-five years in paid occupations. The college women work more than their less educated contemporaries. In spite of many instances where they take jobs which a high school girl might handle successfully, either because they are geographically limited in their search for a job, or because they have not kept up with their field of specialization in the years that they were at home with the children, the majority appear to be working in professions that normally require higher education. Most of them teach. And it seems quite probable that whether they want to or not college graduates will continue to teach in the future. Who else is going to educate their children now that 93 per cent of all women marry and half are married by the time they are twenty? It is hardly to be expected that enough men can be recruited for this unless salary scales are increased beyond the expectations of the optimists.

A college education will probably become increasingly important, also, for the office job. The progress of automation in clerical work promises to do away with a large part of the more mechanical processes which have employed so many high school graduates. Many skilled workers in factories today are sending their sons to college in recognition of the fact that their jobs are likely to be taken over by machines and engineers. The office job, too, increasingly requires professional training.

Our real concern should be, then, not whether college women will ever use their college education, but whether the women will get the education they need before they marry, in order to bring up their children according to the best advice of the specialists; and then, when the youngest child is in school, to follow the children to school and teach, or to establish themselves in some other profession without too long a period of training.

The increasing withdrawals from college before the college course is completed will be discussed later.[11] It is enough to note here that these are primarily due to marriage, and that they are sufficiently large to make it clear that many women are going to return to the labor market sometime in the future without sufficient training for any profession. If young married women are to complete their college course, the colleges themselves will probably have to give them more assistance. Many of the students do try to finish, and the residence colleges no longer refuse to let them continue because they have married. A few hardy souls have remained to graduate, even in the residential women's colleges, after their first baby was born. But most try to finish elsewhere. For these, the colleges might be more generous, either in granting degrees to those who take their senior year at another institution, or granting them to seniors who have completed their first three years somewhere else. Another possibility, often discussed but rarely tried, is to shorten the course for some of the better students, either permitting them to enter college before they have completed the traditional four years of high school, or providing a longer college year or a more intensive course for those capable of handling it at the college level.

Another question that needs rethinking is whether the educational program now being offered is the best for the ends in view. This question has been sharply raised by recent Russian achievements, particularly in the scientific field. This is too large an area to be covered here, but a few points can appropriately be raised in relation to the specific question under discussion—the kind of college course that is most useful in preparing women for professions. There has been a great deal of criticism of the specialized courses oriented toward specific occupations, and with good reason. Many of them have provided training in simple skills, at best, and at worst not even that. I still recall my own experience with such courses in my first year of graduate study when it occurred to me that I had no specific training for a job. I was allowed to take both a secretarial training course and a course in education as part of my work toward a master's degree in economics! I never had any real regrets about the training in typing.

It did much to facilitate my research in later years. But it contributed nothing to my understanding of economics, and there were other ways in which I might have acquired this useful skill. The course in education I abandoned after a few lectures, together with any chance of obtaining a teacher's certificate. I simply could not sit through it. The final outrage was advice on how to arrange chalk around the blackboards, and on the importance of not letting one's hair straggle!

The state and municipal colleges and universities have responded to the desire for occupational training to a marked degree. They have not only taken the responsibility for training teachers for the public schools; they train for private business as well. To illustrate, more than one institution now offers a course leading to a certificate for airline stewardesses. The programs have been improvised by regrouping courses that are given anyway in the schools of transportation and home economics. Their relevance for the purpose in view is not always clear, and it is hard to imagine that some of them could offer anything challenging to an intelligent college student. One of these programs includes courses in airline operation, passenger procedures, home nursing, meal preparation and service, and appropriate dress and personal appearance. Another (the program is not yet standardized) takes care of nursing and food handling in a single course on "air stewardess flight service," expands the "appropriate dress and personal appearance" into two courses on "personality and poise" and "modeling," and adds geography.

Is it necessary to give college courses in such procedures? What do they discuss in a whole semester of modeling? Is nothing to be left to on-the-job training, to imagination and reason? One school of business administration offers four courses in typing—fundamental, elementary, intermediate, and advanced—and six in shorthand. It also offers a course in punch-card equipment. A friend of mine who recently took a required course in visual aids, for a teacher's certificate, said that the only thing she learned that she hadn't already known was how to operate a particular kind of projector, and she thought she might have learned that by reading the directions. In one education department I find three full semester courses in the teaching of driver-safety training—elementary, intermediate, and advanced, in this instance omitting the fundamental. This particular education department offers a total of 328 different courses.

In criticizing this type of training I do not mean to argue that the colleges should ignore their students' concerns for vocational training. On the contrary, I believe that the revulsion against mere technical training has tended to carry some of the liberal arts colleges to the other extreme, condemning any course that may seem to have any practical value for later professional purposes, and trying to persuade the students that they should not even think about professional needs until after graduation. It seems to me that this is unrealistic in view of the facts.

Our women students are not going to graduate schools in great numbers. They will do well if they acquire the A.B. degree before they marry. And their undergraduate studies will provide all the training they are likely to get for the job they are almost sure to hold. Why, then, should we be so reticent about the fact that it is possible to combine a genuine liberal arts course with the requirements for an accredited chemist? That statistics will give one a useful job skill at the same time that it stretches the mind? That one can even acquire a teacher's certificate with the appropriate combination of courses in the liberal arts curriculum, and some practice teaching on the side?

If the colleges that stand for a sound liberal arts training reject all possibilities for combining this with any professional preparation, they are in danger of defeating their own aims. For the job-minded students will gravitate in increasing numbers to the places where specific, but superficial and easily out-dated, vocational training is offered. If the state universities waste the limited time their women students are prepared to spend on higher education by luring them into courses on personality and poise, and requiring them, if they want a teacher's certificate, to take courses in visual aids, they too are likely to defeat the apparent purpose of their training. Such courses can be of little value for immediate use. They may provide the technical requirements for a job, but their value on the job is questionable, at best, and they contribute nothing to preparation for a professional career later in life.

There is increasing emphasis today on the importance of general education as a basis for any professional training, the latter being largely deferred until the graduate years. Even the graduate training is making room, here and there, for a broader base. Notable instances of this shift can be found among the schools of medicine, law, and engineering, and even in the schools of education. They are still far too few; but the trend does emphasize the fact that professional training and general education need not be mutually exclusive.

The judgment of the older college women who have had some occupational experience confirms this view. The results of the many opinion polls that have been taken of college alumnae are not very conclusive. There is little agreement among those who answer, and the proportion replying is usually small and likely to be biased. Here, as elsewhere, the discontented are probably more vocal than the others. The criticism is more often of the choices that they made as students than of the courses that the college had made available. Moreover, those who are regretting the courses they did not take might not have found them as valuable as they imagine. I recall a debate among a group of college instructors on the value of education courses that ended when it was discovered that none of those favoring such courses had ever elected one in their own college course, and all of those who had had such courses regretted them as time wasted.

In spite of these limitations, the results of some of the surveys are worth noting. One of the most extensive studies was made by the American Association of University Women in 1948. A questionnaire was sent to its entire membership and replies were received from over 30,000—approximately 28 per cent of those queried. The majority of the women replying had at some time been teachers, and about half were over forty-five years of age. They had attended a large variety of universities and colleges, but membership in this organization is limited to the graduates of an approved list of institutions which tends to exclude the alumnae of schools giving primarily technical training.

The findings of the study of interest here are that, among the improvements in college training suggested, a broader training was recommended by 12 per cent as compared with 5 per cent urging more specialized training.[12] The largest proportion agreeing on any one point was 14 per cent recommending more vocational and academic counseling. It is also of some interest to note that the group least satisfied with their training were those who had majored in education. The group best satisfied were those who had majored in home economics. The latter had been able to use their training both in professional work and in homemaking.

Another study that is of interest in this connection was made of students of the University of Minnesota in the late thirties, about ten years after the students had graduated or had left the university. In this instance there was enough follow-up to insure a more representative sample than in most studies of this nature. The group included 800 women.[13] Fewer of the women than the men—44 per cent as compared with 56 per cent—were in positions related to their college specialization, apparently because the women had not had specific occupations in mind during their college course to the same extent that the men had had. Nevertheless, approximately four-fifths of the women, as well as the men, considered that their university training had been useful both in getting jobs and in later advancement.[14] The author concludes that the greatest lack in the university experience, as far as vocational needs are concerned, was vocational guidance.[15] This is in agreement with the findings of the American Association of University Women study. What is wanted is not more specialized vocational training but more help in planning college courses with vocational ends in view.

Looking toward the future, there is every indication that an increasing proportion of women, particularly among the older age groups, will work outside of the home. The fact that a larger proportion of women are marrying than formerly, that they are marrying younger, and that they are having more children, has not interrupted this trend. The women, with fewer years on the job than the men, and more restrictions on where they can live, may not be able to add $100,000 to their life earnings as a result of a college degree as the men do; but the most satisfying and remunerative positions for women are in the professions, and the whole range of professions is now open to them. These, more and more, demand college degrees, and often advanced degrees. At the undergraduate level there is a trend away from technical training, and at the same time there is increasing pressure for graduate study.

The woman's dilemma is that early marriage and the care of small children all too often ends her formal education before its completion, and delays the period when professional training will be needed. Even if she does marry late enough to make it possible to complete her training first, her uncertainty as to when, if ever, she will use it makes such training seem relatively unimportant. There is also the risk that knowledge acquired ten years too soon will become obsolete or forgotten before it can be put to use. One solution for this is to acquire the training at a later period of life. This points to expansion of adult training courses. This is often possible, but the married woman is less mobile, geographically, than one with no immediate family, and the opportunity for further study is not always within easy reach. Also, some will not be able to afford the necessary training when the time comes. Another solution is more intensive training in the high school and college years. Both of these should be carefully explored.

Finally, it appears to be important for the liberal arts college to give more attention to vocational guidance, and to put more emphasis on the importance to the students of finding a congenial occupation and making some effort to prepare for it. It might even be hoped that advisors could be found who would occasionally encourage an ambitious and able student to break with tradition and prepare for one of the "men's professions" if it interested her.

More vocational guidance does not mean more specialized and technical training. On the contrary, the best judgment of the educators, and the criticisms of the graduates, both point toward the liberal arts training. Particularly for women who may not enter the job market for fifteen or twenty years, mere technical skills are likely to be useless. It does mean, however, a liberal arts training with some vocational objective in view. In some instances this would give more meaning to the student's education at the time. It would answer the complaint that "college doesn't prepare us for anything." And in the long run it would reduce the wasted ability and the frustrations that occur when an able, college-educated woman takes a position that could easily be handled by a woman of lesser ability, with not more than a high school diploma.

NOTES

[1] H. Martineau, *Society in America* (New York, 1837), vol. 2, p. 257.

[2] National Manpower Council, *Womanpower* (New York, 1957), p. 75.

[3] B'nai B'rith, Vocational Service Bureau, *5000 Women College Graduates* (Washington, 1953), p. 4.

[4] National Manpower Council, *op. cit.*, pp. 221-222.

[5] T. Woody, *A History of Women's Education in the United States* (New York, 1929), vol. 1, p. 361.

[6] S. Kingsbury, "Economic Efficiency of College Women," *Journal of the Association of Collegiate Alumnae*, February 1910, p. 3.

[7] *New York Times*, March 16, 1958, p. 75.

[8] National Manpower Council, *op. cit.*, p. 182.

[9] B'nai B'rith, *op. cit.*, p. 4.

[10] Commission on the Education of Women of the American Council on Education, *The Education of Women*, no. 4, December 1958.

[11] See page 214 below.

[12] P. W. Cautley, *American Association of University Women Study: Members Look at College Education* (Washington, 1949), p. 22.

[13] C. R. Pace, *They Went to College* (Minneapolis, 1941).

[14] *Ibid.*, p. 94.

[15] *Ibid.*, p. 107.

TO ADVANCE THE BOUNDS OF HUMAN KNOWLEDGE HOWEVER
LITTLE IS TO EXERCISE OUR HIGHEST HUMAN FACULTY. THERE
IS NO MORE ALTRUISTIC SATISFACTION, NO PURER DELIGHT.
I AM CONVINCED THAT WE CAN DO NO MORE USEFUL WORK
THAN THIS—TO MAKE IT POSSIBLE FOR THE FEW WOMEN OF
CREATIVE AND CONSTRUCTIVE GENIUS BORN IN ANY GENERA-
TION TO JOIN THE FEW MEN OF GENIUS OF THEIR GENERATION
IN THE SERVICE OF THEIR COMMON RACE.

M. CAREY THOMAS*

10. Scholars and Artists

THE ENGLISH ideal of a "gentleman and a scholar" never took
root in American soil. American men have been expected to earn their
living whether they have inherited wealth or not. It was appropriate
for women to indulge in leisure, circumstances permitting. But there
was no tradition for combining the leisure that was accorded to ladies
with scholarship. And by the time that the necessary education was
available to women the leisure had somehow vanished. Those daughters of the wealthy today who do not marry young are likely to de-
clare their independence by moving to their own apartment, probably
with college friends; and this independence is usually accompanied by
self-support, although as long as they continue formal study, family
assistance is acceptable.

There are women scholars, but like the men they are ordinarily
working women. Nevertheless, they differ from the great majority of
professional women in that they are contributing to knowledge as well

* From M. C. Thomas, "Present Tendencies in Women's College and University Education," *Educational Review*, January 1908, p. 85.

as using it; and any attempt to evaluate the achievements of the higher education of women could hardly pass them by with only casual mention.

How does the number of these women scholars compare with the number of men? What fields attract them? What kind of formal education produces them? What contributions have they made? To answer some of these questions I have turned to the various biographical compilations, beginning with the three volumes of *American Men of Science*[1] and the one volume, *Dictionary of American Scholars*.[2] These four volumes include more than 100,000 biographies of living scholars in all fields of scholarship. Most of the scholars graduated from college in a period when college education for women, including graduate study, was generally accepted and available for those who could afford it and wanted to continue their education that far.

Data have been recorded for all the women listed on the first fifty pages of each hundred in all four volumes. This gave the numbers in Table 13 below.

The great majority of the scholars listed graduated from college between 1900 and 1950, the peak for the women being in the decade

Table 13.

NUMBER OF WOMEN SCHOLARS, 1956

Field of Study	Women in the Sample	Estimated Total of Women Listed	Approximate Number of Men and Women Listed	Women as Percentage of Total
Physical sciences	650	1300	43,500	3
Biological sciences	892	1784	25,000	7
Social and behavioral sciences	664	1328	25,000	5
Humanities	1177	2354	18,000	13
Total	3383	6766	111,500	6

of the 1920's. The number of women enrolled in institutions of higher learning during this period has varied from a little over one-third to a little less than one-half of the total number of students. Obviously the estimated 6 per cent of women among these scholars is far below the percentage of women in the college population. However, the proportion of women enrolled in college who have obtained even an A.B. degree has been consistently lower than the proportion of men enrolled who have obtained the A.B. degree, primarily because of the large number of women attending normal schools which, in the early years of this period, were rarely degree-granting institutions.

When only doctor's degrees are taken into account—and this degree is the usual passport to scholarly careers—the women comprise only 14 per cent of the total.[3] Even 14 per cent, however, is considerably larger than the 6 per cent of women scholars. In short, the proportion of women obtaining doctor's degrees, whose later scholarly achievements led to their being listed in these volumes, was less than half that of the men obtaining doctor's degrees and later being listed. If this proportion can be assumed to hold for the immediate future, it is apparent that the chance of a man's using the doctor's degree for further sustained scholarly work is at least twice the chance of a woman's doing so.

The principle reasons for this are well known. Marriage is likely to prove a handicap to a scholarly career for most women. Between 35 and 40 per cent of the women scholars listed are married, but this is a much smaller proportion of married women than the proportion for women college graduates as a whole. Family obligations limit the woman's opportunity. Even the unmarried women are frequently expected to live in or near the family home. This often prevents them from finding the specialized positions for which they are especially fitted. Moreover, the opportunities for women scholars have been greatly restricted. While the women's colleges have taken the position that the best faculty will be one with a good representation from each sex, the men's colleges have for the most part, assumed that women would be out of place on their faculties. And while coeducational institutions have employed some women, the women are a relatively small minority except in the teachers and junior colleges. Research opportunities are also greater for men than for women.

The fields of concentration of the women scholars are shown in Table 14. The four divisions—represented by the four volumes from which the data were obtained—are given, as well as the special subject within each division attracting the largest number of women scholars. These proportions have been compared with the fields of concentration of women students of the class of 1956. The differences are accounted for in part by long-term trends in student choices. More than half of the scholars obtained their A.B. degrees before 1930. The larger proportion of social science majors among the recent graduates coincides with an increase in student interest in these fields in the last half century. The proportion of women specializing in science has declined over the past fifty years, as the figures for recent graduates indicate, but in no period has science attracted as large a proportion of women students as that found among the women scholars. Nor do the figures for scholars reflect the extent of the election of the humanities as fields of concentration.

The larger part of the differences between recent graduates and the older scholar group is due not to changing student interests, but to professional opportunities, and the fact that students with no strong professional motives are more likely to choose the humanities (and to a lesser extent the social sciences) than the physical and biological sciences. This is particularly apparent in the biological sciences. There has never been anything like one-fourth of the women students specializing in this field, although one-fourth of the scholars are in this group. The same influence is at work in the field of psychology. The trend in this field is upward, and yet the proportion of scholars in psychology exceeds the proportion of recent students majoring in this field. Subjects not listed in Table 14 that were listed by more than one hundred scholars in the sample as their fields of concentration are, in order of the number of scholars, physiology, history, botany, mathematics, bacteriology, French, and sociology.

Table 14.

PERCENTAGE DISTRIBUTION OF WOMEN SCHOLARS AND RECENT GRADUATES IN SELECTED FIELDS OF STUDY[a]

Fields	Women Scholars		1956 Women Graduates	
Humanities	34.8		48.6	
English		12.3		24.1
Biological sciences	26.4		7.3	
Zoology		5.9		[b]
Social and behavioral sciences	19.6		36.7	
Psychology		10.0		6.1
Physical sciences	19.2		7.4	
Chemistry		10.2		2.6

[a] The classification for women scholars follows that used in the *American Men of Science* and *Directory of American Scholars*. The subdivisions of each group are those with the largest proportion of scholars. The data for 1956 graduates are from the United States Office of Education, Circular no. 499, *Earned Degrees, 1955-1956*. Only those women taking nonprofessional courses have been included for this comparison since few of the scholars have professional degrees. The proportion of 1956 women graduates taking nonprofessional courses was approximately 37 per cent of the total number of women graduates.

[b] The large number of students whose field of concentration was biology makes it impossible to obtain a comparable figure. Only 0.4 per cent specifically majored in zoology.

The test of a "scholar" used in the compilation of the volumes from which these data were taken is membership in the faculty of any university or college, a research position in government, private business, or a private research organization, or published research regardless of present occupation. Thus some private consultants and practicing physicians are included, although the occupation as such would not entitle them to being included. The following data on occupations represent the present occupation or, for retired members, the last occupation listed.

More than two-thirds of the women held positions on university and college faculties, about one-third of this group teaching in women's colleges and two-thirds in coeducational institutions. Research occupied all but 4 per cent of the remainder. These proportions vary greatly with the field of study. In the humanities, 95 per cent were engaged in college teaching. The only fields in which the number of women engaged in research exceeded the number teaching were bacteriology (60 per cent), chemistry (57 per cent), and psychology (53 per cent).

These data make it clear that an appreciable number of women have continued their education to a point where they themselves are contributing to the accumulation of knowlege. It is also apparent that the chance of men students going on to scholarly pursuits is very much greater than the chance of women using their education in this way. The enrollment figures for the fifty years during which most of these scholars graduated from college show that approximately four out of every ten students were women. But women scholars account for only one out of sixteen. Even when the women continue their education as far as the Ph.D., they are less likely to use their education for further scholarship than the men who obtain this degree. As noted earlier, women received 14 per cent of the Ph.D. degrees granted during this period, but they account for only 6 per cent of the scholars. Family responsibilities and discrimination in many professional fields are the principal reasons for this. There may also be differences in scholarly motivation, although these would hardly account for the failure of the women who have obtained Ph.D. degrees to continue in productive scholarship.

There has been a good deal of interest, particularly recently, in the kind of educational institution that fosters scholarship. The evidence indicates that the number of scholars whose undergraduate work was in the small liberal arts colleges is out of proportion to the enrollment in these colleges. It is also apparent that among this group of institutions a small number of individual colleges far outdistance the rest.

The women's colleges themselves have sometimes claimed that their emphasis on the quality of teaching stimulates student interest in learning beyond that found in the average institution of higher education, and trains the students in research while still at the undergraduate level. If this is true it is to be expected that a larger proportion of their students will continue with graduate study than the proportion from other institutions. To test these claims I have compared the number of women scholars obtaining their first degrees from different types of institutions with the enrollment in these institutions over the period from 1900 to 1950. I have also tabulated separately the graduates of the eight largest women's liberal arts colleges that were in operation during the entire period. All of these are eastern colleges.[4] The results are given in Table 15.

The data in Table 15 show that the women's colleges as a whole accounted for 16 per cent of all women students enrolled and 34 per cent of all women scholars. In other words, they have produced more than twice as many women scholars as might be expected from their proportion of enrollments. When both the public women's colleges and the Catholic women's colleges are excluded from the figures, the remaining women's colleges, with 8 per cent of the enrollment, account for 25 per cent of the scholars, or a little over three times their share.

The considerably smaller proportion of scholars among the public and (to a lesser degree) the Roman Catholic women's colleges are largely attributable to the emphasis of these colleges on teacher training. Many of the public women's colleges started as normal schools. And preparation for teaching in secondary and elementary schools requires a master's degree at best, and usually, in the earlier period, no degree at all. These colleges have also emphasized nursing and other technical training that does not ordinarily lead to advanced study and research. The same factors explain the great discrepancy between the proportions for the women's colleges and the coeducational institutions. Most of the women preparing specifically for professions have gone to the large universities which offer specialized training at the undergraduate level.

The eight women's liberal arts colleges that have been separately tabulated accounted, as a group, for 2 per cent of enrollment and 17 per cent of the scholars. All of these produced several times their

Table 15.

COMPARISON OF ENROLLMENT AND SCHOLARS IN SELECTED WOMEN'S COLLEGES AND GROUPS OF COLLEGES

Colleges	Percentage of Women Enrolled in All Colleges 1900–1950[a]	Percentage of Living Women Scholars	Ratio of Percentage of Women Students Enrolled to Percentage of Women Scholars
All women's colleges	16.3	34.1	1: 2.1
Public women's colleges	4.7	3.6	1: 0.8
Private women's colleges	11.6	30.5	1: 2.6
Catholic women's colleges	3.4	5.3	1: 1.6
Non-Catholic women's colleges	8.2	25.2	1: 3.1
Eight selected women's colleges	2.0	17.5	1: 8.75
Other non-Catholic women's colleges	6.2	7.7	1: 1.2
Eight individual colleges:			
Bryn Mawr	0.12	1.78	1:14.8
Mount Holyoke	0.24	3.14	1:13.1
Barnard	0.20	2.38	1:11.9
Vassar	0.29	2.79	1: 9.6
Radcliffe	0.17	1.32	1: 7.7
Wellesley	0.36	2.62	1: 7.3
Goucher	0.16	1.12	1: 7.0
Smith	0.48	2.35	1: 4.9

[a] In obtaining these percentages, only undergraduate women in degree-granting colleges have been used.

"share" of scholars, but the differences among them are marked, varying from five times the average for Smith to 15 times the average for Bryn Mawr. It is not surprising to find Bryn Mawr at the top of the list. It was the only independent women's college to start with a graduate school, and it was never hampered by a preparatory department. Also, Carey Thomas in her long administration stressed scholarship more than most of the college presidents of the time. Moreover, the proportion of the faculty with doctor's degrees has been higher over the first half of this century than the proportion found in any other college of this group excepting Radcliffe.

It is not so easy to account for Smith's position at the bottom of the list. Smith started without a preparatory department, and with the same requirements for entrance as the leading men's colleges of the period. Both Seelye and Nielson had high standards of scholarship; the college developed a certain amount of graduate work; the proportion of faculty with doctor's degrees has compared favorably with the proportion for both Mount Holyoke and Vassar, and has been considerably higher than the proportion for Wellesley. Carey Thomas, making a tour of the eastern women's colleges just before Bryn Mawr opened, reported that Smith had no productive scholars on its faculty, and the faculty's claims for Smith's superiority rested largely on the high entrance requirements.[5] But this period is too early to have had much effect on Smith's relatively low rating for scholars living in mid-twentieth century, unless it established a precedent and a stereotype that has affected the college's later development.

Radcliffe's position is also difficult to account for. It appears to have had even more of the factors that should lead to scholarly interests and attitudes than the other colleges under consideration. With the Harvard faculty at its disposal, Radcliffe had more faculty with doctor's degrees, and more distinguished scholars among the faculty, than any of the other seven women's colleges. It also had its own graduate school—likewise provided by the Harvard faculty. In many ways Radciffe resembles Barnard. Both are coordinate colleges attached to universities with outstanding graduate schools. Barnard has its own faculty, as Radcliffe never had, but it has drawn on the Columbia faculty to a considerable extent and its students have had access to courses elsewhere in the university. It has been suggested that repetition of the courses prepared for the Harvard students resulted in the Radcliffe students getting something less than equal instruction, and that the inferior library facilities for Radcliffe students may have discouraged the continuation of studies to the graduate level, but these are mere conjectures. It is, perhaps, worth noting that the first Radcliffe students had to obtain books from the library by messenger after the library closed in the evening, and the books were returned by messenger when the library opened in the morning. Whether the students stayed up all night to read them is not recorded. Library facilities have greatly improved over the years, but the Radcliffe women are still excluded from the Harvard undergraduate men's library. The explanation offered by the librarian, as late as the 1940's, was that the building had many alcoves and policing would be too expensive.[6]

The detailed data for the eight colleges provide evidence that the influence of individual faculty members is an important factor in encouraging scholarship. Mount Holyoke has excelled, in the number of scholars, in chemistry, zoology, physiology, and English; Vassar in chemistry and psychology; Barnard in psychology alone; Bryn Mawr in the humanities as a whole; and Goucher in the physical and biological sciences. The other colleges do not show the same concentration of scholars in a limited number of fields, but for the colleges where such concentration appears it can be traced in each instance to one or more outstanding teachers and scholars in that field at the time that the largest number of these scholars were undergraduates.

There is some evidence, also, that the presence of large numbers of women scholars on the faculties of the women's colleges has been influential in developing scholars among their students. Not only are women faculty more likely to have faith in the intellectual capacity of women students and encourage them to go on with graduate study; they also serve as "models" for their students. They are living evidence that scholarship is not a masculine monopoly. There is, however, no close correlation between the number of women on the faculty and the number of scholars that have come from different institutions. And unless the women scholars on the faculty are outstanding, their value as models is doubtful. The quality of the faculty is unquestionably of more importance than their sex.

Another point of interest in the data for individual colleges is the changes over the entire period. Bryn Mawr and Goucher, for example, have suffered a sharp decline in the number of scholars in the younger group. Radcliffe, on the contrary, has shown a marked increase in scholars recently. Radcliffe's rise coincides with the shift from separate classes to complete coeducation with the Harvard students. The data presented here reflect the status of these colleges at an earlier period, since very few scholars listed are graduates of the postwar period.

A study of recent graduates gives a quite different ranking of the women's colleges in this respect. This study covers the graduates of 1946 and later, the test of a "scholar" being a Ph.D. degree from a list of the 25 largest degree-granting universities, a substantial fellowship from one of these institutions, or fellowships from certain private foundations or from specified government sources.[7] The scholars as thus defined have been related to the number of graduates of the colleges from which the scholars obtained their first degrees.

This study finds that twelve institutions, including both women's colleges and coeducational institutions, produced 10 women scholars or more per 1000 women graduates in this period. Bryn Mawr still leads the list with 40 per 1000. Barnard has risen from third place for the older scholars to second place for the younger; and Radcliffe has risen from fifth place to third. Vassar remains fourth in both. Three other institutions follow for the younger scholars, and then Mount Holyoke and Smith. Wellesley and Goucher do not appear in this list at all.[8]

As a possible indicator of future scholars, it is worth noting the colleges recently selected by the recipients of the National Merit Scholarships. In 1956 Radcliffe headed the list for women recipients with 14 merit scholars and 30 receiving certificates of merit. Wellesley came second, followed by Smith, Bryn Mawr, and Mount Holyoke. The institutions listed, which include all that were chosen by three or more of these scholars, do not include Barnard, Goucher, or Vassar.[9] Radcliffe again headed the list in 1957. Thus it is clear that the institutions that attract or produce the largest number of scholars in one period do not necessarily hold their position.

I noted above that Radcliffe's rise coincides with her coeducational status. I would not argue that coeducation is directly responsible for the shift, although the quality of instruction may have improved now that lectures do not have to be repeated to the women in separate groups. It seems probable that the important factor here is Radcliffe's growing popularity with women students. To what extent coeducation is responsible for this popularity is not clear. Whatever the cause, however, it has given the college the opportunity to select a better group of students than the other colleges in this group now have. There is, of course, no guarantee that Radcliffe's National Merit Scholars will forego early marriage and devote themselves, married or not, to scholarly pursuits. But the quality of students is certainly the most important factor in producing scholars and it seems reasonable to expect that Radcliffe will lead in this as long as present trends hold.

The discussion thus far has been limited to the eight women's colleges. In order to determine whether the high standing of this group is peculiar to women's colleges, data were tabulated for women scholars that had graduated from three coeducational liberal arts colleges —Swarthmore, Carleton, and Oberlin. The results indicate that it is the liberal arts college—not specifically women's colleges—that produces scholars in large numbers. Oberlin ranked below Smith, but it still produced three times the number that its enrollment would account for; Carleton ranked above Smith with six times its quota; and Swarthmore outdistanced even Bryn Mawr with eighteen times its quota. These data are for women students only.

It is unfortunate that the all-important factor—the quality of scholarship—cannot be measured readily. However, the 1944 edition of *American Men of Science* includes a separate list of 1,000 distinguished scholars, selected by their colleagues. This list contains 29 women— 3 per cent of the total.[10] The women scientists listed in the volume as a whole comprise nearly 7 per cent of the total. Thus the proportion of women among the scientists of distinction is much smaller than even their proportion of the scholars as a whole. There is other scattered evidence that this is true in all fields of scholarship. Whether there are fewer geniuses among women, or they have been held back by limited opportunities, or whether their achievements have not received the recognition they merit can still be debated. The two last are certainly contributing factors. It should be recalled that while Maria Mitchell received a medal for discovering a comet, the English astronomer, Caroline Herschel, had failed to receive recognition for a similar achievement a little earlier because she was a woman. The number of women scientists is too small to draw any conclusions as to whether women are more likely to reach the top in one field than another.

A recent study of Radcliffe Ph.D. recipients throws some light on this question. It shows that the women in college and university faculties do not publish to the same degree as men. This is notably true in the textbook field. While prejudice on the one hand, and marriage and family responsibilities on the other, are obvious reasons for the failure of women to go as far as men in their chosen fields, there are other factors. One of these, the Radcliffe study concludes, is that men with families are likely to be under greater financial pressure than their women colleagues. Textbooks bring in additional income and scholarly publications assist in promotions.[11] Many of the women, on the contrary (although fewer than is sometimes assumed), have only themselves to support and find it easier to forego further advancement for the sake of more leisure.

Some women have argued that they are handicapped, as compared with the men, because they have no wives to keep house for them. My own observation has been, however, that men with wives and children are apt to have as many home responsibilities as their unmarried women colleagues. Certainly many women have been able to surmount this obstacle. One woman in the Radcliffe study explains her own lack of publications by the fact that her mother lives with her and (although her mother does most of the cooking) this takes up all the margin of time that might otherwise have gone toward research in winter; and, because her mother is with her, visiting relatives fill the summer months.[12] Yet Vera Micheles Dean and Cecilia Payne-Gaposchkin, who are cited by the Radcliffe Report as outstanding in their publication records, have had the continuing responsibility of their own children—not merely visiting nieces and nephews. Gaposchkin is one of the 29 distinguished women scientists cited earlier.

Another, and apparently more important, reason for the poorer record of the women, which is suggested by the Radcliffe Report, is the feeling among women that research and publication will not bring the same recognition for them that comparable achievements bring for men. This, it is pointed out, is a real handicap whether the feeling is justified or not in individual cases. "No one can do first-rate work, a lot of it and over a long period of time, if she is obsessed or seriously bothered with problems of status and discrimination. Even if these problems were removed, the psychological basis would remain.[13] This handicap should diminish with time as the discrimination lessens.

Finally, there is some evidence that women in college teaching and research positions are assigned heavier teaching loads and more extra duties not directly relevant to research than men. Whether this is part of the pattern of discrimination or whether women are more willing than men, the result is to reduce the time available for research.

In order to obtain some quantitative measure of differences in the rate of advancement of men and women in academic positions, I have made a tabulation of University of Chicago Ph.D. recipients teaching in colleges and universities as of 1939. These are men and women with the same graduate training, and while it does not reflect the present situation, it does include many of the scholars in the above tabulation and gives some measure of earlier differences. The results are given in Table 16.

These data show a considerable lag in advancement of the women behind the men in all age groups. The differential appears to be somewhat less, however, for the youngest group. At least the proportion of instructors shows a greater differential for the two older groups.

One final factor of interest in relation to the women scholars is whether they are increasing in number. One test of this is the record of the number of women obtaining doctor's degrees. In 1900, 21

Table 16.

UNIVERSITY OF CHICAGO PH.D.s TEACHING IN
UNIVERSITIES AND COLLEGES, 1938–1939[a]

| | | | Date of Receiving Degrees | | | |
| | Before 1911 | | 1911–1925 | | 1926–1938 | |
	Men	Women	Men	Women	Men	Women
Number	236	20	679	91	1009	231
Percent with rank of:						
Professor	94.0	85.0	78.4	56.0	43.2	32.4
Associate and						
Assistant Prof.	5.5	5.0	21.2	40.7	42.0	43.7
Instructor	0.5	10.0	0.4	3.3	14.8	23.8
Total	100.0	100.0	100.0	100.0	100.0	100.0

[a] University of Chicago, *Register of Doctors of Philosophy, 1938-39* (Chicago, 1939).

women received such degrees. In 1920 the number was 93; in 1940, 429. This last figure was more than doubled in 1956, when 885 women received the Ph.D. or its equivalent. But here as in other areas of higher education the women are not keeping pace with the men. Women received 16 per cent of the doctor's degrees in 1920 and 10 per cent in 1956.

A second test of trends is the number of women on college and university faculties. These, like the Ph.D. degrees, have increased in absolute numbers but not in proportion to the men. The proportion of women reached a peak of 28 per cent in 1940. It had declined to 23 per cent in 1954.[14] The percentage of women on the faculties of the six independent women's colleges whose output of scholars was discussed earlier in this chapter declined from 73 to 60 per cent between 1940 and 1957. Barnard and Radcliffe have been excluded from this comparison since part or all of their faculty come from the universities with which they are affiliated.

A third test of the trend of women scholars is the proportion of women among the scholars listed in the different editions of *American Men of Science* and the *Directory of American Scholars*. The latter was first published in 1942. Taking this volume and the seventh edition of *American Men of Science* (1944), I found that women comprised 8 per cent of the approximately 46,000 scholars listed in these volumes. This compares with 6 per cent in the 1957 editions.

All these tests show a marked decline in the proportion of women among American scholars. If present trends continue, it is to be expected that women will contribute a decreasing share to the advancement of knowledge in this country. The prejudices against women scholars have diminished with time, and opportunities for women in this field have increased in consequence. But women are now faced with a new handicap of their own choosing—increasingly early marriages and larger families.

Women have found it easier in the past to achieve recognition in the arts than in scholarly pursuits. As actresses and singers they fill essential roles that depend on their sex. Women poets, painters, and pianists are more likely to be accepted on their merits than women chemists, physicists, and philosophers. But training in the arts, however prolonged and exacting, has not usually been based on a college degree.

The college curriculum in the early years of women's education was better adapted to training scholars than creative writers, musicians, painters, and other artists. The early Greek education included poetry, music, and the drama. Music was one of the seven liberal arts of the medieval church. But literature survived in the classical curriculum, as developed in the early American colleges, only in the classical languages. Music disappeared entirely at this time.

The women's colleges were more tolerant than the men's in this respect. English literature received considerable attention, even in the early courses of study; and while art and music were rarely offered for credit they were at least available as special studies. The first Vassar catalogue features the college's thirty-one pianos, and the art gallery, even listing individually all of the five to six hundred paintings and drawings to be found there. With time, both art and music became a regular part of the curriculum in all the women's colleges, although restrictions were placed on courses in the applied arts that were not found in other fields. Dramatic production appears later, and even the dance. These developments are not peculiar to the women's colleges, but the women's colleges have tended to lead in these fields. This has unquestionably contributed to intelligent appreciation of the arts; but the extent to which it has provided training that is useful for artists is less certain. The specialized schools of art and music compete strongly for incipient artists in these fields. For creative writing, however, the colleges have been more successful in attracting future authors.

One of the first consequences of permitting girls to go beyond the three R's in their formal schooling was an outburst of women authors. Writing was something that could be done at home, and there was a growing literate audience among women, who had at least a minimum of leisure. There was only one Emily Dickinson, but there were many women who could get their poems published in the magazines and newspapers of the day. Sarah Josepha Hale was unique as a woman editor, but she encouraged other women to contribute poems, short stories, and serious essays to her *Ladies' Magazine* and *Godey's Lady's Book*. More than half of the approximately 700 women listed in the first *Who's Who in America* (1899) were authors.

It is often assumed that the creative artist will not submit to the discipline and the many restrictions of a college course. Specific instances of this can be cited. According to Catherine Bowen's biographer, when a relative predicted that she had "a forehead that will go to Bryn Mawr and write a book" she replied: "Never, never to Bryn Mawr! . . . Never to any of their stuffy colleges."[15] And she has written books without benefit of college studies. One of Vassar's distinguished poets, Muriel Rukeyser, found two years ample for her purposes. But Edna St. Vincent Millay, without being a strict conformist, met all of Vassar's requirements and obtained her degree—

with a little special cooperation from the faculty and administration. The majority of women authors today are college graduates.

Most of the earlier women authors had no higher education. Only 12 per cent of some two hundred authors born in the first half of the nineteenth century and listed in the 1899 *Who's Who* had had any college education. But more than one-third of those born in the third quarter of the century had some higher education. And a sample of approximately 200 authors born since 1900 shows that four out of five have attended college, three out of five have graduated, and one in six has had some graduate study.[16]

The women's colleges have attracted or produced more than their quota of the college educated women writers. Using the same tests as that applied to women scholars, the eight colleges account for fourteen times the number to be expected from their enrollments. This is a much better record than the ratio of nine times found for the women scholars who graduated from these eight colleges. This is to be explained in part, but only in part, by the fact that the writers are a somewhat older group than the scientists so that more of them went to college when these particular colleges played a more important part in women's education than they do today. The record for the authors is not as complete as that for the scholars, and the number of cases is smaller—approximately 400 as compared with 3,400. Consequently, the ratio for the authors cannot be assumed to be exact. But allowing for this it is still true that the differences between these colleges and other institutions is not a chance difference.

For the individual colleges the ratios are more unstable. Two or three cases would change them appreciably. Nevertheless it is possible to divide the eight colleges into three groups with some assurance. The top group is comprised of Barnard, Bryn Mawr, Radcliffe, and Vassar—all with ratios of approximately 25 times the number to be expected. Smith and Wellesley form a middle group with a ratio of approximately 10 times. Mount Holyoke and Goucher are at the bottom. Not one of the more than 400 writers in the sample obtained an A. B. degree from Goucher, and only one obtained an A. B. from

Mount Holyoke. Goucher excelled in the sciences. It is the only one of these eight colleges which had as many as three graduates among the 29 distinguished women scientists noted above. It apparently did not attract or train writers successfully, however. Mount Holyoke, also, had its greatest success in science, although it did turn out a large number of scholars in English. Barnard, Bryn Mawr, and Vassar are in the first half of these colleges in both categories, although the scholars from both Barnard and Vassar have been largely in the behavioral and physical sciences.

The three coeducational colleges whose graduates compared favorably in numbers with those of the women's colleges among the scholars are in the same group as Goucher and Mount Holyoke among the writers. Oberlin and Swarthmore each have one graduate in the group. Carleton has none at all.

College education has played a relatively minor role in the education of the women who have been successful in the other arts. Only four of the 140 actresses, artists, and musicians listed in the 1899 *Who's Who in America* had any college education at all. Two of these were artists and two were musicians. For the contemporary group the number with college records has increased, with 32 per cent of the artists and 27 per cent of the actresses and singers having some college education.[17] However, only one out of every three attending college remained to obtain a degree. And those with graduate work can be counted on the fingers of one hand. The numbers that have attended schools of art or music or who have studied with private teachers is, on the contrary, very large. These are not areas in which the liberal arts education appears to have made important contributions.

None of the 185 contemporary artists, actresses, and singers listed in the compilations used for these data attended Mount Holyoke or Wellesley. The other six women's colleges separately tabulated can claim one or two each. The numbers are too small to relate them to enrollment, but it is clear that these colleges have not excelled in this area.

The decline in the proportion of women among both scholars and writers appears in other fields. Women comprised 8 per cent of all the individuals listed in the first edition of *Who's Who in America* and between 4 and 5 per cent in the 48th edition. This is due in part to the increased space allotted to business records in the latter volume; but insofar as *Who's Who* records can be taken to represent people of importance in America today (and I would be the first to emphasize that they have some limitations for this purpose), women are playing a decreasing role. This statement needs many qualifications, but these will have to wait for later discussion.

NOTES

[1] Jaques Cattell, ed., 9th edition. New York, 1956.
[2] Jaques Cattell, ed., 3rd edition. New York, 1957.
[3] Approximately three-fourths of the scholars listed have doctor's degrees.
[4] The actual procedure was as follows: Enrollment figures were obtained for every tenth year from 1900 to 1950 and these were totalled. The enrollment figures used are those for undergraduates in degree-granting colleges. Since enrollment figures are not classified in this way for all decades in the Reports of the Office of Education, it was necessary to estimate these in part. However, the margin of error is too small to be responsible for the marked differences among the groups. This period was used because most of the scholars graduated from college between 1900 and 1950. The total enrollments for these six "tenth years" were used to determine the proportion of women attending each college or group of colleges. Since the trends in enrollment in the different institutions were fairly steady the fact that only one year in ten was used should not distort the results appreciably. The fact that the list of scholars does not represent the completed record of all graduates during the period—some having died and others having not yet achieved the status used by the editors of these volumes—is more troublesome, the early and late years having less weight among the scholars than they should, compared with the middle group. The enrollment figures are, of course, complete. However, a breakdown by decades shows that the proportion of scholars in different groups remains fairly steady over this period. That is, the groups of institutions that show a greater than average or less than average proportion of scholars maintain this position throughout the period. And the largest group of scholars—most of whom are still living and have also "arrived"—who graduated during the 1920's, shows much the same characteristics as the total group. A complete record would probably change the proportions a little, but in every test I have been able to make the marked differences among the groups of colleges shown in Table 15 appear. For the eight individual colleges a complete tabulation of all the scholars listed was made since the smaller number of cases for these (the group as a whole represents only 2 per cent of total enrollments) made this desirable.

[5] E. Finch, *Carey Thomas of Bryn Mawr* (New York, 1947), p. 140.

[6] J. A. Lewis, "Harvard Goes Coed, But Incognito," *New York Times Magazine*, May 1, 1949, p. 38.

[7] R. H. Knapp and J. J. Greenbaum, *The Younger American Scholar: His Collegiate Origins* (Middletown, 1953), pp. 8-9.

[8] *Ibid.*, p. 70.

[9] J. L. Holland and J. M. Stalmaker, "An Honorary Scholastic Award," *Journal of Higher Education*, October 1957, pp. 361-368.

[10] Three of these 29 obtained their A.B. degrees at Goucher, and two each from Bryn Mawr, Smith, and Vassar.

[11] *Graduate Education for Women, The Radcliffe Ph.D.* A Report by a Faculty-Trustee Committee (Cambridge, 1956), pp. 45-46.

[12] *Ibid.*, p. 47.

[13] *Ibid.*, p. 51.

[14] It has recently been reported that the percentage of women on the faculties of institutions of higher learning in Russia is 35. (Commission on the Education of Women of the American Council on Education, *The Education of Women.* No. 4, December 1958.)

[15] S. J. Kunitz, *Twentieth Century Authors*, supplement (New York, 1955), p. 104.

[16] The authors used for this were compiled from S. J. Kunitz, *op. cit.* H. R. Warfel, *American Novelists of Today* (New York, 1951), lists of poets taken from recent collections of poems of younger American poets, and a sample from *Who's Who in America* for 1954-1955, covering approximately one-third of the listings in this volume.

[17] Pianists, composers, and other musicians are not included here because of the very small numbers found in *Who's Who* and other biographical collections.

IT HAS BEEN SAID . . . THAT AN EDUCATION FOR WOMEN
WHICH SHARPENS INTELLECTUAL CURIOSITY AND QUICKENS
THE IMAGINATION IS EITHER A WASTE OF TIME OR A SOURCE
OF FRUSTRATION, SINCE THE ROLE OF WOMEN AS WIVES AND
MOTHERS WILL PREVENT THEM FROM ENJOYING ANY OF
THEIR INTELLECTUAL OR CULTURAL INTERESTS. A COLLEGE
EDUCATION IN THE LIBERAL ARTS IS SAID TO BE EITHER UN-
NECESSARY OR POTENTIALLY HARMFUL. I FIND THIS ATTITUDE
INSULTING, BOTH TO WOMEN AND TO EDUCATION.

HAROLD TAYLOR*

11. Homemakers and Civic Workers

THE FACT that homemaking is woman's most important role
has never been seriously questioned either by those arguing in favor
of college education for women or by those opposing it. Those opposing higher education for women have usually expressed the fear
that it will encourage them to pursue independent careers, foregoing
marriage; or if they marry, that it will make them dissatisfied with
the homemaker's lot. Those promoting higher education have, on the
contrary, insisted that college women make better wives and mothers
than their less educated sisters. Even those who have been concerned
with the rights and interests of unmarried women have never argued
that higher education might encourage women to remain single, except as it occasionally offered a reasonably satisfactory alternative
when the only available young men were not entirely acceptable.

The majority of college women have always married, but by the
turn of the century it was clear that the proportion of college women
who did not marry was greater than that for noncollege women. And

* From H. Taylor, *On Education and Freedom* (New York, 1954), p. 165.

to make matters worse, the proportion of unmarried college women was increasing. At one point the unmarried were nearly half of the total. Moreover, the number of children of college women was small. Not even those who married had enough children, on the average, to replace themselves. And since they were presumably a superior group the consequences were alarming. This started a whole new debate on the advisability of educating women. Some of the literature on the subject was almost hysterical. A few writers forgot, in their distress, to allow for the fact that it takes some years to find a husband and produce several children—particularly in those days of late marriages. But even the defendants could not explain away the trends.

These trends are clearly seen in the figures of Table 17. The data cover the longest period of any records I have been able to find, and are reasonably accurate for the groups represented. The Mount Holyoke figures include part of the seminary period as well as the college, but the differences in the age groups and the type of student attending the two appears to be small. The figures for both colleges show a downward trend, both for marriages and the number of children, until the end of the nineteenth century. There was an upturn in the number of marriages in the first quarter of the twentieth century, but even in this period college women did not have enough children to replace their group.

The trend in both marriages and birth rate was downward for the population as a whole during the late nineteenth century and early twentieth century. If we take as an index the number of children under five years of age per 1,000 white women 20 to 44 years old, as reported by the Census (and this is the only figure available that is comparable from decade to decade), it shows a steady decline from 905 in 1860 to 666 in 1900 and 419 in 1940. Moreover, the daughters of the well-to-do, from which group the colleges largely drew, had fewer children than the poor, whether they went to college or not.[1] But the basic criticism remained true. The birth rate for all women was substantially higher throughout this period than that for college

Table 17.

TRENDS IN MARRIAGES AND SIZE OF FAMILIES
AMONG COLLEGE WOMEN[a]

Classes	Mount Holyoke Alumnae[b]		Classes	Vassar Alumnae[c]	
	Per cent Married	Number of Children Per Married Woman		Per cent Married	Number of Children Per Married Woman
Before 1864	77.5	2.7			
1864–1873	72.1	1.9	1867–1871	61.9	2.4
1874–1883	57.1	2.6	1872–1881	54.3	2.1
1884–1893	48.2	2.0	1882–1891	55.8	2.1
1894–1903	52.0	2.1	1892–1901	56.4	2.0
1904–1913	52.0	2.1	1902–1911	60.6	2.2
1912–1921	57.9	2.0	1912–1921	75.0	2.1
1922–1931	57.4				

[a] The later figures are incomplete, particularly for children.

[b] Sophia Maranski, "A Census of Mount Holyoke Alumnae," *Mount Holyoke Alumnae Quarterly*, October 1924, p. 154; and Department of Economics and Sociology, Mount Holyoke College, "Mount Holyoke Alumnae Census," January 1939 (mim.).

[c] Mabel Newcomer, "Marriages and Children of Vassar College Alumnae," *Vassar Quarterly*, May 1931, pp. 99-100; and Margaret Myers and Mabel Newcomer, "Marriages and Children of Vassar Alumnae," *Vassar Alumnae Magazine*, April 1939, pp. 17-18.

women. And the college women did not have enough children for replacement.

It was never entirely clear, of course, that higher education discouraged marriage and large families. Those who married very young never got to college; and there were other selective factors. Those who failed to marry young—or ever—were likely to teach, and a college education was useful to that end. One serious study of marriages among college women, published some years ago, showed that the proportion of marriages among Vassar graduates was higher than the proportion among Stanford women graduates. The author concluded that coeducation discouraged marriage more than segregated education. What he apparently did not know was that the Stanford graduates were heavily weighted with school teachers who had returned to college after many years of teaching in order to get ahead in their profession, whereas most of the Vassar graduates were completing an uninterrupted schooling at the average age of 21 or 22. Also, it was sometimes claimed that in the days when higher education was not widely accepted, parents sent their less marriageable daughters to college. In short, it was not entirely that higher education discouraged marriage. Those who, for whatever reason, did not marry were more likely to go to college than the others.

The relative importance of the different factors that resulted in fewer marriages among college women than others has never been successfully measured, but the debate is over. The situation is now reversed. Marriage and children may interfere with college education, but the college education does not interfere with marriage. According to Zapoleon, 90 per cent of college graduates 25 years out are married.[2] The Vassar statistics show 90 per cent married in less time than this. Sweet Briar reports that 100 per cent of the Class of 1945 was married eight years out, and had an average of two children apiece nine years after graduation—as many as the Mount Holyoke and Vassar married alumnae of fifty years ago ever had! All of the members of the Sweet Briar Class of 1930 also eventually married, but it took them twenty years to do what the Class of 1945 had done in eight; and they had no more children at the end of twenty-three years than the Class of 1945 had produced at the end of nine years.[3] Such instances could be multiplied. But the phenomenon is too obvious to require further elaboration. Earlier marriages and larger families are apparent among all groups, and are in no way peculiar to college women. But no one is worrying today about college women failing to replace themselves.

The change in the life cycle of the average woman in the United States has been summarized as follows:[4]

Median age when:	1890	1957
She leaves school	14	18
She marries	22	20
Her last child is born	32	26
Her youngest child goes to school	39	32
Her youngest child marries	55	48
Her husband dies	53	61
She dies	68	77

This is a revolutionary change. The period between leaving school and marrying has been reduced from eight to two years, and at the other end of her life the average woman lives 45 years after her youngest child starts to school as compared with 29 years in the earlier period. At the same time there is less work to be done at home than there was seventy years ago. The typical college graduate necessarily marries a little later than the average. She cannot ordinarily complete her college course and marry before she is 21 years old. But she will probably make up for this slight delay by living until she is 80.

This change in the timing of marriage and the family responsibilities for the average woman, and the fact that the proportion of college women who marry has increased so markedly, raises new problems for higher education. The college woman of earlier years had time to complete her course before she married. She even had time to continue with professional training and probably work at her profession, at least for a little while. The median age of marriage for those Vassar alumnae of the first forty years of the college's existence who married was between 27 and 28. This had dropped to 24 by the 1930's, and today it is around 22. This means that those who finish college have little opportunity for either professional training or job experience before they marry. And of course many drop out of college to marry without getting even the first degree. For the ten years ending in 1925, and including World War I, at Vassar withdrawals for marriage ranged from none to two at the most during the college year. During and since World War II they have ranged from 10 to 16 a year. This does not include the number withdrawing during the summer. These figures are not available for the earlier period but in 1957 there were 26 summer withdrawals on account of marriage.

Another indicator of the extent to which marriage interrupts the college course is provided by the announcements of engagements and marriages in the newspapers. I kept a record of these announcements as they appeared in the society pages of the *New York Times* over a period of several weeks in the winter of 1957-1958. For more than 1,000 fiancées and brides with a record of attendance at some four-year college, 52 per cent had graduated and 17 per cent more were seniors. These presumably will finish their course. Of the remaining 31 per cent, 15 per cent had dropped out earlier and 16 per cent were below the senior year. It seems improbable that many of these will finish.

The consequences of this are not only that many do not get even such training as the undergraduate course provides for a profession, but that for those who do graduate, interest centers on the more immediate problems of homemaking. The need for professional training and the opportunity for professional work will probably come later— in their 30's or 40's. There is neither time before marriage for such training, nor any apparent urgency. Fifteen or twenty years is a long way off. Marriage is the more immediate concern.

The first problem of the college is, then, a matter of timing. Should more opportunity be offered young women to accelerate their college course? Some institutions are experimenting with this for both men and women. Men also marry younger, and are subject to military service besides. Those universities on the quarter system make it relatively easy for students to complete their course in something less than four years. The standard long vacation may be needed by some students in order to earn money to continue their course; and others use it to gain valuable work experience. But judging from their summer activities, few students need it for recuperation or meditation. Other possibilities are to admit students to college before they have completed their high school course, or to permit students to elect more than the normal number of courses year by year. These alternatives are open of course, only to the better students; but even for these, few colleges provide any real assistance in accelerating.

Another approach to the problem is to encourage students to continue their college education after marriage. The coeducational colleges are taking special steps to assist in this. Stanford University, for instance, has recently built 250 apartments for their married students, and has plans for several times that number. The university authorities are assuming that married students are a permanent and important part of the student body. They report that one-fifth of their students are now married and they expect this proportion to grow to more than one-third. These, of course, are mostly men, but a good many of their wives are also studying. This is no solution for a women's college, but the women's colleges could be more flexible in granting credits for courses taken elsewhere.

The A.B. degree seems to be a reasonable goal for women students to strive for before they are engulfed in family obligations. Graduate professional training for most will probably have to wait until the children are in school. There will be more time then, and with the chance to use their training in the immediate future there is more incentive, and less worry that it may prove out of date or be forgotten. The problem at that time is likely to be one of geographic limitations. The married woman must find opportunity both for training and for jobs within reach of a home the location of which is determined by her husband's work. Fortunately, in our urban society the number of institutions of higher learning is growing and a great many women live within reach of one. Also, there are sometimes adult education classes that provide a fair substitute for training in some skills, although without degrees. Some of the residence colleges still make it needlessly difficult for members of the local community to take occasional courses. These could make a real contribution to the solution of this problem if they revised their policies. This would include opening courses in men's and women's colleges to the opposite sex if they are residents in the area.

These are some of the possibilities that need further exploration;

and some of the promising developments that might well be expanded. For if married college women are to spend some twenty-five years of their lives in paid occupations, it will prevent much frustration and waste of talent if they spend those years in professional pursuits and not as typists and saleswomen.

The function of a college education in preparing for homemaking itself is less clear. In the early period it was accepted as the mother's obligation to prepare her daughter for marriage and homemaking. Home economics as a college subject was not unknown, but in spite of the support received for such study by some of the earliest advocates of the higher education of women, its great popularity came only when its value as professional training was recognized. The most that was expected of higher education for women in this domain was that it should not make women feel that they were wasting their talents on the daily routine of the home. Nor has this attitude changed greatly. The *Fortune* opinion poll of 1949 reports that the parents who wanted their daughters to go to college put preparation for homemaking low on their list of the things they hoped their daughters would get from college training.[5] It is true that many parents would like the college "to do something" about training for marriage. But they are more concerned that college will not spoil them—the women, of course, not the men—for family life.

Today, courses on marriage and the family, and child psychology, and consumer economics, are regarded as appropriate subjects of study in a liberal arts course, but it is assumed that these have a wider interest than training for family life. And there is usually no specific major for homemakers. When the issue is raised it is argued that the undergraduate liberal arts course is designed to train the mind, broaden horizons, and acquaint young people with their cultural heritage, and that this is the best foundation for any career. Specific professional and technical training will come later, whether on the job or in graduate schools. And while many people would grant homemaking the dignity of a profession it is assumed that in this instance on-the-job training is the best preparation.

It is argued that the college-trained woman, equipped with the appropriate manuals, whether cook books or books on child care, will learn quickly enough. She knows how to look things up and how to follow directions; and she will "use her head" when the directions don't quite fit the case. She will not spend sleepless nights worrying because Johnny at the age of four fits the manual's description of a three-year-old in some of his behavior and acts like a five-year-old in other ways. She will be able to allow for deviations; she will know how to adapt and improvise.

But a great deal more is expected of her education than this. Those who believe that the early years of childhood are the all important ones want well-educated mothers. If an A.B. degree is required for school teachers, it is none too good for mothers. Also, the college educated wife is expected to be able to hold up her end of the conversation, whether alone with her husband at dinner, or at one of those combined business and social functions where both husband and wife are being inspected with the husband's promotion in view. And she will have "inner resources" which will make for contentment when routine household chores are unavoidable. All this should come with the diploma, whether she specializes in Greek, psychology, or physics.

There are dissenting voices, of course. And when the dissent comes from married college women it must be taken seriously. Turning to what the college-educated homemakers themselves think about their education, about one in four of the women who responded to the American Association of University Women questionnaire of 1948 felt that there should have been more college preparation for one or another aspect of married life. However, there was no clear agreement on the specific aspects of homemaking that they thought college should train for. Perhaps this is inevitable in view of the diversity of skills demanded of the combined job of wife, mother, and housekeeper. Also, they were often expressing regret as to their choice of college courses rather than criticizing the college for not providing opportunity.

One in five of these women mentioned the specific value of their college training in marriage and homemaking careers. They particularly emphasized its value to them as mothers. The specific factors that they stressed as contributing to successful marriage, apart from children, were that it gave them similar interests to those of their college-trained husbands, or enabled them to "speak the same language." Some mentioned the fact that their education had helped to make them "social assets" to their husbands. Comparatively few mentioned its contribution to their housekeeping, although the ones who most consistently mentioned the value of college education were the majors in home economics.[6]

A more intensive inquiry made of 65 Vassar alumnae from different age groups in the late 1930's found that half of them considered that their education had been a great help to them as homemakers. One-sixth reported real difficulties in adapting to family life, however.[7] The difficulties appear to have arisen in part from lack of technical skills, but even more from a feeling that they were wasting their talents on menial tasks. The extent to which the college education was held responsible for this was not completely clear. Some specifically blamed the college training, where others absolved the college from blame for their troubles.

Those who credited the college education with being useful for homemaking mentioned such things as learning how to attack new and changing situations; learning how to look things up in books; the ability to keep up with college educated husbands; and help in bringing up children. In contrast to the American Association of University Women report, the Vassar Alumnae laid more emphasis on the value of their education in keeping up with their husbands, and less on its value to them as mothers.[8]

Considering all sources, the criticism is less of the content of college courses and the learning of skills, and more of the attitudes toward homemaking which they acquired at college. The complaint is that college education has made them think that they are too good for the daily household chores. They have a sense of guilt if they are not actively engaged in community affairs, even when there are three small children at home and no hired help. And they feel that they do not have the recognition as homemakers that is accorded to the professional woman.

It is difficult to assess this type of complaint. Actually, the great majority of college wives appear to be reasonably content, whether because or in spite of college. The contented are usually less vocal than the others, but the comments of two who are both contented and articulate are worth summarizing in this connection.

The first one married after obtaining a Ph.D. and teaching briefly in college. She not only settled happily into married life, but deliberately made a fulltime job out of homemaking by dismissing the maid when her children were small. She had to be at home anyway, she explains, and there was not enough to keep her busy when a maid was around. She did not feel above household chores. On the contrary, she points out that even the professions have their share of dull routine and even dirty work. She argues that monotonous manual work is to be preferred to monotonous mental work. "A teacher grading papers must give as much attention to the fortieth as to the first. A woman washing dishes can think about something else." She found plenty to challenge and interest her in the variety of her duties. Also, she found time for serious reading. She did not lose contact with the outside world. And when the children were old enough she took an active part in community affairs.[9]

The second college housewife is still in the midst of coping with young children—four, ranging from one to eight years. Yet without benefit of household help she has still, miraculously, found time to express in print her satisfaction with a liberal arts education as preparation for homemaking.[10] She particularly values the training in "the technique of learning" and the "diversity of subject matter covered." She is quite specific in her application of these to the daily job, and she concludes: "The career of homemaker and mother of young children is the most satisfying, interesting, and challenging that a woman can have. The mother with an understanding of the liberal arts, and realization of the importance of the work she is doing, is able to maintain her perspective and integrity in an extremely demanding and confining situation."[11]

Obviously much depends on the individual temperament. In the course of one study which we made of community activities of Vassar alumnae some years ago, we received a complaining letter from one alumna because we had failed to ask about the "really important thing," namely children. She had had one child, and she explained that her time was currently taken up with two grandchildren (although they did not live with her). Another woman replying to our inquiry listed many community activities in the years immediately following college and again when she was older, but with a gap of some twenty-five years between, which she did not explain. Our curiosity led us to the alumnae files where we found that she was the mother of nine children. We had not asked about children and she had found it possible to tell us only what we apparently wanted to know. She felt no need to protest.

The only evidence that college-educated housewives may be more restless than their high school sisters is their greater tendency to work outside the home. But this can be attributed, at least in part, to the fact that the job alternative, for those who prefer it, is at once more attractive and more remunerative than that open to the high school graduates. A recent college graduate with two small children told me a short time ago that she had to earn at least $5,000 to break even financially, taking into account extra household help and additional income-tax liability. "But," she added, "I like the job, and of course I can make more than that." In short, it seems reasonable to assume that the college women have options which the less educated lack, so that they can give full time to homemaking or not, as suits their temperament.

The daily routine of the mother of small children with no hired help, even when all the time-saving equipment is at hand, is easily a fulltime job. The washing machine and the drier only insure that the laundry is done at home. The dishwasher and the vacuum cleaner, the cake mixes and the strained baby foods, save time that is used to drive husbands to their offices and the older children to their music and dancing and swimming lessons, and the dentist. Papering and painting are now so easy to do with all the improvements in paint and equipment, and skilled workmen are so expensive, that a whole new field of home activities has opened up for the more ambitious. And if there are any stretches of time not otherwise occupied, there is always some community activity where the homemaker can be useful.

The skills required for successful homemaking are easily equal to those of many professions. But while we pay lip service to the dignity of motherhood, *Who's Who* does not list wives and mothers of distinction. There is, of course, the mother of the year, but she usually has to live a long time and have a good many famous sons to achieve it. The award comes long after the job is done and it is soon forgotten. It is hard to get public recognition for a job which is in its nature so personal and private. The work of homemaker concerns only the members of the immediate family. Even these have no experience with better or worse wives, mothers, and housekeepers. There can hardly be distinguished members of such a vocation.

The apology of the returning alumna who explains that she is "only a homemaker" stems partly from this; but not entirely. Rightly or wrongly, something more is expected of the college graduate. Referring back to the current life cycle of the average woman, she has some 45 years ahead of her after the youngest child is in school. What of these? The fact that such large numbers of college women do combine marriage and professions, or spend a large part of their time in community activities, lends support to the fact that such expectations are not unreasonable. Nor does it necessarily follow that the children suffer from such activities. If the result is a more contented mother, and one with a wider circle of interests, the children will probably be happier, too. Very little evidence has been found on this score, but it is worth noting that one of the findings of the Mellon Foundation at Vassar College is that the most important factor distinguishing good students from poor ones is that the mothers of the good students "had intellectual interests and aspirations."[12] And the working mothers reported by Agnes Rogers mention, among other advantages of the job, that it has increased their own contentment and this has made them better mothers. They also mention the greater self-reliance of the children and the children's pride in their mother's profession.

Community activities are in a very real sense a natural extension of the homemaker's duties. Fluoridation of the city water supply may do more for the children's teeth than regular trips to the dentist. And when the children are in school it becomes important to join the PTA, and perhaps to run for the school board. Also, more is expected of the homemaker's community activities than self-interest. There are community centers for underprivileged children that need volunteers, either as board members or leaders in charge of group activities. There are all the church-supported functions. There is the League of Women Voters with projects that require all the research and organizing skills learned at college. There is volunteer work with political parties. The list is long. Whether the motive is protection of the family, concern for the underprivileged, or simply social contacts, most housewives with time on their hands—and a good many others who don't know how the time is to be found—will become involved.

When the higher education of women was still in its pioneering state, training for social responsibility was not the explicit aim of any institution of higher learning. Even college men in this early period were not encouraged by the authorities to participate in public affairs. On the contrary it was assumed that students were subject only to the laws of the college and were exempt from government controls. When off campus they could steal fruit or break windows with impunity. Quincy, president of Harvard from 1828 to 1845 after having spent many years in political life, was apparently the first college president to insist that students obey the laws of the state. Wayland, president of Brown, took the same position a few years later.[13] This was the beginning of training for citizenship, although it was not listed among the institutions' aims. As Conant, former president of Harvard, has noted, education for citizenship represents the modern approach to education.[14]

Government at this time was primarily to maintain law and order. Voluntary cooperation, often made palatable by being coupled with social festivities, took care of many group needs. Charity was linked with the church. America was still essentially rural, and those in need could presumably look to their neighbors for help.

Women nursed the sick and carried baskets of food to the poor. They formed Ladies' Aid Societies that raised money for the churches; they sewed for the needy. No special training was required for such budding community enterprises. The women had no place, of course, in political activities. Benjamin Rush urged that women must be instructed in government and liberty and the obligations of patriotism if these were to be made effectual.[15] But they not only could not vote; they could not speak in public. "Public speech was outside a mystic geometrical entity called 'women's sphere.' The religious called it unscriptural for a woman, the cultured thought it unseemly, the cynical found in it material for their bitterest sneers."[16] A visitor to Mount Holyoke Female Seminary in the early 1840's reported that, much to his surprise, everything was in the best of taste with one exception: "Twelve young ladies, without parents, rising in a crowded church to receive a broad diploma with its collegiate seal presented to my view the least attractive spectacle of a most interesting day."[17] The young ladies had not uttered a word.

Oberlin, concerned as to the reputation of its early women students, did not permit them to appear before a mixed audience. When Lucy Stone addressed a small local meeting she was called before the Ladies' Board of Managers and reprimanded.[18] She was later invited to write an essay for commencement, but when she found that she would not be allowed to read it herself she declined the honor. If she could not read she would not write.[19] Oberlin relaxed its rules to permit women students to read their own essays in 1859, but as late as 1870 the authorities were startled when one young lady dared to discard her manuscript after the first sentence and look at her audience as she addressed them.[20]

Vassar's Prospectus of 1865 notes that there will be voluntary associations for religious improvement, such as "Societies of Missionary Correspondence and Inquiry," and sewing circles for charitable purposes.[21] But "oratory and debate (whether public or private) are not feminine accomplishments; and there will be nothing in the College arrangements to encourage the practise of them."[22] In spite of this, private debates were in progress in the early 1870's; interclass debates began in the 1890's; and the first intercollegiate debate took place in 1902. This was with Wellesley, and the Wellesley authorities specified that it must be on their campus, and participants must obtain special health certificates. Vassar, with fewer safeguards, won![23]

The college authorities were particularly cautious in endorsing the woman suffrage movement. Vassar's conservatism in this respect has been recounted earlier.[24] As late as 1891 Lucy Stone was complaining that only men were asked to speak to Mount Holyoke students.[25] And the Mount Holyoke students voted against woman suffrage, 185 to 114, in 1895.[26] It was not long after, however, that a College Equal Suffrage League was thriving, and President Woolley publicly endorsed the cause in 1906, as did President Thomas of Bryn Mawr. The other women's colleges still held back. A majority of Wellesley students voted against equal suffrage as late as 1912, but at the same time they had a flourishing Equal Suffrage League.

It is obvious that the majority of college women were not active supporters of the movement. But the colleges furnished the leaders in the movement just the same, except for those whose schooling was over before colleges were open to them. Even these were educated in the best seminaries and academies of the time. The colleges were educating women to participate in public affairs in spite of themselves. The students had learned how to find the necessary information and to organize their thoughts clearly. And they had, after the earliest days, debated controversial issues before large audiences. This was an area where education counted.

The first women's organizations were mostly for philanthropy and education. In these fields, too, the college education helped, and the college authorities were more cooperative. They had always accepted responsibility for educating teachers. And later they undertook to do something about social work. Courses in "charities and corrections" appeared in some college catalogues in the late 1880's and 1890's, and they spread rapidly in the early years of this century. These were hardly adequate preparation for professional social work, but they did much to arouse interest in this area, and they did in fact provide about all of the formal training that many of the volunteer workers and some of the professionals ever had. College Settlement Associations vied with College Christian Associations for the interest and support of women undergraduates.

On the whole, however, the specific course offerings have had little to do with later volunteer activities. Community and civic service has been determined more by the apparent needs of the time and place than any specialized training. In the early days church work predominated. But as the churches emphasized, more and more, the social responsibilities imposed by Christianity, social and educational activities frequently stemmed from religious affiliations. Of all the larger women's organizations functioning today, the Young Women's Christian Association is the oldest, dating from the middle of the nineteenth century. Social work came later. And active participation in politics and government followed the granting of suffrage.

A record of nearly three thousand Vassar alumnae who were asked to list their unpaid activities in the early 1930's shows that two-thirds of these volunteer activities were in social work for the younger group, and one-half for the older group.[27] The alumnae reporting were those who studied economics and sociology in college, which accounts in part for the high proportion of those engaged in social work. But this does not account for the increased interest in volunteer social work in the later period. Other activities included war work during World War I (28 per cent); work with civic and educational organizations (19 per cent); and government service (3 per cent). The PTA and the League of Women Voters predominated among the educational and civic organizations, and most of the unpaid government service was on school and library boards.

Today there is less interest in social work than formerly, in spite of the growing study of sociology. The major interests of the sociologists themselves are in other areas. And there is relatively greater need for the volunteers elsewhere. Social work is increasingly a professional job. Moreover, the general prosperity and the introduction of a comprehensive social security system have decreased needs in this area.

I have found no studies of current volunteer activities that provide extensive quantitative data; but judging from membership trends in different organizations, and what one sees and hears and reads, there appears to be some revival of church work, and a marked increase in educational and civic activities. Married college women, particularly, are found increasingly in the PTA and on the school boards. A considerable number are working with their political parties, and some are turning up in a wide variety of elected offices. About half of our increasing number of Congresswomen are college graduates; and a few of those rare officials, lady mayors, are also college graduates.

There is no indication that either early marriage or large families have diminished these activities. The Wellesley mother of four, cited above, has found time to take a leading role in organizing a local church and a cooperative nursery school. Among my own acquaintances, one mother of five young children serves on the local school board, and most of the more active members of the local League of Women Voters are mothers of young children. Unpaid community service is preeminently the job of the married woman. These activities are necessarily less rigid in their demands than paid occupations. They can take up as much or as little time as the homemaker can spare, and the time of meetings can be adjusted to her schedule. Also, being one step removed from her husband's business, the wife can afford to take the less conventional position. A man's business relations are less likely to suffer from his wife's espousal of unpopular causes than from his own.

The findings of the 1948 survey of the American Association of University Women support the claim that community affairs are primarily the homemaker's job, although the record of all college women is impressive. Eighty-nine per cent of the married women with children reported community activities, compared with 80 per cent of the married women with no children and 78 per cent of unmarried women. It is of interest to note, also, that those with extracurricular activities in college were more active in community affairs than the others. It is the well-recognized division between the doers and the inert.

Some of the members of the older generation are complaining that few among the younger generation are interested in anything but their immediate circle of family and friends. They do not want to participate in the larger world. The churches appear to be stressing, more and more, the personal importance of religious beliefs rather than the social responsibilities which are assumed by Christian brotherhood. The term "retreat from the world" appears again and again. And a Barnard senior, Class of 1958, in answer to a request to characterize her generation, writes, "Silent. Because we are so self-centered."[28]

Whether or not this is true can be measured better ten or twenty years from now. My own guess, based on admittedly inadequate data, is that there is a change in the nature rather than the amount of civic activities. It seems to me that the members of the younger generation have lowered their sights only in the sense that they are concentrating less on international affairs and more on local matters. Concern for the welfare of their own families may lead them into community problems of education and health rather than international problems. And pressing as international problems are it is not unrealistic to assume that, being a parttime amateur tied to a limited geographic area, the homemaker will achieve more in the local than in a wider arena. And the local experience may well lead to wider interests later, and more ability to cope with them.

I have sometimes suspected that the people who overlook the problem on their doorstep as too petty to concern them, and lose sleep worrying about Russia or the Near or Far East, are evading responsibility. They might solve the problem on their doorstep if they were prepared to put some time and thought on it. There is very little they can do about Russia, as long as they are at home with the children, except to worry. Even the woman without family responsibilities is likely to make more progress at the local than at the national or international level. World affairs are still largely outside of "women's sphere." I would not discourage the ambitious from trying. It is not impossible, as a few women have demonstrated. And it is all important. But I do not think that we can charge the younger generation with either lack of concern or lack of action because they have chosen to run for the city council or to ring door bells to persuade local voters to approve the school bond issue instead of wringing their hands over Russian scientific progress.

Although no exact figures are available as to the proportion of volunteer workers that are college trained, there is ample evidence that the college women hold volunteer positions out of proportion to their numbers. This is in part the direct result of their college training. It makes them more articulate. They know how to write a properly documented official report, or a clear and convincing argument for a cause. They can speak effectively on a public platform. And, as they themselves continually testify: "College gave me a social conscience." They sometimes add, a little plaintively: "It never lets me rest."

The colleges cannot take full credit for this. It is true that training for citizenship appears with increasing frequency among the college aims. And the citizens' responsibility extends far beyond voting intelligently on election day. This is the usual argument for subsidizing education at any level, and particularly from public funds. Moreover, many of the faculty in the social sciences, and also in other fields, accept this as an important objective, and demonstrate it by participating actively in community affairs themselves. Also, the liberal arts training makes for greater understanding and greater competence in working on civic problems. Nevertheless, Eleanor Roosevelt, the woman who is preeminent in this field today, never went to college.

Nor did two recent presidents of the National League of Women Voters, Anna Lord Strauss and Percy Maxim Lee, both of whom have a distinguished record in a variety of civic activities. Others could be cited.

There are ways of acquiring the necessary skills without obtaining an A.B. degree, and one of the reasons for the good record of college women in civic affairs is that they come in larger numbers than others from families where the level of income and education is high, and the quality of training they have had, both at home and in private schools, has been much better than that available to the average girl. This does not mean that college education does not make an important contribution. For many, particularly those whose home and school training has been inadequate in this area, the college years can make the difference.

It is of interest to examine the education of those women who have made their mark in civic affairs. Unlike homemaking this is a field in which public recognition can be attained. To test this I have taken the women listed in *Who's Who in America, 1954–55,* whose achievements have been primarily in the field of volunteer services. Four out of five of the 647 found in this category are college women. And again, as for the scholars and the writers, the larger eastern women's colleges can claim more than their quota. Using the average enrollment figures as a test of the number of alumnae that could be expected, on the average, to achieve distinction, Bryn Mawr, Barnard, and Vassar head the list, in the order named, with 23 to 17 times the expected quota. The other five colleges, Radcliffe, Smith, Wellesley, Goucher, and Mount Holyoke, again in the order named, have from 10 to 5 times the expected quota. In the replies to the American Association of University Women questionnaires of 1948, the graduates of the women's colleges mention the value of their college training for community affairs more often than the graduates of coeducational institutions.[29] Pace's study of the graduates of the University of Minnesota shows that neither men nor women were very active in civic affairs. This was in the 1930's.

In conclusion, the average college woman today appears to be a better wife and mother, a better housekeeper, and a more active and better community worker than the average noncollege woman. And there is some evidence that the college training itself has contributed to this end. Among those college homemakers who have recorded their own convictions with respect to these matters, the number who believe their education has been helpful for meeting the varied demands made on the homemaker exceeds the number of dissenters.

There appears to be little demand for more specialized courses oriented either to the homemakers' needs or those of the civic workers. In short, there is no evidence that anything in particular should be done about women's education to make the homemakers and the community workers happier and more effective individuals. This does not mean that the educational program is beyond improvement; only that with its infinite variety there is no one glaring omission.

With regard to the new problem posed by the early age of marriage there is the difficulty of getting a college education of any kind. Are the women who drop out at the end of the sophomore year to marry going to regret, in later years, not having finished their college course? Are those who marry when they graduate from high school going to wonder if they have missed something important? And are their college-educated husbands going to regret that they didn't marry a college woman? If the colleges themselves are convinced of the value of their offering, what can they do to increase the number of women completing at least the undergraduate course? These are the important unanswered questions in this sphere.

NOTES

[1] One study stated that members of the Junior League who did not go to college married in the same proportions as college women. The way in which these figures were obtained is not given in detail, but there is some indication that the low proportion of married women was partly due to failure to take the age of members into account. (M. Lee, "College Graduates and Civilization," *Harper's Magazine*, May 1931, p. 721.)

[2] M. Zapoleon, *The College Girl Looks Ahead* (New York, 1956), pp. 2-3.

[3] E. Lloyd-Jones, "Our Dear Amazing Daughters," *Journal of the American Association of University Women,* March 1957, p. 158.

[4] P. C. Glick, "The Life Cycle of the Family," *Marriage and Family Living,* February 1955, p. 4.

[5] E. Roper, "The Public Looks at Higher Education," *Fortune Magazine Supplement,* June 1949, p. 259.

[6] P. W. Cautley, *American Association of University Wowen Study: Members Look at College Education* (Washington, 1949), *passim.*

[7] Agnes Rogers, *Vassar Women* (Poughkeepsie, 1940), pp. 155-156.

[8] *Ibid.,* p. 168.

[9] H. B. Fitt, "In Praise of Domesticity," in *College Women and the Social Sciences* (New York, 1934).

[10] C. P. Beebee, "How Does a B.A. Help to Raise Them?" *Wellesley Alumnae Magazine,* May 1958, pp. 215 ff.

[11] *Ibid.,* p. 228.

[12] N. Sanford, "Is Education Wasted on Women?" *Ladies Home Journal,* May 1957, p. 198.

[13] F. and H. L. Wayland, *A Memoir of the Life and Labors of Francis Wayland, D.D., LL. D.* (New York, 1862), vol. 1, p. 264.

[14] J. B. Conant, *Education in a Divided World* (Cambridge, 1949), p. 75.

[15] B. Rush, "Of the Mode of Education Proper in a Republic." (1798).

[16] F. J. Hosford, *Father Shipherd's Magna Charta* (Boston, 1937), p. 81

[17] Quoted in *ibid.,* p. 82.

[18] *Ibid.,* p. 88.

[19] *Ibid.,* p. 95.

[20] *Ibid.,* pp. 100-102.

[21] P. 15.

[22] P. 18.

[23] *Vassar Miscellany Monthly,* 1915, pp. 144 ff.

[24] See page 18 above.

[25] A. C. Cole, *A Hundred Years of Mount Holyoke College* (New Haven, 1940), p. 182.

[26] *Ibid.,* p. 266

[27] Classes of 1917-1931 and 1892-1916 respectively. M. Newcomer and R. G. Hutchinson, "Occupations of Vassar Alumnae," *College Women and the Social Sciences* (New York, 1934), p. 321.

[28] A. B. Kaplan, "Are They a Generation?" *Barnard Alumnae Magazine,* July 1958, p. 9.

[29] P. W. Cautley, *op. cit.,* p. 40.

I FIND MYSELF WONDERING WHETHER OUR GENERATION WAS
NOT THE ONLY GENERATION OF WOMEN WHICH EVER FOUND
ITSELF. WE CAME LATE ENOUGH TO ESCAPE THE SELF-CON-
SCIOUSNESS AND BELLIGERENCE OF THE PIONEERS, TO TAKE
EDUCATION AND TRAINING FOR GRANTED. WE CAME EARLY
ENOUGH TO TAKE EQUALLY FOR GRANTED PROFESSIONAL POSI-
TIONS IN WHICH WE COULD MAKE FULL USE OF OUR TRAINING.
THIS WAS OUR DOUBLE GLORY.

MARJORIE NICOLSON*

12. Progress Report

THE MORE important developments of a century of higher education for women have already been recounted. At this point it should
only be necessary to summarize the significant changes, and try to indicate where we are on a road that has no ending. We have reached and
passed some of the mile posts that the pioneers set as goals. Many
obstacles have been surmounted. But we have not arrived. There are
always new goals and new obstacles ahead.

Today there is general acceptance of the fact that women in
approximately the same numbers as men are able to meet the most
exacting standards set by our universities and colleges. It can still
be debated whether the apparent shortage of geniuses among women
is due to sex differences or social attitudes, but we have never thought
of limiting higher education to geniuses. Neither intelligence nor desire
for a college education are masculine prerogatives. It is not unusual
for intellectuals to be ridiculed, but not specifically women intellect-

* From M. Nicolson, "The Rights and Privileges Pertaining Thereto. . . ."
A University Between Two Centuries. University of Michigan (Ann Arbor, 1937),
p. 414.

233

uals. The term "bluestocking" no longer has any currency. The "high-brow" has no gender. And the "egghead" has a distinctly masculine connotation.

Simone de Beauvoir has said: "How to make the wife at once a servant and a companion is one of the problems he will seek to solve."[1] For the American college man today this has apparently been decided largely in favor of the companion. It is true that some girls "play dumb" in the presence of a boy friend. But at the same time others are giving as their principal reason for wanting a college education the desire to be a real companion to a college-educated husband.

Men are not upset by attending classes with women. They can concentrate on what the professor is saying if they want to. Even if they are outnumbered by women they can usually take it in their stride. They, as well as the women students, regard coeducation as "natural." Moreover, the girl friend is likely to be a classmate. There used to be some prestige from choosing one's girl friend from another college, if she was a college girl at all. But I was recently told by a Harvard senior that it was easier to date a Radcliffe girl, and that the old prejudice was breaking down. And I have been told that the president of a men's college with no women's institution close at hand has complained that the academic work is suffering because the men spend so much time ranging far and wide in search of dates.

More and more college men regard a college-educated wife as an asset, socially and economically. The young business executive is likely to be promoted faster if he has a college wife. And the wife who is working while her husband completes his graduate studies can usually get a better job if she has an A.B. degree. It also saves time if one's wife can make out the income tax return, and can advise on how to vote. There are still a good many husbands, of course, who insist on exercising their masculine prerogatives, but the cost is high. And a recent study of marriages shows that the happiest are those where the educational level of husband and wife is the same.[2]

There is almost complete acceptance of women's right to higher education. Women may study today in any of more than nine hundred institutions that offer at least a four-year course leading to a bachelor's degree. There are even more institutions open to women than to men, since the women's colleges outnumber the men's. When Elmira opened one hundred years ago there were very few institutions where women could obtain a college education, although those open to men were between one and two hundred. Under these conditions the founding of women's colleges not only offered an important addition to opportunities for women to pursue their education at least to a bachelor's degree; it also dramatized the movement. Today the decline in the number of both men's and women's colleges (except for Catholic institutions) has occurred almost without comment. Even the alumni and students of individual men's and women's colleges have raised few protests when the shift to coeducation was made. The coeducational trend appears to have complete public acceptance. The undergraduate institutions are largely coeducational; and most of the best graduate schools of medicine, law, and even engineering are now open to women, although these are still men's professions in practice. There can be no complaint as to the number of opportunities for women to pursue their education at any level and in any field they may choose.

There is not, however, general acceptance of the idea that higher education is just as important for women as for men. In recent years the most disappointing development, to those most concerned with the higher education of women, is the failure of women to keep pace with men in college enrollments. In 1920 there were almost as many women as men students in our institutions of higher learning; and while the proportion of young women who go to college has increased substantially in the past forty years, it has fallen so far behind the increase in the numbers of young men who go to college that there are now nearly two men for every woman enrolled.

In current discussions of higher education there appears to be either the tacit assumption that the number of women going to college is increasing as much as the number of men, or that women's claims to education are of a lower order of importance than men's. It is occasionally proposed that one way to meet the shortage of educational facilities might be to give preference to men, since women will not use their education anyway. I have heard educators, even in women's colleges, express surprise, and even disbelief, when I have mentioned the fact that the proportion of women among current college and university enrollments is much smaller than it was in the 1920's. And I have heard other educators approve the idea of giving preference to men. One dean of a teachers college told me that they were wasting taxpayers' money on women students who would "just get married." It is not, of course, the first job of a teachers college to educate homemakers; but he does not seem to know that marriage does not mean the end of a woman's professional career; that something like half of the women teaching today are married women.

The failure of women to keep pace with men in higher education is not from lack of adequate preparation. The problem a century ago was the problem of finding students with good basic training in the classics and mathematics. This was so general for boys as well as girls that all but the elite among the colleges were maintaining preparatory departments. But the girls' preparation was much less adequate than the boys'. Even the daughters of the well-to-do who had continued their schooling well into their teens were more likely to be skilled in embroidery and musical performance than in mathematics, Latin, or even French. This has long since ceased to be a special problem of women's education. More girls than boys graduate from high school today. And there are well-established entrance requirements and systems of admission. The problem today for women is lack of motivation. The women themselves are not convinced that higher education is as important for them as for the men.

The reasons for this are many. The most obvious is that women marry so much younger than they did forty years ago that many drop out of college after a year or two, or don't find it worth while to start. If one has the choice between marriage and college, marriage is almost sure to win. The educational system has taken little cognizance of this change. There is more than the usual concern for the waste of student time, whether in simple technical training or in courses of diluted content. It is easy to condemn the course in typing, but the conventional liberal arts curriculum far too often conceals courses of indubitable liberal arts content, watered down to the requirements of students whose interests and activities are primarily extracurricular. Some streamlining of the curriculum can be expected in time. Teacher shortages and financial pressures as well as the apparent waste of student time are working toward that end.

There have also been some attempts to break the tradition of a sixteen year course from first grade to the A.B. degree. The free elective system, combined with some flexibility in the number of courses carried at one time, was the first step taken by the colleges to permit students to complete the degree requirements in less than four years. The growing number of summer sessions and the occasional introduction of a quarter or three-term system have also contributed to this end. Today, partly as a result of concern for our shortage of scientists and engineers, exceptional students are occasionally permitted to enter college after three years of high school. Most of these changes have been made, however, with the men's needs in view. Military service does not apply to women, and little is expected of them in the fields of engineering and science.

In some ways, however, this is more important for women than for men, once it is conceded that college education for women is important. It is true that men only are subject to military service, but government assistance for their education has in some measure offset this handicap, and the assumption that the husband's education has priority over the wife's gives the man a distinct advantage. Also, women marry younger than men. An additional reason, often noted, for making it possible for women to shorten the period of their education is the fact that they mature more rapidly than the men. Yet I have found no women's college that has taken important steps to help the abler students, at least, to get their education and marry early, too.

A second reason for the smaller number of women than men in

college is that neither the women nor their parents are convinced that education is as important for them as for their brothers. This is closely tied to the occupational drive, of course. And as the earning period for the average woman tends to be deferred to middle age, the economic value of the education becomes less clear. Not only will the direct financial returns be smaller and later for the women than for the men, but the immediate educational cost falls in larger part on the women's parents, since the earning power of women students is lower than that of men, and they are reluctant to borrow.

The facts that education has always been subsidized in this country, whether by philanthropists, taxpayers, or teachers, and that its unstandardized and intangible nature makes it difficult to value it, militate against the willingness of parents to pay what it costs, even when they can afford to do so. It is easier for the average man to judge the quality of a specific make of car or a television set than the quality of education provided by a particular college. The result is likely to be that the car must be of the best but a second-rate college will do. A recent article written by a father on the problems of educating his daughter mentions the financial sacrifices the family has made. The specific instances he lists are driving the family car for five years, and his wife's giving up a new winter coat for a year or two. These are not very impressive sacrifices to faculty members who are likely to get their cars only after someone else has driven them for five years, and whose wives do well to get a new winter coat once in a college generation.

A third reason for the women lagging behind the men in going to college is the fact that the great majority of students—men and women both—think of their education as an aid to occupational advancement. This is nothing new. One of the compelling reasons for educating women in the first place was the need for teachers. What is new is that the changed life cycle of the women tends to defer professional and vocational activities to middle age, whereas formerly they sought such work immediately after leaving school. This makes the need for college education less obvious to the seventeen-year-old when she is faced with deciding whether or not to continue her education beyond the high school. There is, of course, one relatively new factor working in favor of a college education—namely, that this may improve a girl's social position, and not only make her a social asset to her future husband but even improve her chances of marriage. Women marry above their social class more often than men. It is true that men sometimes marry the boss's daughter, but women can marry the boss.

This motive alone is not likely to lead to much serious study, and is partly responsible for the large withdrawals at the end of the sophomore year. But some students who have had no more serious interests than this for further study when they have entered college have become interested "in spite of themselves." And others, who have had serious interests from the first, may be reassured that this will not interfere with their chances of finding a husband.

The prominence given to economic considerations has increased with recent trends. The great growth in college enrollments will not come from the wealthy or professional families. Among the very wealthy, where both economic and social status are assured, the daughters are frequently educated by private tutors and foreign travel rather than by college training. But the majority of the daughters of the well-to-do and the well-educated have gone to college as a matter of course if they were bright enough. Thus, if there is to be any large increase in the proportion of girls who continue their formal education after graduating from high school, this will have to come largely from the daughters of manual workers. Many of these go to college today, but primarily where vocational training at the undergraduate level—such as nursing, secretarial work, and teaching—is available. Widespread interest in a more general education is not apparent. And the residential liberal arts colleges have not attracted any considerable number of women students from these groups.

As the engineer replaces the skilled worker in our industrial plants, the importance of college education for sons is becoming more apparent to the blue-collar workers. But as education becomes more expensive, and as the girls marry earlier, it seems quite probable that education for daughters will continue to be considered a marginal luxury, if it is considered at all. This is particularly true because the office job is readily available and quite satisfactory for the short interval between high school graduation and marriage.

The women's colleges have made some effort to reach the daughters of low-income families, but without much success. Their admissions policies have sometimes militated against this end. In spite of good intentions they have sometimes taken into account whether the girl from a different social background "will be happy" at their particular college. One women's college quietly excluded Negroes for many years because the administration honestly believed that Negro students would be happier in a different kind of college. And more than one college has hesitated to give full scholarship to an admittedly brilliant girl from a working class family because she might not make friends easily or might prove socially inept. This stems partly from the tradition that it is an important function of the higher education of women to turn out ladies, and for this end it is safer to begin with girls from wealthy or well-educated families. It is partly because in the closely guarded atmosphere of the residential college, some individualists and rebels, or the merely uncouth, probably will not, in fact, be happy.

It is clear that if women are not keeping up with men at the undergraduate level, the lag will be reflected in graduate study too. The number of women obtaining Ph.D. degrees increases year by year, but not as rapidly as the number of men. In 1920 women obtained one in seven of the doctor's degrees conferred. In 1956 they obtained only one in ten.

As the total number of students increases, the women may lose some of the ground they have gained in the past century. Many of the better coeducational colleges accept a larger proportion of the men than of the women who apply. The women must be better. And obtaining fellowships for graduate study, or even admission to the best graduate schools, becomes more difficult for women, in particular, as the number of students multiplies. The women themselves are partly responsible for this. They sometimes take very lightly any obligation to use an expensive and subsidized education when the opportunity of marriage presents itself.

The evidence now available indicates that the majority of women will use their specialized graduate education at some time in their lives. But it cannot be denied that they are poorer risks than men. And as long as this expensive education is subsidized, and facilities are inadequate at best, there is good reason for setting a somewhat higher standard for women than for men at the graduate level.

The debate as to whether women's education should differ from men's has been settled not so much by agreement among the educators as by the free elective system and the prevalence of coeducation. The women students, as well as the men, have been able to shape the curriculum to their needs and interests through free choice of courses and institutions. The results show that the women are interested in every field, like the men. They also show that the interests of the majority of women are somewhat different from the interests of the majority of men. This is largely due to job opportunities and social pressures. The distinction between men's and women's fields is not quite as sharp as it used to be, but it is still true that women rarely go into engineering, for example, because engineering is supposed to be a "man's field." This attitude not only makes it difficult for a woman to succeed in this area. She is likely to regard it as so unsuitable that she never gives it consideration at all, just as she is often convinced that women "can't do mathematics." If she is job-minded she is very likely to follow one of the well-trodden paths leading to teaching, nursing, library, or secretarial work. These are the "women's professions."

Quite aside from professional considerations, however, women have shown a greater interest than men in the arts. In this area social attitudes deter the men. The arts are tinged with effeminacy in the popular thinking. Male college students are sometimes apologetic about enjoying music or poetry. For women, on the contrary, these are "natural" interests. And the very fact that college education is not supposed to be as important for women as for men leaves the women freer to follow where fancy leads. It is largely because of this that the women students, both in women's colleges and in coeducational institutions, are often credited with preserving the liberal arts tradition in a period when technical training was increasingly demanded by the men, and the monetary value of higher education was emphasized.

The early women's colleges, except as they stressed the arts and the biological sciences, did little to cater to women's special interests. Those, like Simmons, that have concerned themselves primarily with women's professional training, came late. It was the state universities, sensitive to public demand, that developed schools of education and home economics. Even the introduction of courses on the family, and social work, which have been of special interest to women, cannot be credited to the women's colleges. Having taken a firm position on the desirability of higher education of women, they conformed in everything else. One battle at a time was enough. But the early precedent is not the only reason why many of the older and larger women's colleges have both avoided and belittled vocational courses. The pressure from their students for such work has never been great. And when concessions have been made to "women's interests" by the administration, the students have sometimes been scornful. The vocational and homemaking training, as it has usually been offered, has not afforded sufficient challenge to the better students.

As the proportion of young people going to college increases there has been some concern that the ability of the average student will be lower. Thus far the evidence shows that this has not occurred. A college education used to be largely for the children of the professional and well-to-do families. Today, for men in particular, it is reaching a much wider circle. This is less true for women, but there is no indication that the quality of women students has declined either. The fact that there is less pressure for women than for men to go to college has undoubtedly resulted in greater selectivity among those who apply. The educators' problem is not the quality of the women who go to college, but how to attract at least a larger proportion of the top tenth of the girls from high schools, the majority of whom even now do not seek a college education.

The extracurricular education of women probably reached its highest development in the women's residential colleges. The fact that there were no men to be presidents of the study bodies and editors of campus newspapers gave women opportunities for leadership and responsibility that were rarely open to them elsewhere. And the fact that they were less free than men to stray from the college campus gave them more time for such activities. They developed student self-government early. Also they never became absorbed in intercollegiate athletics and so had more time for musical and dramatic performance and literary productions. Nor did they neglect political and social discussions.

These activities have diminished in importance because of the more frequent and extended weekends today. And also because the high school, the summer job, and the academic courses have gradually encroached on this field so that it no longer offers the novelty or the educational value that it had when girls had been more sheltered before coming to college. The college itself, in the earlier days, had misgivings about women speaking from a platform even when it was a college platform, and did not permit them to leave the campus without a chaperon.

To sum up, all the old arguments against higher education of women have been answered. Women have proved that they have the mental capacity and the physical endurance needed for a college education. They have made their mark in the professions, the arts, and scholarship. They have also retained their feminine charm. They marry and they have large families of healthy children. They are the backbone of the community services. But having achieved all this they are themselves questioning the value of the college degree. The challenge of pioneering is gone. The immediate value of higher education for homemaking is not altogether clear. The more remote value of college training for professional work can scarcely be perceived on the distant horizon.

More than this, while women's sphere has been enlarged and no longer has the old, sharply defined boundaries, it is still a limitation to be observed. In the field of learning, men's judgments still have a degree of authenticity that women's judgments lack. George Eliot's comment is still true: "A man's mind—what there is of it—has always the advantage of being masculine, . . . even his ignorance is of a sounder quality."[3] Women themselves prefer men professors. In the university that I attended it was not difficult to avoid women professors, but I took some pride in achieving this just the same. Women's colleges (but not men's) insist on "balance" on the faculty. Many women prefer men physicians and men lawyers. Few would vote for a woman for president of the United States, no matter what her qualifications might be. More men than women are to be found among the presidents and trustees of women's colleges. Men are more influential than women, and only men can be trusted with important matters of finance. Is the struggle worthwhile for ambitious women when the pleasant alternative of a home of one's own is always there?

This is the new front on which the battle lines will be drawn—if indeed enough recruits can be found for such a battle, or even a minor skirmish. I would not belittle the achievements of a century of higher education for women. I am even inclined to think that only a minor skirmish is needed for the next step. But there is no cause for complacency either. In these days many people are insisting that our greatest waste of resources is in brain power. If this is conceded, then it must be conceded that the larger part of that waste is women's brain power.

NOTES

[1] Simone de Beauvoir, *The Second Sex* (New York, 1953), p. 81.
[2] Mirra Komarovsky, *Women in the Modern World* (Boston, 1953), p. 86.
[3] George Eliot, *Middlemarch*, Bk. I, Ch. 1.

OUR COLLEGES SHOULD NOT BE MONUMENTS TO THE DEAD
BUT WORKSHOPS FOR THE LIVING. THERE IS NO BEAUTY IN
UNFITNESS.

MARIA MITCHELL*

13. What Next?

IT IS ALWAYS easier to evaluate the past than the present. Time
gives perspective. The nonessentials fade, and the important achievements stand out clearly. New beliefs and institutions, on the contrary,
have not been tested by time. It is hard to believe that we could have
such quaint ideas as our ancestors had one hundred years ago, but
our descendants one hundred years hence will doubtless see them that
way.

Even the task of evaluating the present, however, is simple compared with the future. For the present one can at least choose from
among known facts. But if we are not to drift, deal with the future
we must. And while the risks of forecasting are many, it is not just
a guessing game. If we can make up our minds what we want the
future to be, we can in some measure shape it to that end.

The men and women who decided a century or more ago that
women had the same right to a college education as men made their
plans and fought their battles against heavy odds. It was convictions
—not chance—that proved important. Women's right to higher education is now accepted. But how many men and women today are

* From H. Wright, *Maria Mitchell: Sweeper in the Sky* (New York, 1949),
p. 192.

245

convinced that a college education is just as important for women as for men? And how many are concerned over the waste of our national resources when they are told that among the top 10 per cent of our high school seniors the proportion of girls with no plans for going to college is more than double that for boys? Is the higher education of women wasted, or is it a waste not to educate more of the ablest young women than we do? These are things that we could and should make up our minds about, but I find few people who have any real convictions either way. We are not planning for the future. We are drifting.

Nor have we made up our minds what the education of women is for. Is it just a privilege which we are prepared to grant, to be taken advantage of or not as each individual happens to decide? Or is it as important to our society to have highly educated women as men? And if it is important, how are we going to persuade the women and their families of that importance? Also, if it is important —important for what? Are women to be only transmitters of knowledge, as mothers and teachers? Or are exceptional women to be encouraged, as exceptional men are encouraged, to make their contributions to the store of human knowledge and culture as scholars and artists? And if we are going to encourage women in creative thinking, research, and expression, are we going to encourage them to explore any field that catches their fancy, or only those which social usage has designated as of feminine concern? And what of the women's colleges? Have they outlived their usefulness? Or have they still a unique contribution to make to the rich and varied pattern of American higher education?

Too few people, it seems to me, are giving these matters much thought. Far too many are assuming that all the problems of higher education of women were settled long ago. The educators of women have been too long on the defensive. We have protested too often that college education won't hurt women any; that it may even make them better wives and mothers, and improve their social position; that men, more and more, prefer college-educated wives. We have suggested too rarely that the acquisition of knowledge can be a road to women's own fulfillment and independence, or a way to advance human welfare. We seldom encourage our students to break with tradition, to question the stereotype. Too many are saying: "Women are admittedly intelligent, but science is not their forte." "Higher education is useful for career women, but it is largely wasted on homemakers." "Some college education may be a social asset for a woman, but it is a luxury that the average family cannot afford." Meanwhile, the overcrowding of the universities and colleges threatens increased discrimination against women students. The fact that women with professional training have not used it as regularly as men for professional ends appears to justify giving preference to men, both in admission and in conferring fellowships.

Many of those immediately concerned, of course, are aware of these problems. The National Manpower Council's study, *Womanpower*, makes it clear that college women, more than noncollege women, are working outside of the home in increasing numbers and for long periods of their lives. This is a relatively new development. The Commission on the Education of Women of the American Council on Education is contributing much to public understanding of the problems. The Secretary of Health, Education and Welfare, Arthur S. Flemming, has recently pointed out (January 1959) that there are more unused resources of brain power among women than among men. And the dearth of women scientists and engineers, in particular, is frequently noted.

It is quite generally recognized that more highly trained scholars are needed, whether in science or elsewhere. And the statistics show that a much smaller proportion of the ablest women than of the ablest men have continued their studies to the point of obtaining advanced degrees. Marie Curie is not the only woman who has made important contributions in the scientific field, but the small number of women among distinguished scientists threatens to grow smaller. Meanwhile there is a shortage of good scientists. There is need for scholars in other fields. My own conviction is that the need to advance the frontiers of knowledge in the complex field of the social sciences is at least as important as the need for further scientific research. It might be easier to capture women's interest here than in science. It seems likely that the interval of homemaking, combined with community activities, may sharpen interest and promote understanding in this area, rather than proving a handicap. In the humanities, also, the record shows that there is room for women's contribution.

Changing the stereotypes will not be easy, but innovators have never sought a life of ease. Mary Lyon is said to have told her students to "learn to sit with energy." We accuse the younger generation of being conformists, but what challenge have we offered them? It is time for those who believe in the positive values of higher education for women to abandon their defensive position; to set their goals; and to make plans for attaining these ends.

No simple blueprints can be offered for this. On the contrary, there are probably many routes to the same goals, and it can be left to the educators and the students to choose their own way of arriving, once they are convinced of the value of goals. Having been somewhat critical, however, of what seems to me apathy and lack of understanding on the part of the general public, and even some of the educators immediately concerned, I feel that some positive suggestions are called for.

I begin with the assumption that the present pattern of the average American woman's life is likely to continue for the predictable future. The three changes that affect the problem of education are (1) earlier and nearly universal marriage; (2) the growing tendency for married women, and more particularly those with college training, to work outside of the home; and (3) taking up one's profession again—or even going into it for the first time—in middle age after the children are in school. The factors responsible for these changes seem likely to endure. It has become eminently respectable for the wife to support her husband while he completes his training, and add to the family income at any time in order to maintain high standards of living.

It is also easier than it used to be, with the labor saving devices now available, to manage a household and pursue a profession at the same time.

I am assuming, further, that this changed pattern of life has not made higher education of women less important than it used to be, or less important than the higher education of men. Many will not agree with this, but for those who do agree I make the following suggestions as to areas where more experimentation might well prove rewarding.

The educators themselves might take a fresh look at their offerings with these changed conditions in mind. If women are to be persuaded to go to college in the same proportions as men, and to obtain at least the first degree before they become absorbed in family responsibilities, they must be convinced that such education is important both for family life and for a profession, and they must be assisted by more flexibility in college schedules and requirements. I am not suggesting lower standards than now prevail. On the contrary I should hope that some standards, now so low that they only waste students' time, would be stiffened.

One of the first steps for the educators appears to be the reconciliation of the apparent conflict between the liberal arts and the professional training. Those who deplore training for professions as the guiding motive of the college undergraduate are either assuming that such training is of a limited and technical character that makes little demand on the intellect, or they associate the scholar with the gentleman—or lady. Either concept is an anachronism. More and more the leaders in professional education are recognizing the importance of more liberal arts training at the undergraduate level. Both the law schools and the medical schools are continually urging more training in the liberal arts. The normal school has been replaced by the teachers college, which has expanded "subject matter" training. And the home economists have revised their courses of study to resemble more closely those in the liberal arts program. In short, those concerned with training for specific professions are acknowl-

edging the importance, for their purposes, of the more general training. But most schools have not gone nearly as far as the leaders advise
in introducing liberal arts courses, particularly at the undergraduate
level. It is generally conceded that the state universities have yielded
too readily to pressures for technical job training. This is not peculiar
to the education of women students, but there is some evidence that
the training for "women's professions" is likely to be more superficial
and less demanding than the training for "men's professions." The
education of airline hostesses, it seems to me, could be safely left to
the airlines; and most secretarial skills could be left to the high
school commercial courses and the ubiquitous private business schools.
I am an enthusiast for the use of visual aids at all levels of instruction, but is it necessary to give special—and required—courses in
the comparatively simple techniques required?

Many of the liberal arts colleges have erred in the other direction,
either ignoring or belittling the desire for vocational training. If, instead, they were to recognize this as a legitimate reason for such
education, for women as well as for men, and would attempt to make
it clear to their students that the training they are providing at
the undergraduate level is the soundest base for a future profession;
and if, in addition, they were to give the students real guidance in
orienting their liberal arts course toward specific professional ends,
it seems probable that more of the women students would attempt
to finish their course. Merely stating the importance of such preparation is not enough, with so many pressures the other way. A colleague
of mine, who is fairly emphatic about this matter when talking with
her students, had one returning alumna complain: "Why didn't you
tell us that what you were saying was so?"

More stress on professional training would, of course, require the
frank recognition that some courses are better than others for one or
another end. It is one thing to point out that a broad base is so important that the student who has majored in art history, say, can
still prepare herself to be a psychologist without repeating an entire
undergraduate course. It is quite another to imply that the major

in art history will get her to her goal as fast as a major in psychology.

I am not suggesting that the universities and colleges which give specific professional courses abandon them completely for the liberal arts training, or that the liberal arts colleges introduce technical training at the undergraduate level, together with rigid sequences of study. On the contrary, there is reason to believe that widely varied types of institutions are desirable. But the professional training might profitably offer more subject matter and fewer techniques. And the liberal arts colleges might provide more advice and guidance looking toward a profession. If wise and impartial advisors can be found to help a student to formulate her goals and start her on her way—I know these are not easy to find—instructors in her field of concentration should be able to guide her from that point forward. The process might well be simplified if most of the universities and colleges were to reduce their course offerings. Many would profit, in my judgment, by cutting them in half. The students would be less confused in choosing their free electives, and the college would save money. It is always easier to add new courses than to abandon old ones; but many courses have outlived such usefulness as they may once have had. Now that women are prepared to give so little time to higher education it is important that that time be well spent.

More might be done, also, to assist students who marry before graduation to complete their undergraduate course. Many of these find themselves within reach of another university or college, than the one where they first studied, but they are rarely encouraged to enroll, and they are often deterred by rigid requirements. Institutions with high standards sometimes refuse to give credit for work done at an institution the quality of whose work they question. Yet these same institutions sometimes accept foreign students as provisional juniors simply because of the difficulties of measuring the quality of their earlier education. Such students are granted a degree on the completion of two years of work of the quality demanded for the other students. Is it out of the question to give this privilege to American women too? The risk, after all, is theirs. A real effort on the part of the women's colleges to reach such individuals might offset the dropouts they suffer because the women students marry and leave in order to live with their husbands. Some colleges are cautiously providing that they will give degrees to students who complete their senior year elsewhere, but only at selected institutions. Reluctance to bestow a degree for a senior year at a college with different standards is understandable, but the college where the student completes her senior year might consider granting the degree for those who complete it successfully, even though the first three years were spent elsewhere. This, today, is frequently refused.

It might also be worthwhile to explore the possibility of permitting the best students, at least, to complete their education through the undergraduate course in less than the standard sixteen years. Devices for achieving this are an extended school year, such as the quarter system, and permitting exceptional students to enter college after three years of high school, or to carry heavier than normal programs in college itself. These are well known but little used, whether because exceptions in individual cases require value judgments or because traditions tend to become sacred is not clear. Women mature earlier than men, and they marry younger. Might they not be encouraged, more frequently than they are today, to compress their education into fifteen years, say, if they have the desire and the ability to do so?

Another difficulty that stands in the way of higher education for women more than for men is the cost of education. Parents have always been reluctant to meet the full cost of such education. The majority have thought of it as an investment that must bring clear financial rewards. The intangible returns that do not lend themselves to such a test are likely to be regarded as a marginal luxury or overlooked altogether. This has always militated against educating women at the expense of their parents, although it has favored their being educated at public expense to provide cheap teachers for the public schools. In the earlier period even parents could often see the value of educating daughters so that they could support themselves the rest of their lives or until they married. But today when they marry so early, or get an office job with a high school diploma, the financial value of educating them is not so clear. The women themselves are less able to work their way through college than the men, and less willing to borrow.

The private colleges have provided generous scholarships. But the residential schools housing most of their women students have done very little to provide for differential living costs, or to reduce the costs for some in other ways. And few institutions encourage payments on the installment plan. Education is, perhaps, the only expensive commodity today that is not regularly sold "on time." If education that was guaranteed to last a life time could be purchased in small monthly installments spread over a period of, say, ten years, the parents might be persuaded to pay more of what it costs even for daughters. Colleges have the obligation not to waste funds, and to see to it that the education they provide is all they claim; but the parents will still have to be persuaded that it is worth what it costs.

Further, if the daughters of the blue-collar classes are to be attracted to the private liberal arts colleges, the colleges themselves— and more particularly the women's colleges—will have to change the stereotypes: namely, that they are for the daughters of the well-to-do; that they are training ladies, and perhaps scholars, but not homemakers and professional women. If the women's colleges want more brilliant students, and students with more varied backgrounds, as they say they do, the manual workers' families appear to be the most likely place to find them. It is certainly an area that needs more exploration than it has received to date. The financial barrier does not appear to be great. Family incomes compare favorably with those of many professional families. The problem, rather, is one of incentives and attitudes.

In time the office jobs at the high-school-diploma level may become less plentiful as office automation progresses. At the same time it is to be hoped that teaching positions will not only be plentiful but also better paid. Under these conditions the importance of college education for daughters may be as clear to blue-collar families as it is today for their sons. By that time, the fathers, of course, may have been transformed into engineers, with a college education and the professional attitude toward higher education. It may also become increasingly apparent, if present trends continue, that preparation for jobs later in life is important for women.

Much of the preparation for professional work may have to be left until the children are in school. At this point there seems to be no lack of incentive, and except in those families where the woman is the sole support of the family, the additional time and cost of such training appears to be justified by the fact that it leads directly to a more challenging and remunerative occupation than would otherwise be available. The greatest obstacle at this point is the geographical limitation. The wife and mother must get her education within commuting distance of home. Urbanization and improved transportation, coupled with the multiplication of colleges and universities, makes this possible for large numbers of older women. They are sometimes deterred from attending a residence college, however, because regulations and schedules are not geared to their needs, and the emphasis on residence is likely to make them feel unwelcome. They will be accepted by the college if they can make the necessary adjustments; but I believe that the majority of residence colleges could be more cordial and more helpful than they now are in assisting women to complete their college courses. Also, they might find that the result was to give the college some of that diversity in its student body that it has been seeking.

There is still the problem of training more women scholars. We cannot afford to depend on men alone for advancing the frontiers of knowledge and developing the arts. Whether or not there are as many geniuses among women as men is not important. There are some, and we cannot afford to pass them by; geniuses of either sex are rare. But if women scholars are to be encouraged, it is important first to break down the belief that men's and women's intellectual interests and abilities are quite different. Also more opportunities must be available to women on university faculties and in research institutions. If the balance of men and women on a women's college faculty is educationally sound, might not men's colleges and the coeducational institutions find it equally sound?

As for the women's colleges, I have sometimes prophesied that they will be converted to coeducational institutions or die in another twenty years. I am convinced that the usual case that is made for them has no validity today. Some are not even asserting that they have positive values. They are arguing, it seems to me, that they are just as good as coeducational colleges. A book, *Educate a Woman,* which was issued by the Woman's College of the University of North Carolina to celebrate its fiftieth anniversary in 1942, ends with a full-page picture of a young woman marching arm in arm with two young men. It is entitled "The Woman's College Faces the Future." This apparently was not intended to imply that the future lies in coeducation. I assume that it was merely to indicate that the life of a student at a women's college is not the life of a nun. But this is hardly a justification for a women's college.

Yet I believe that women's colleges still have an important role to play. They, more than coeducational institutions, are in a position to dramatize the changing needs in the higher education of women today, and to lead in providing for them. If the women's colleges themselves fail to adapt to these changing needs, it is hardly to be expected that coeducational institutions will give special consideration to women, or even give them the same consideration as men.

Unfortunately, there are no new women's colleges, and little likelihood that one will be founded for this purpose. And it has never been easy for long-established institutions, incrusted by time with outmoded customs, to slough off the shell of tradition and grow with the times. It has usually been easier to start afresh with a new institution. Many of the women's colleges have been stirring uneasily. There has been more than the usual study by committees and long debates in faculty meetings. But thus far the results of such deliberation have been disappointingly few. Most of the revisions, however desirable, have been of a minor nature; and majority votes have frequently been obtained by logrolling rather than a clear consensus. There appears to be no real agreement, and even no real conviction of need for drastic changes. Yet I believe the problems are no greater than those faced by the original founders of women's colleges, and I can hope that some of the women's colleges will provide the leadership to assess these new needs and provide for them.

The educators' task is not limited to the transmission of knowledge. They must also make the reasons for learning clear. If young women can be convinced of the importance of a college education; if, more specifically, they know why it is important for themselves and for human welfare, I would trust them to get that education even if it should mean deferring marriage—or at least babies—for a little while. And I would trust the modern young men, who are so helpful about the housework and the care of the babies, to cooperate in this venture too.

Bibliographical Note

THE SOURCES used in this study are widely varied, extending from the *Decennial Census* of the United States to casual comments of undergraduates, but for those interested in pursuing the subject of this book further a statement of the sources that I have found most useful may be helpful.

For the early history of women's education, Thomas Woody, *History of Women's Education in the United States* (New York, Science Press, 1929, 2 vols.) has proved invaluable. And for the development of the liberal arts curriculum, I have found R. Freeman Butts, *The College Charts Its Course* (New York, McGraw Hill, 1939), and George P. Schmidt, *The Liberal Arts College* (New Brunswick, Rutgers University Press, 1957), the most useful general accounts. For the basic theories of education I have depended on such classics as John Dewey, *Democracy and Education* (New York, Macmillan, 1916) and Alfred Whitehead, *Aims of Education* (New York,

Macmillan, 1929). For differing current points of view on the higher education of women I have found the best statements in Harold Taylor, *On Education and Freedom* (New York, Abelard-Schuman, 1954) and Lynn White, *Educating Our Daughters* (New York, Harper, 1950). Mirra Komarovsky, *Women in the Modern World*, (Boston, Little-Brown, 1953) and Kate Mueller, *Educating Women for a Changing World* (Minneapolis, University of Minnesota Press, 1954) also make interesting and important contributions to the question from a somewhat different approach.

The basic statistics come largely from the statistics of higher education included in the annual, or biennial reports of the United States Commissioner of Education from 1870 to date, and from a number of special studies made under the auspices of the United States Office of Education. Data on occupations of women come largely from the United States *Decennial Census* and from National Manpower Council, *Wowanpower* (New York, Columbia University Press, 1957). These sources have been supplemented by many special studies of the occupations of college women, made both by national organizations and by specific colleges that have gathered data on their own alumnae.

For the educational programs it has been necessary to draw heavily on the college catalogues and the annual reports of the presidents of the various colleges. The recent facts and figures concerning such matters as applications for admissions and the reasons for converting from a men's or women's college to a coeducational institution, have been obtained by correspondence with individual college officials.

The biographies of women leaders and educators and the individual college histories that I have found useful are too numerous to list. I cannot refrain, however, from stating that most of the college histories have contributed relatively little for the purpose in hand, and are hardly a credit to the institutions they are designed to extol. Too many are anecdotal in nature, and give more space to the buildings and their donors, and to extracurricular activities, than to the basic educational purposes and programs of the institution. There are, however, honorable exceptions among which, for the women's colleges, Arthur C. Cole, *A Hundred Years of Mount Holyoke College* (New Haven, Yale University Press, 1940) is outstanding.

Opinion surveys and factual inquiries that I have found particularly useful are the American Association of University Women survey of its membership in 1948, the *Fortune* survey: Elmo Roper, "The Public Looks at Higher Education," (June 1949), B'nai B'rith, Vocational Service Bureau, *5000 Women College Graduates* (Washington, 1953), and the Radcliffe Committee on Graduate Education for Women, *The Radcliffe Ph.D.* (Cambridge, Harvard University Press, 1956). Alumnae magazines for individual colleges have also proved very useful for presenting student and alumnae viewpoints.

Index